THE MORMON
TREK WEST

THE MORMON TREK WEST

JOSEPH E. BROWN

PHOTOGRAPHS BY
DAN GURAVICH

Introduction by Stanley B. Kimball
HISTORIAN, MORMON PIONEER TRAIL FOUNDATION

DOUBLEDAY & COMPANY, INC.
GARDEN CITY, NEW YORK
1980

PHOTO CREDITS

Page xvii, page xviii bottom, page xxi bottom, C.W. Carter Collection, Church Archives, The Church of Jesus Christ of Latter-day Saints

Page xviii top, page xix top, center, bottom, page xx top, center, bottom, page xxi top, page xxii bottom, page xxiii, Church Archives, The Church of Jesus Christ of Latter-day Saints

Page xxii top, Culver Pictures, Inc.

Page xxiv top, bottom, Marsena Cannon Collection, Church Archives, The Church of Jesus Christ of Latter-day Saints

Acknowledgments

The author and the photographer wish to extend sincere thanks to the following people whose assistance was invaluable in the preparation of this book: Grant Heath, External Communications Department, and Dr. Glen M. Leonard, Historical Department, The Church of Jesus Christ of Latter-day Saints; Dr. LeRoy Kimball, President, Nauvoo Restoration, Inc.; Dr. Stanley B. Kimball, Historian, Mormon Pioneer Trail Foundation; and the late Paul Henderson.

Library of Congress Cataloging in Publication Data

Brown, Joseph E. 1929–
The Mormon trek west.
Includes index.
1. Mormon trail. 2. Mormons and mormonism—History. I. Title.
F593.B785 917.8'04'2
ISBN: 0-385-13030-9
Library of Congress Catalog Card Number 77-16900

BOOK DESIGN BY M FRANKLIN-PLYMPTON

PHOTOGRAPHIC LAYOUTS DESIGNED BY ADELE SCHEFF

PRINTED IN THE UNITED STATES OF AMERICA
FIRST EDITION

To the memory of the Pioneers

Contents

Introduction

Since its beginning, in 1846, The Great Trek has captivated the fancy of both Mormons and non-Mormons, and the Mormon Trail is quite probably the most written-up trail in all history. Dozens, perhaps hundreds, of contemporary journals were kept during the twenty-two years the Mormons trod it. Scores of books, hundreds of articles, and thousands of stories have been written about it. (I, myself, have contributed well over a hundred.)

All this fascination with The Great Trek is well deserved. Interest has never been greater than it is today.

Until recently, one could gauge the interest in this particular American trail by asking the late Paul Henderson of Bridgport, Nebraska, about his guest book. Paul, a great trail expert, who in his eighties had himself become a monument along the road, was consulted by all serious students, writers, and photographers of the trail, including the co-makers of this book.

The belief that this famous trail was a Mormon creation or discovery is mistaken. It may be that of the thousands of miles of trails and roads the Mormons used during their migrations from 1831 through 1868, from New York to California, they actually blazed less than one mile. This one bit of authenticated trail-blazing lies between Donner Hill and the mouth of Emigration Canyon, just east of Salt Lake City. The Mormons were not looking for a place in the history books. They had a job to do and they did it as easily and as expeditiously as possible, always using the best roads available. But whether the trail should rightfully be called the Mormon Trail or the Great Platte River Road, the Oregon Trail, the California Trail, or something else, Wallace Stegner said, I believe accurately, "By the improvements they made in it, they earned the right to put their name on the trail they used. . . ."

Prior to The Great Trek, the Mormons had had little experience in moving masses of people and livestock over long distances. What training they had acquired was in 1834 during the Zion's Camp March from Kirtland, Ohio, to Liberty, Missouri. This nine hundred mile journey to redress wrongs done to their brethren by mobs and militia in Jackson County, Missouri, redressed no wrongs after all, but it helped train them for their final exodus west.

The additional skills they learned while crossing Iowa in 1846 not only made easier the much longer part of the trek from the Missouri River to the Valley of the Great Salt Lake in 1847, but they also set the pattern for building and colonizing the Great Basin.

It is a curious fact that the Mormons, who did not want to go west in the first place, were the most successful in doing so. Mormons were not typical westering Americans: whereas others went for a new identity, adventure, furs, land, or gold, they were driven west for their religious beliefs. The pioneer group was not concerned just with getting themselves safely settled but in making the road easier for others to follow. Furthermore, the Mormons transplanted a whole people, a whole culture, not just isolated, unrelated individuals. They moved as villages on wheels and differed profoundly from the Oregon and California migrations. Consequently, the Mormons became the most systematic, organized, disciplined, and successful pioneers in United States history.

The experience of the trail, the crossing of the plains turned into a great event not only in the lives of the pioneers but in the minds of their descendants. It became a rite of passage, the final test of faith. The contemporary U.S. Mormon is proud of nothing in his heritage more than that one or more of his ancestors "crossed the plains." Today a special mythology and clouds of glory surround these pioneers. The most important honor societies in Mormondom are the Sons and Daughters of the Utah Pioneers.

The Mormon Trek West is a skillful blending of beautiful photography and beautiful writing. Mr. Guravich might well have had in mind producing something like "The Illustrated Emigrants' Guide" or "The Illustrated William Clayton's Journal." (Clayton's *Guide* and *Journal* are the best original single sources for The Great Trek.) He has carefully framed every photograph so that the hand of man is never visible. One can almost believe he was with Clayton during those exciting days.

Mr. Brown is a professional writer of great skill, and he has followed the trail himself. His text, derived almost exclusively from contemporary journals, is eminently readable. Mormon and non-Mormon alike will appreciate his artistry.

One notable strength of the text is the thorough attention paid to the background of The Great Trek—a background that unobtrusively extends back to Joseph Smith's grandfather. Too often this genesis is missing in other studies of the trail, but without, for example, the explanation of the Missouri persecutions, neither the Illinois experience nor the exodus itself can be understood properly.

The story commences with Charles Shumway, a real person standing in the snow on February 4, 1846, dejectedly looking from Nauvoo, Illinois, across the mighty Mississippi into Iowa, that Mormon Mesopotamia between the Mississippi and Missouri rivers, into his future, into his fate.

The whole text is neatly held together by continual reference to Shumway and his family. We follow them, their trials and triumphs, across three future states and into the Great Basin, through the fiftieth anniversary of the trek in 1897, and to his death the following year.

The Great Trek must be divided into two parts: across Iowa in 1846 and across the Great Plains in 1847. The three hundred-mile-long Iowa portion was the worst. In the beginning the weather was terrible, and the Saints, a mixed group of men, women, and children, were inexperienced and often unprepared. Most of the trail deaths took place in Iowa. It required a month to cover the first hundred miles—an average of three per day.

By March 1 the Mormons were ready to quit their staging round on Sugar Creek in Lee County, Iowa, six miles west of the Mississippi, where they had been gathering since February 4. No accurate record was kept of how many wagons and people were at Sugar Creek that March 1—estimates vary from four to five hundred wagons and from three to five thousand individuals. Five hundred wagons and three thousand people is probably close to the truth. The ubiquitous whitetops, or covered wagons, of the era were ideal for such travel. Families en route could live in, on, and under these animal-drawn mobile homes, and at the end of the trail, they could become temporary homes until real houses could be erected.

The Saints used all kinds of wagons and carriages and all sorts of draft animals, especially horses, mules, and oxen. They often preferred the latter when they were available, for oxen had great strength and patience and were easy to keep, they did not fight mud or quicksand, and they required no expensive and complicated harness. The science of "oxteamology" consisted of little more than walking along the left side of the lead oxen with a whip, prod, or goad urging them on and guiding them, and was considerably simpler than handling the reins of horses or mules. With gentle oxen, widows with children could and did (with a little help, especially during the morning yoking up) transport themselves and their possessions successfully all the way to the Valley of the Great Salt Lake.

What from the start was known as the "Camp of Israel" began to lumber out about noon to the "gee-haws" of teamsters and the yells of herdsmen and children. Thereafter, Old Testament parallels to a Zion, a Chosen People, an Exodus, a Mt. Pisgah, a Jordan River, a Dead Sea, and to being "in the tops of the mountains," and making the desert blossom like the rose were noted, devised, cherished, and handed down. The Mormons resembled ancient Israel in other ways: they were divided into groups of fifties and tens and, at times, were factious and whiny. To keep the camp together, or at least to keep in touch with the various leaders, Brigham Young and Heber C. Kimball appointed mounted couriers to ride back and forth and arranged for different-colored signal flags to communicate messages and call meetings.

Mormons had and have a strong penchant for making the best of things. Throughout the pioneering period they sang around campfires, listened to brass-band concerts, and danced—they loved square and line dances, Virginia reels, Copenhagen jigs, polkas, and especially quadrilles. (Round dances, particularly the new waltz, were a bit suspect.)

As far as Bloomfield, Iowa, the pioneers used established old territorial roads. Thereafter they followed primitive roads and Potawatomi traces to an Indian agent's settlement on the Missouri at present-day Council Bluffs. En route they founded several permanent way stations and first blessed a sick animal, and William Clayton wrote the words to "Come, Come Ye Saints," the Mormon Marseillaise.

Later that June, the pioneers arrived on the Missouri River, where they set up their Winter Quarters. Contrary to myth, the 1847 part of the trek, covering approximately 1,073 miles, was neither one long and unending trail of tears nor a trail of fire. Over the decades Mormons have emphasized the tragedies of the trail. Tragedies there were, however. Between 1847 and the building of the railroad in 1869, perhaps as many as six thousand died along the trail from exhaustion, exposure, disease, and lack of food. (Few were killed by Indians.) To the vast majority, though, the experience was positive. Nobody knows how many Mormons migrated west during those years, but eighty thousand in over ten thousand vehicles is a close estimate.

The route west of Winter Quarters requires some explanation. The simplest way of following the pioneers (and most subsequent Mormon immigrants) from "civilization to sundown" is to divide the trail into four sections and relate them to the Oregon Trail, the "Main Street to the West." They followed generally what is sometimes called the Great Platte River Road, which had always been regarded as the most advantageous approach to the easiest crossing of the Rocky Mountains. The trail had been blazed by Indians, trappers, fur traders, and other immigrants such as the Marcus Whitman party, which went to Oregon in 1836, and the Stevens-Townsend-Murphy group, which first took wagons over the Sierras in 1844.

The Oregon Trail started at Independence, Missouri, and crossed Kansas, Nebraska, Wyoming, and Idaho. The first section of the Mormon Trail was from Winter Quarters generally along the north bank of the Platte River to near present-day Kearney, Nebraska. Up to this point the Mormon Trail and the Oregon Trail of the late 1840s were entirely separate. The second portion of the Mormon Trail was from Kearney to Fort Laramie, Wyoming. Along this section the two trails followed the Platte, the Mormons on the north bank and the Oregonians on the south. Since in the 1840s the favored route to Oregon and California was along the south bank of the Platte, it might appear that the Mormons pioneered the north-bank trail, but actually during the 1820s and 1830s the north bank had been the preferred way, used by fur trappers and missionaries. As late as 1846, the famous historian Francis Parkman took the northern route to South Pass.

The third section of the trail was from Fort Laramie to Fort Bridger. Here the Mormons followed the Oregon Trail proper for 397 miles. The fourth and final section started at Fort Bridger, where the Oregon Trail turned north and where the Mormons left the Oregon Trail and picked up the year-old Reed-Donner track through the Rockies into the Salt Lake Valley.

From Winter Quarters, they had followed the broad, flat valley of the Platte for some six hundred miles and the beneficent little Sweetwater for about ninety-three more, all the while enjoying an increasingly rugged and beautiful land, and traversing finally a series of defiles and canyons from Coyote Creek to the famous Emigration. Topographically the trail had led across the Central Lowlands, over the Great Plains into the Wyoming Basin, through the middle Rocky Mountains, into the Great Basin. The Mormons passed along river valleys, across plains, deserts, and mountains, over several inland seas of grasslands and sagebrush steppes, and through western forests of Douglas fir and scrub oak. They were entering the empire of the buffalo, wolf, antelope, bear, coyote, goat, elk, fox, raccoon, rabbit, gray squirrel, and prairie dog; the prairie hen, wild turkey, snipe, goose, duck, crane, swan, great blue heron, and quail; the bee, grasshopper, and firefly; the rattlesnake, copperhead, lizard, and turtle; the grayling, catfish, and trout. They traversed the domain of various grasses from the stubby buffalo through the prairie, wheat, needle, sandhill, up to the five-foot-tall bluestem. Seasonally the area was a piebald garden of sunflowers, daisies, gayfeather, and butterfly milkweed.

For the 143 men, three women, and two children who left Winter Quarters, the pioneer trek of 1847 was mostly a great adventure with a dramatic ending. One hundred and eleven days later, as everyone knows, Brigham Young entered the valley and declared, "This is the place."

Stanley B. Kimball
Historian, Mormon Pioneer
Trail Foundation

THE MORMON
TREK WEST

Lucian R. Foster moved to Nauvoo in the autumn of 1843 and established a daguerreotype gallery on Main Street. Foster probably took this view of the Nauvoo Temple and city early in 1846 as the city was being evacuated. The daguerreotype is looking northeast from Foster's gallery. Utah photographer Charles W. Carter made a wet-plate copy of the original and thus preserved Foster's rare early view.

This engraving of the Nauvoo Peninsula was "drawn after nature" about 1845, before completion of the Nauvoo Temple. The view is from across the Mississippi River. (From *United States Illustrated*, published in New York, 1854 or 1855.)

The Nauvoo Temple, completed in 1846 just as the Latter-day Saints were leaving for the West, was badly damaged by fire on October 9, 1848. A year and a half later (May 27, 1850), a tornado toppled the weakened walls, leaving only the front wall intact and portions of the side and back walls standing. Residents of Nauvoo began using the stones for building material, and when artist Frederick Piercy visited Nauvoo in 1853 en route to Salt Lake City, he sketched this view, published in *Route from Liverpool to Great Salt Lake Valley*, edited by James Linforth (Liverpool, England: Franklin D. Richards, 1855), as a steel engraving.

Brigham Young

William Clayton

Orson Pratt

Charles Shumway

Wilford Woodruff

Heber C. Kimball

Between Nauvoo and Salt Lake City, the Latter-day Saints established a staging center for their wagon trains in western Iowa. After Brigham Young evacuated Winter Quarters, in 1846, the camp known as Miller's Hollow was renamed in honor of Thomas L. Kane, a friend to the Mormons, and grew into a community with a peak population of five thousand. Kanesville flourished until 1853, when the Mormons sold their farms and businesses to others and joined the migration to Utah. Frederick Piercy made the sketch from which this engraving was prepared in 1853, as Kanesville was being abandoned. It was published in his *Route from Liverpool to Great Salt Valley* (1855).

Wagon trains followed the Mormon trail to Utah until the completion of the transcontinental railroad, in 1869. This view of Mormon emigrants was taken by Charles W. Carter in Echo Canyon in 1867. Poles for the transcontinental telegraph (joined at Salt Lake City in October 1861) are visible in the picture.

Buffalo herds covered the prairie when the Pioneer Company set out for the West.

The title page and an interior page of William Clayton's guidebook for the Mormons who followed the trail-blazing Pioneers.

THE

LATTER-DAY SAINTS'

EMIGRANTS' GUIDE:

BEING A

TABLE OF DISTANCES,

SHOWING ALL THE

SPRINGS, CRFEKS, RIVERS, HILLS, MOUNTAINS,
CAMPING PL .CES, AND ALL OTHER NOTABLE PLACES,

FROM COUNCIL BLUFFS,

TO THE

VALLEY OF THE GREAT SALT LAKE.

ALSO, THE

LATITUDES, LONGITUDES AND ALTITUDES
OF THE PROMINENT POINTS ON THE ROUTE.

TOGETHER WITH REMARKS ON THE NATURE OF THE LAND, TIMBER, GRASS, &c.

THE WHOLE ROUTE HAVING BEEN CAREFULLY MEASURED BY A ROADOMETER, AND THE DISTANCE FROM POINT TO POINT, IN ENGLISH MILES, ACCURATELY SHOWN.

BY W. CLAYTON.

ST. LOUIS:
MO. REPUBLICAN STEAM POWER PRESS—CHAMBERS & KNAPP.
1848.

PROMINENT POINTS AND REMARKS	DIST. miles.	From W Qrs. miles.	From C of G S L miles.
5th small creek from the last. - - After crossing this, you ascend a high bluff, the top of which is a succession of hills and hollows for five miles. The road is good, but crooked.	4¾	574½	456½
"La Bonte" river, 30 feet wide, 2 ft. deep. Good place to camp—plenty of timber, grass, and water. There is also a good chance, a mile further. Plenty of wild mint on the creek.	8¼	582¾	448¼
Branch of La Bonte, 10 feet wide, 18 inches deep. - - . - - Doubtful about water. Steep banks. You have now traveled near a mile over this dark, red sand, and will find it continue three and a half miles further.	5	587¾	443¼
Very small creek. - - - - Little chance for grass, and less for water. One mile beyond this, you ascend another bluff, but the road is tolerably straight and good. Look out for toads with horns and tails.	6¼	594	437
Very small creek. - - - - Very poor chance for camping.	6¼	600¼	430¾
Very small creek. - - - - The road runs down the channel of this creek, near two hundred yards, but there is little grass on it.	½	600¾	430¼
A La Prele river, one rod wide, 2 ft. deep. Current rapid—good place to camp. Land between creeks mostly sandy and barren, Road from here to the Platte very uneven, being a succession of hills and hollows.	1½	602¼	428¾
Small creek. - - - - - No place to camp—doubtful for water.	4¼	606½	424½
Box Elder creek, 5 feet wide. - - Clear water, and plenty—but not much grass. Not very good to cross, banks being steep. Some timber on it.	1	607½	423½
Fourche Boise river, 30 feet wide, 2 feet. deep: Lat. 42° 51′ 5″. - - Current rapid. Plenty of good grass and timber.	3¼	610¾	420¼
North fork of Platte river. - - - Not much grass here. You will now find a sandy road and heavy traveling.	4	614¾	416¼
"Deer Creek," 30 feet wide, two feet deep: Lat. 42° 52′ 50″: Altitude, 4,864 feet Lovely place to camp. Swift current, clear water, and abundance of fish. Nice grove of timber on the banks, and a coal mine about a quarter of a mile up, on the east side. After this, you will find sandy roads for nine miles, but not much grass.	5	619¾	411¼
Deep hollow, or ravine—steep banks. -	2½	622¼	408¾
Sudden bend in the road. - - - To avoid a deep ravine.	5¾	628	403
Grove of timber on the banks of the river. Good chance to camp. Lat. 42° 51′ 47″.	1	629	402
Crooked, muddy creek, 12 ft. wide, 1 deep. Not good to cross—steep banks. Plenty of grass, but no wood.	1	630	401
Muddy creek, 3 feet wide. - - - Soft banks and bad to cross. Considerable small timber, but little grass. After this, good but crooked road.	5¾	635¾	395¼
Deep gulf. - - - - -	2¾	638½	392½

When Frederick Piercy arrived in the Salt Lake Valley, in 1853, he found the six-year-old Mormon capital a flourishing agricultural and commercial center. Visible in this detailed sketch, looking down Main Street from the north, are Brigham Young's farm buildings and first home (White House), far left; the Heber C. Kimball property, foreground, in the shadow; the Deseret Store and Tithing Office, the two large buildings on the left, at Main and South Temple; the Council House, across the street to the right; public-works shops on Temple Square behind an incomplete wall intended to enclose the square; and the Old Tabernacle (1852) on the Square, far left. Most of the buildings at this time were of sunbaked brick (adobe) or logs. The sketch was published in *Route from Liverpool* (1855).

Salt Lake City's Main Street, 132 feet wide and lined with irrigation ditches, is seen here in a view from atop the Council House in 1862. The view, by Utah photographer Marsena Cannon, shows the telegraph office (first building on the left) and business houses in a burgeoning commercial district between South Temple Street and South Second Street.

Three of Brigham Young's homes are seen in this view by Marsena Cannon, Utah's first resident photographer. The buildings are, from left, the Lion House (built 1855–56), Brigham Young's office, the Beehive House (1853–55), and beyond the Eagle Gate, the White House (1852). The Beehive House was the "official" residence; all were built of stuccoed adobe brick.

1

Exodus

Charles Shumway tugged the collar of his jacket tightly around his throat and clapped his mittened hands together in the bitter morning cold. Walking beside his ox-drawn wagon, he had arrived early at the Nauvoo ferry dock that morning, February 4, 1846. He was the first of a wave of refugee-emigrants anxiously awaiting the flat-bottomed boats that would float the wagons and their sagging loads of humanity and possessions across the river from Illinois to the eastern shore of Iowa Territory.

As a backdrop for a major exodus, a westward migration that was to become one of the most important and dramatic in American history, Nauvoo's weather could not have been worse. For days, the temperature had struggled to climb above zero. Ice floes choked the Mississippi. Deceptively beautiful, they drifted past the wharf like frozen white clouds, then disappeared around a bend downriver. Shumway flinched as the wind forced the bone-numbing cold through even the thickest part of his clothing.

The hardest part was the waiting. Physical immobility, nagging apprehension over the unknown that lay across the river past the boundaries of the United States, and the knowledge that to remain meant harm or even death only worsened his discomfort. Though the ice appeared innocent, each floe could slash a wooden ferry's hull as a knife could cut butter. Only when several floes clogged together, leaving a clear opening in their wake, did the ferrymasters dare attempt to negotiate the river, even though the Iowa shore was tantalizingly visible.

Occasionally, as he waited in the near-zero weather at the foot of Parley Street, Shumway gazed wistfully back at the city stretching gently up the hill to the east.

Under its winter mantle of snow, Nauvoo seemed peaceful and undisturbed, although even in the early morning there were flurries of activity. Five blocks east, at the corner of Parley and Granger Streets, Webb's Wagon and Blacksmith Shop was a noisy beehive; for weeks, its occupants had toiled far into the night hammering red-hot iron into wheels needed by the hundreds of covered wagons that would take the emigrants west. The Webb shop was as busy as usual this morning; rising heat from the blazing forge had melted a neat circle of snow from the roof above.

Not far away stood the two-story brick building that housed the printing shop of the *Times and Seasons,* Nauvoo's newspaper. Purchased the year before by Elias Smith, business manager of the Mormon Church Printing Office, the building now had two additional functions. It served as the Nauvoo post office, and it doubled as a real estate office from which most of the property of those preparing to flee the city was being sold, usually at a staggering loss.

Charles Shumway was equally familiar with the snow-covered one- and two-story building on Main Street between Kimball and Munson Streets, where a native Kentuckian, Jonathan Browning, converted to the faith of the young and expanding Church of Jesus Christ of Latter-day Saints, had begun to design and make the first of the repeating rifles that would earn him, and later a son, John Moses Browning, a worldwide reputation. Even as early as February 1846, the elder Browning had turned out several dozen guns for the Nauvoo Police Department, of which Shumway was a member. The guns had served two purposes. They were used when necessary to enforce the local law. And perhaps more important, since Nauvoo's local crime rate was among the country's lowest, they were useful in defending the community against an increasing onslaught of terrorism from outside, from which Nauvoo enjoyed little respite.

In February 1846, Nauvoo was a city under pressure. Its citizens were about to take flight in the dead of winter toward a destination not precisely known.

Only seven years before the morning Charles Shumway waited at the ferry landing, the rolling Mississippi riverbank was little more than a mosquito-infested swamp. It was a site scarcely suited for a city, but that hardly deterred its settlers. Where there was a will there seemed a way, and the fact that no one else wanted the land only made it more attractive to Nauvoo's founders.

After all, they had already been driven out of two other states. Perhaps here, on the very frontier of America, far from metropolitan centers, they would find the peaceful sanctuary that had so long eluded them, a place where they could build their Zion.

Under the leadership of Joseph Smith, the first of an eventual population of twelve thousand Mormons drained the bogs. They laid out a grid of streets. They erected homes and shops, and the beginnings of a magnificent temple. In the rich, black alluvial soil beside the townsite, they planted corn, other grains, and orchards. Under their efforts, Nauvoo prospered, and by February 1846, the city had truly earned its name; in Hebrew, Nauvoo means "beautiful place."

During the first years, life in Nauvoo had been pleasant. There had been corn-husking parties, dinners in private homes, quilting bees. Citizens shared in house-raisings and summer swims in the cocoa-colored Mississippi. There had been cruises aboard Captain Dan Jones's *Maid of Iowa*, at least one circus, and on the Fourth of July, the community had turned out to watch the gaudily festooned Nauvoo Legion (the only private army in America) re-enact famous battles of American history, and to hear Captain Pitt's brass band play stirring anthems and church hymns.

There were other towns in Illinois along the Mississippi, but few could compare with Nauvoo, a town almost as large as Chicago. Months after the February exodus had begun, in fact, a visiting U. S. Army officer, Colonel Thomas L. Kane, could find little but praise for the city.

Ascending the upper Mississippi in the autumn, when the waters were low [Kane later wrote], I was compelled to travel by land past the region of the Rapids. . . . My eye wearied everywhere to see sordid, vagabond and idle settlers, a country marred, without being improved, by their careless hands. I was descending the last hillside upon my journey when a landscape in de-lightful contrast broke upon my view. Half encircled by a bend of the river, a beautiful city lay glittering in the fresh morning sun; its bright, new dwellings, set in cool green gardens, ranging up around a stately dome-shaped hill, which was covered by a noble white edifice, whose high tapering spire was radiant with white and gold. The city appeared to cover several miles; and beyond it, in the background, there rolled off a fair country, chequered by the careful lines of fruitful industry. The unmistakable marks of industry, enterprise and educated wealth everywhere, made the scene one of singular and most striking beauty.

The "noble white edifice" described by Kane was the Nauvoo temple. It was by far the most prominent landmark in the city, or, for that matter, in the entire state of Illinois. Its cornerstone had been laid nearly five years earlier, in April 1841, on a gently rising hill east of the community and by 1846 the temple was a scene of vigorous activity. If anything, work had even increased while most of Nauvoo's citizens prepared for the forced exodus into Iowa Territory and beyond.

The temple was indeed an imposing structure. At the time of its completion, in May 1846, it was the largest and most widely known building north of St. Louis and west of Cincinnati. It measured 128 feet east to west and 88 feet north to south. Its main structure rose 60 feet above ground level, its tower and spire an additional

98½ feet. Native gray limestone, quarried near Nauvoo, provided material for its massive walls, and although it embodied elements from classical, medieval, Renaissance, and nineteenth-century architecture, it was unique in form and appearance. America's frontier had witnessed nothing quite like it.

The most striking external characteristics were huge moon stones, which formed the base of the pilasters or buttresses, unique sun stones with faces, surmounted by hands holding trumpets or horns of plenty, and star stones on the frieze. Each of these decorative stones, thirty in all, was hand-tooled and polished.

Although non-Mormon visitors to Nauvoo estimated the temple's value at between one half and one and a half million dollars if constructed conventionally elsewhere in America, a considerable part of the materials and labor was donated. No one appreciated this better than Charles Shumway. Although he had amassed considerable wealth as a sawmill operator since he had been converted to the LDS faith, in 1841, and had settled in Nauvoo, he had turned over the lion's share of his profits to Brigham Young, the brilliant leader of the church after the murder of its founder, Joseph Smith, at the hands of a mob in nearby Carthage. Shumway specified that his donation was to be used in temple building.

Without the kind of donation that Shumway had made, it is doubtful the temple could have been completed nearly as soon as it was. It was built by a people whose community bank was empty at the time: Its construction, in fact, began when the nation was still in the economic doldrums created by the Panic of 1837, and it was completed at a time when every spare Mormon penny was desperately needed to finance the great trek West.

Gold and silver specie were almost unknown in this frontier section of the United States; much voluntary labor and material, and a substantial dosage of plain old devoted faith, had to take its place. Those who worked on the temple were paid not with money but with something of equal value. Their "wages" were donations of china and glassware, watches, clothing, furniture, household goods, and the crops of Nauvoo farms. Each man and boy in Nauvoo was expected to contribute a tenth of his labor on the building, and each family a like percentage of its worldly goods.

One might wonder why a people preparing to flee their city would continue to pour such effort into temple-building. Nauvoo's citizens, however, were possessed of an iron-willed stubbornness and a relentless faith. Just as Joseph Smith's martyrdom, two years earlier, had welded the Mormons into a more cohesive group than ever, so the mob's pressure on Nauvoo merely accelerated their efforts to complete the temple as quickly as possible.

To a Mormon, then as now, the temple is far more than a building. It is a special religious sanctuary within which certain sacred ordinances of Jesus Christ are performed which have a value in the eternal world. Among these are vicarious baptism for the dead, and marriage for eternity as well as the present. It is also a material manifestation of the Mormon's spiritual devotion and religious convictions. Little did it matter to those in Nauvoo, apparently, that the Temple would probably soon be destroyed by the same enemies who had hounded and terrorized them, burned and pillaged their homes and farms, and even murdered a few of their number, in the past two bitter years. They went on building.

As Charles Shumway awaited the safe moment to ford the Mississippi, another, related exodus was beginning eleven hundred miles away, on the Eastern Seaboard. The fact that both began the same day — February 4, 1846 — was entirely coincidental. When LDS Elder Samuel Brannan had the previous December announced plans for a group of Mormon Saints to travel by ship around Cape Horn to California, the sailing was scheduled for January 24, 1846. But because there were many delays in preparing the ship *Brooklyn* for the voyage, two major migrations in Mormon history happened to be launched, "by land as well as by sea," almost at the same moment. The risks were nearly equal.

To Nauvoo's Mormons, nearly fifteen hundred miles of prairie and mountains lay to the west, much of it frozen solid in winter and fraught with perils. Although the route had been traversed many times by earlier explorers, it was still largely untamed country. What Brannan's Saints faced, nearly seven decades before the opening of the Panama Canal, was a passage encircling two thirds of the land in the Western Hemisphere, including the rounding of the gale-swept Cape.

By late 1845, thousands of Mormons, many of them recent converts to the church, were living on the East Coast. Some had converged upon New York from the other eastern states and Canada, many more from England, where proselyting LDS missionaries had been active for several years. Elder Orson Pratt, of the Council of the Twelve Apostles, who was presiding in the eastern states, had heard of the Nauvoo Mormons' accelerated migration schedule. On November 8, 1845, he called upon those in the eastern states to head westward, via the water route, by early spring.

"We do not want one Saint left in the United States after that time," he said. "Let every branch in the East, West, North, or South be determined to flee out of 'Babylon,' either by land or sea, as soon as then."

Considering the number of Mormons in the East, that might take some doing, Pratt conceded. "If all want to go," he reasoned, "charter half [a dozen] or a dozen vessels and fill each with passengers, and the fare among so many will be but a trifle."

Sam Brannan was the logical choice to head the seagoing phase of the Saints' westward emigration. A born organizer, he had a strong personality and a forceful way of command; he became one of the most colorful and powerful men of the American West.

In December 1845, Brannan announced details of the *Brooklyn's* scheduled passage. He had chartered the 450-ton vessel for twelve hundred dollars per month; the fare was fixed at fifty dollars per adult, with an additional twenty-five dollars added on for provisions; children over five and under fourteen would be charged half fare.

Three hundred persons signed up for the passage, most of them farmers and mechanics from the eastern states; 238—including two or three non-Mormons— were aboard when the *Brooklyn* set sail. Judging by the *Brooklyn*'s cargo manifest, her passengers had no intention of ever returning to the East. It listed everything from farm and mechanical tools—plows, hoes, shovels, spades, plow-irons, scythes, nails, glass, and blacksmith, carpenter, and millwright implements, "enough for 800 men"—to a complete printing press, on which *The Prophet* had been printed in the East. Her hold bulged with dry goods, twine, brass, copper, iron, tin, and crockery ware; 179 volumes of Harper's *Family Library*, a gift from one J. M. Vancott, shared space with spelling books, histories, arithmetic manuals, and volumes on astronomy, grammar, and geography.

Taking no chances, Brannan had provisioned the vessel for a voyage of six or seven months, to San Francisco via Hawaii (then the Sandwich Islands). But except for a few storms, good weather prevailed, even around Cape Horn, and the *Brooklyn* arrived in San Francisco the following July, only five months and twenty days after her departure.

When the *Brooklyn* sailed, in February, what is now California was a part of Mexico. But the hostilities that had simmered between the United States and Mexico flared into full-scale war in May, about the time the *Brooklyn*'s passengers were spending a brief sojourn in the Juan Fernández Islands, famous as the place where Alexander Selkirk (Robinson Crusoe) spent his lonely exile from 1704 to 1709.

When Brannan's Saints landed at Yerba Buena, in San Francisco Bay, not the flag of Mexico but the Stars and Stripes of the United States was flying overhead. Mexico had surrendered California during the *Brooklyn*'s days at sea, and once again the Saints found themselves on American soil. They did not try again to escape it. Brannan's group became actively engaged in the early settlement of California under the American flag; Mormons participated in the discovery of gold in California's mother lode, which touched off the rush of western emigration, and involved themselves in the real estate bonanza that spawned San Francisco, where a street today remains named for Brannan.

Brannan had shared the conviction of Mormon leader Joseph Smith and, later, Brigham Young, that only in the West, beyond the borders of the United States itself, were the Saints to find their Zion. Where he differed with them was the place. Brannan plainly preferred California, regardless of who owned its soil. He regarded the Great Salt Lake Valley of Utah as only so much worthless desert.

A shrewd businessman, Brannan himself invested in mines, milling and railroads and became a large-scale distiller (no doubt to the disgust of the avidly temperate Mormons who later settled in Utah, from which Brannan could not tempt them to budge). He was one of the West's richest men, but he fell on hard times, lost his fortune, and died in Sonora, Mexico, in 1889. By then, Mormondom was sinking solid roots in the Great Salt Lake Valley, the at-last-realized Zion that had been only a flimsy but fervently prayed-for dream that wintry February morning in 1846.

Charles Shumway decided that conditions were at last safe enough to begin the Mississippi crossing. Each flat-bottomed ferry, propelled by paddle wheels, could carry one wagon, but, considering the load of the wagons, even this seemed a bit precarious. Aboard were men, women and children, horses, oxen, pigs, chickens. They held feather beds, farm implements, rocking chairs, books, sacks of flour and of beans, casks of water, bundles of clothing, firearms, carpenter's tools. Though Conestoga wagons were in vogue at the time, the Saints had built wagons of their own specifications that would more nearly fit their needs. The homemade wagons also saved money, and every penny saved was a penny earmarked for such lifesaving items as food, tools, and warm clothing.

With Shumway's wagon in the lead, the ferries crossed the river one by one, depositing each wagon on the Iowa shore, then returned to Nauvoo. Halting only when the weather closed down, the ferrymen worked tirelessly throughout the first day and for days to come. Gales buffeted the frail craft. Not all the ferrymen were skillful at judging the swift current and the drifting ice; more than one boat and its wagon swamped and sank to the bottom. Terrified oxen kicked holes in the sides of the wagons, and children screamed at the din. One of the accidents nearly drowned a man and two boys whose skiff, crossing behind a flatboat, swamped because of inexperienced overloading. The flatboat found itself in trouble as well. According to a version of the crossing written by Brigham Young, ". . . a filthy wicked man squirted some tobacco juice into the eyes of one of the startled oxen attached to Thomas Grover's wagon," and the oxen kicked one of the boat's sideboards out. The boat sank as it approached the Iowa shore. Although all human occupants of both craft were rescued, the two oxen drowned and the flatboat's precious cargo was damaged or lost.

On the Iowa shore, Charles Shumway waited until a few wagons had gathered, then set out across the snow-covered Iowa prairie to Sugar Creek, six miles to the southwest. The wagonmasters who followed could not mistake the new trail that was being blazed—the wagon ruts that deeply penetrated the snow and led into the wilderness beyond.

After the warm and safe comfort of their homes in Nauvoo, the camp at well-timbered Sugar Creek was eerie, hostile, forbidding. Here the first pioneers pitched a camp. The timber made an excellent windbreak, but it could not banish the noises of strange animals rustling through the snow-covered underbrush, the blasts of icy chill, or their own thoughts.

Between February 4 and March 1, when the main body of Saints had assembled and the Sugar Creek camp was broken, the camp assumed the appearance of a white city, the first of a series of semipermanent settlements that would eventually stretch the width of Iowa. Those who had not pitched tents felled timber to be used as the frames of rude huts whose walls were bed quilts, bark, or brush. Mealtimes were catch-as-catch-can affairs, consisting of warming up food held over campfires in pans. The cold, punctuated by severe snowstorms, lasted for days, and the people, hastened out of Nauvoo before they were fully prepared to go, underwent great suffering. In many cases, their meager food supplies were exhausted in a few days; mothers spent many a sleepless night holding their children in front of a roaring fire merely to keep them from freezing to death.

Nine babies were born that first night in Sugar Creek. Eliza R. Snow, whose wagon arrived at the camp later and who kept an eloquent diary of the trip, described the conditions under which those births occurred. A widow of the martyred Joseph Smith and soon to be a wife of his successor, Brigham Young, she wrote:

We had been preceded from Nauvoo by thousands and I was informed that on the first night of the encampment, nine children were born into the world, and from that time as we journeyed onward mothers gave birth to offspring under almost every variety of circumstances imaginable, execpt those to which they had been accustomed; some in tents, others in wagons—in rainstorms and in snowstorms. I heard of one birth which occurred under the rude shelter of a hut, the sides of which were formed of blankets fastened to poles stuck in the ground, with a bark roof through which the rain was dripping; kind sisters stood holding dishes to catch the water as it fell, thus protecting the newcomer and its mother from a shower bath as the little innocent first entered on the stage of human life.

In a later description, she added:

Many of our sisters walked all day, rain or shine, and at night prepared suppers for their families, with no sheltering tents; and then made their beds in and under wagons that contained their earthly all. How frequently, with intense sympathy and admiration, I watched the mother, when, forgetful of her own fatigue and destitution, she took unwearied pains to fix up, in the most palatable form, the allotted portion of food, and as she dealt it out was cheering the hearts of her homeless children, while, as I truly believed, her own was lifted to God in fervent prayer that their lives might be preserved.

By mid-February, the string of wagons from Nauvoo to Sugar Creek was almost a solid line. On February 6, Bishop George Miller and his family crossed the Mississippi with their six wagons. John Smith, Joseph Smith's uncle and president of the Nauvoo LDS Stake, followed with his family two days later. The exodus was slowed temporarily when the river ice began to freeze solid in late February (though various histories disagree on the exact date) but resumed when the ice was solid enough to proceed in even greater safety than aboard the flimsy ferries.

Brigham, who had remained in Nauvoo to supervise last-minute preparations for the evacuation, crossed the river with his family on February 15, accompanied by the families of Willard Richards and George A. Smith. He moved four miles ahead with his wagon until he arrived at a low bluff where he paused to await those who had followed. "I helped them up the hill with my own hands," Young later wrote. "At dusk started on, and reached Sugar Creek about 8 p.m., having traveled nine miles. The roads were very bad."

Toward the end of February, the weather turned extremely cold. In the Sugar Creek camp there was intense misery and suffering. By month's end, Sugar Creek held more than five thousand inhabitants. In an account of the migration, pioneer John R. Young later described life in Sugar Creek and what was happening at the same time in Nauvoo:

By the first of March over five thousand exiles were shivering behind the meager shelter of wagon covers and tents, and the winter-stripped groves that lined the creek. Their sufferings have never been adequately told; and to realize how cruel and ill-timed was this forced exodus, one has only to be reminded that in one night nine children were born under these distressing conditions.

By ascending a nearby hill we could look back upon the beautiful city and see the splendid temple we had reared in our poverty at a cost of one and a half million dollars. Moreover, on a clear, calm morning we could hear:

> The silvery notes of the temple bell
> That we loved so deep and well;
> And a pang of grief would swell the heart
> And the scalding tears in anguish start
> As we silently gazed on our dear old
>   homes.

Although there was no panic in the evacuation from Nauvoo, the increasing westward activity across the river began to create a mushrooming momentum; no one wanted to be left behind. Although from the very start the Mormons had been told that only by carefully conserving their resources and by creating new ones along the way could they survive their major undertaking, many of the pioneers in late February set out woefully unprepared. During the last two weeks of the month, for instance, more than eight hundred reported to Sugar Creek with barely enough provisions for themselves and their stock for three weeks. Brigham and the other apostles carried enough for a year, and it became obvious toward the end of February that some major reorganization was called for. That would come when the Saints reached the Chariton River, farther west.

2

Genesis

The early nineteenth century was a time of sweeping religious reform in America. Thousands of discontented Americans struck out against existing creeds, doctrines, and secular teachings. They groped for new and challenging ideas, and the constantly westward-shifting American frontier and its spirit of freedom only served to stoke the fires of religious liberalism.

Content with their own beliefs, however, other thousands of Americans preferred the status quo. Often those who questioned long-accepted doctrines were viewed as dangerous heretics rather than religious reformers following a freedom of choice for which Americans had fought only a generation or so earlier. Sometimes harassed, sometimes physically abused, the reformers nevertheless managed to establish fully thirty new churches in America between the dawn of the nineteenth century and 1830, the year The Church of Jesus Christ of Latter-day Saints—the "Mormon Church"—came into existence. Usually, the formation of a new church was accompanied by a physical move to new territory. In New England, for example, Roger Williams saved his radical religious views—and perhaps his neck—by fleeing with his followers to found the colony of Rhode Island. The Reverend Thomas Hooker, at odds with Boston's Puritans, also fled, in the country's first "covered wagons," to establish the colony of Connecticut.

As a persecuted, driven people, the Mormons were certainly not alone, then, in the first part of the nineteenth century, but it would defy the most patient historian to find a case in which the persecution was more intense or terrifying. At first the church's detractors seemed satisfied with humiliating and taunting the Mormons; it did not stop there, however. The murders of Joseph Smith and his brother Hyrum, shot by an Illinois mob, eventually forced the Mormons to cross the Mississippi from Nauvoo, organize the trek at Sugar Creek, and strike out for Utah's Great Salt Lake Valley, fifteen hundred miles beyond.

Joseph Smith's grandfather, Asael Smith, had expressed unhappiness with existing creeds and religions long before the future leader of the Mormon Church was born, and had himself become a westward-moving refugee. For example, after taking a persecuted Quaker into his home and thus arousing the wrath of the people of Topsfield, Massachusetts, he sold his home and moved west rather than yield to his antagonists. Joseph's father, Joseph Smith, Sr., was so dissatisfied with existing churches that he refused to join any of them, but his wife, Lucy Mack Smith, remembered later, "My husband's mind became excited upon the subject of religion." Joseph's mother was just as independent. None of the many churches she visited seemed to satisfy her, nor could she find a minister with whose views she could agree. Once, for instance, she attended a Presbyterian service ". . . in the full expectation of hearing that which my soul desired—the Word of Life," but left a disillusioned woman. "When the minister commenced speaking," Lucy Smith later recalled, "I fixed my mind with deep attention upon the spirit and matter of his discourse; but after hearing him through, I returned home convinced that he neither understood nor appreciated the subject upon which he spoke, and I said in my heart that there was not then upon the earth the religion which I sought."

A typical New England couple of English-Scottish extraction whose parents had fought in the American Revolution, Joseph Smith, Sr., and Lucy Mack Smith in 1816 moved to the vicinity of Palmyra, New York. It was there, on the frontier of America, that Joseph, at the age of fourteen and one of eight Smith children, as confused and perplexed as his parents had been before him, began, in 1819, to visit a virgin forest where he hoped solitude and prayer would provide the answers he sought. On one such visit, an event occurred that was to overwhelm Joseph, irrevocably change his life, and set into motion a series of events that would consume him until the day he died.

What happened is perhaps best described by Joseph himself:

It was on the morning of a beautiful, clear day, early in the spring of eighteen hundred and twenty. It was the first time in my life that I had made such an attempt, to ask God for guidance, for amidst all my anxieties I had never as yet made the attempt to pray vocally.

After I had retired to the place where I had previously designed to go, having looked around me, and finding myself alone, I kneeled down and began to offer up the desires of my heart to God. I had scarcely done so, when immediately I was seized upon by some power which entirely overcame me, and had such an astonishing influence over me as to bind my tongue so that I could not speak. Thick darkness gathered around me, and it seemed to me for a time as if I were doomed to sudden destruction. But, exerting all my powers to call upon God to deliver me out of the power of this enemy which had seized upon me, and at the very moment when I was ready to sink into despair and abandon myself to destruction—not to an imaginary ruin, but to the power of some actual being from the unseen world, who had such marvelous power as I had never before felt in any being—just at this moment of great alarm, I saw a pillar of light exactly over my head, above the brightness of the sun, which descended gradually until it fell upon me.

It no sooner appeared than I found myself delivered from the enemy which held me bound. When the light rested upon me, I saw two Personages, whose brightness and glory defy all description, standing above me in the air. One of them spake unto me, calling me by name, and said, pointing to the other—

"This is my beloved Son. Hear him!"

My object in going to inquire of the Lord was to know which of all the sects was right, that I might know which to join. No sooner, therefore, did I get possession of myself, so as to be able to speak, than I asked the Personages who stood above me in the light, which of all the sects was right—and which I should join. I was answered that I must join none of them, for they were all wrong, and the personage who addressed me said that all their creeds were an abomination in his sight; that those professors were all corrupt; that "they draw near to me with their lips, but their hearts are far from me; they teach for doctrines the commandments of men; having a form of godliness, but they deny the power thereof." He again forbade me to join with any of them: and many other things did He say unto me, which I cannot write at this time. When I came to myself again, I found myself lying on my back, looking up into heaven. When the light had departed, I had no strength; but soon recovering in some degree, I went home.

Few if any ministers appreciated being told that the creed their church follows is "an abomination" and that those who believe it are "all wrong," especially by a teenage boy, and the irritation expressed at Joseph from Palmyra pulpits in the days that followed was certainly understandable. But the annoyance, for the moment anyway, was only that; except for a few eastern newspapers that poked fun at Joseph's "vision" and a few raised eyebrows on Palmyra sidewalks whenever young Joseph passed by, little commotion was made about the boy's pronouncement. Visions and dreams were hardly considered rare in early-nineteenth-century America; Joseph's father himself was a staunch believer in them, and his life was influenced by such mental fancies.

But although Joseph had declared all existing creeds "wrong," he did nothing to promulgate his newfound belief for the next three and a half years. He continued to work on his father's farm, although in writing about this period later he admitted that the experience in the grove had matured him rapidly, and he expressed remorse over some behavior of his earlier life. "I frequently fell into many foolish errors," he later wrote, "and displayed the weakness of my youth and the foibles of human nature; which I am sorry to say, led me into diverse temptations, offensive in the sight of God."

Little attention was paid to Joseph Smith, in fact, for another eight years, until the publication of a book so startling and controversial it thrust him suddenly into the national limelight. The book was the Book of Mormon.

What the Book of Mormon preached was cause enough for consternation among its early readers. But how it came to be in the first place—young Joseph's story, anyway—made it almost overnight the best-read and most loudly hooted book on the western frontier.

The publication of the book had its antecedents in an event that occurred the evening of September 21, 1823, as Joseph, having retired for the night in his parents' home, began praying to God. Specifically, he asked forgiveness for the sins and follies he had listed in writing following his first vision.

While in the act of calling upon God, he later related, Joseph discovered a light appearing in his room. The light grew in intensity, and when it was very bright, a "glorious personage" appeared as if standing on air and wearing a white robe.

Calling Joseph by name, he said that he was Moroni, a messenger sent from the presence of God. God had work for Joseph to do. The angel said that there was a book deposited, written upon gold plates with an account of the former inhabitants of this continent and containing the fullness of the everlasting Gospel as delivered by the Savior to these ancients. There were two stones in silver bows fastened to a breastplate, the angel continued; these constituted the Urim and Thummim and were deposited with the plates. The possession and use of these stones made one a "seer" in ancient times, whom God had prepared for translating the book.

Moroni, according to Joseph, quoted from the prophecies of the Old Testament, with variations from the way they read in existing Bibles.

Moroni told Joseph that later, when he obtained the plates and stones, he should show them to no person except those he was commanded to show them to. If Joseph disobeyed, the angel cautioned, he would be destroyed. As Moroni spoke, a "distinct vision" opened to Joseph's mind of the place where the plates were deposited.

The light then gathered about this personage, Joseph remembered, until the room was again dark and the apparition ascended into heaven.

As Joseph mused on what had happened, the heavenly messenger reappeared, relating again precisely the first message, and informed the boy of the "grievous judgements" to come to earth in this generation.

Joseph was visited by the messenger a third time that night with the same message. This time, he cautioned Joseph not to be tempted by Satan, that the plates should be used only to glorify God and build up his kingdom.

The next day, Joseph encountered Moroni again. Too tired to work, the boy was sent home from his father's fields. While trying to cross a fence, Joseph fell helpless to the ground and was again surrounded by the "heavenly light." This time, Joseph wrote, he was told to relate his vision and the commandments to his father. Joseph obeyed, and his father said he should do as commanded.

"I left the field, and went to the place where the messenger had told me the plates were deposited; and owing to the distinctiveness of the vision which I had had concerning it, I knew the place the instant I arrived there."

The place where the commandment led Joseph is a hill of considerable size about four miles south of Palmyra. Today, one of the most impressive monuments in western New York stands there. Bathed in floodlights by night, visited by tens of thousands every year, it marks The Hill Comorah, known locally as "Mormon Hill." It was there, in 1823, that Joseph saw, as he had seen in his vision, the weathered surface of a rounded stone, the edges of which were covered with soil and grass. Using a pole as a lever, as he recorded the event later, Joseph raised the stone to find a box beneath it. In the bottom of the box were two stones laid crosswise, upon which lay the plates described in the vision.

Eagerly, Joseph reached into the box but quickly withdrew his arm as a shock of electricity coursed through it. Two further attempts produced the same painful result. When Joseph cried aloud in his bewilderment, he recalled later, the Angel Moroni appeared beside him as he had in the vision the previous evening. When Joseph asked why he could not touch the plates without being shocked, Moroni replied, "Because you have not kept the commandments of the Lord."

Humbled and repentant, Joseph now kneeled, admitting to himself that perhaps in his journey to the hill thoughts of wealth, ease, and fame had dominated his mind instead of the loftier goal specified in his vision. It was obvious to Joseph that the plates would not be his, at least not yet, and he agreed to the Angel Moroni's admonition that he must return to The Hill Comorah each year on the same day. On his fourth pilgrimage to the hill—September 22, 1827—the "gold book," which was the finest tangible evidence of "Mormonism," was delivered to him with specific charges for its care.

"The same heavenly messenger delivered them up to me," Joseph later wrote, "with this charge: That I should be responsible for them; that if I should let them go carelessly, or through any neglect of mine, I should be cut off; but that if I would use all my endeavors to preserve them until he, the messenger, should call for them, they should be protected."

That would take some tall doing. Whereas the vision in Joseph's room had produced only mockery among his peers, Joseph's report that he had received gold plates that had lain hidden in a hillside for fourteen hundred years was the first in a series of events that eventually tossed his church into perpetual flight from its enemies and led him to martyrdom. According to Joseph's own account of what followed, ". . . as soon as the news of this discovery was made known, false reports, misrepresentations, and slander flew as on the wings of the wind in every direction; the house was frequently beset by mobs and evil designing persons. Several times I was shot at, and very narrowly escaped, and every device was made use of to get the plates away from me." That description is found in the famous Wentworth Letter, a condensed history of his life and the history of the church as sent to John Wentworth, editor and proprietor of the Chicago *Democrat*.

According to his mother, Joseph managed to thwart the would-be thieves by moving the plates from one hiding place to another. First he secreted them in a hollow birch log, later in a chest in his father's home, still later beneath the hearthstone in the family living room, and finally in a cooper's shop across the street from where the Smiths lived.

Joseph by now had reached adulthood. Two months before receiving the plates, he married Emma Hale, of Harmony Township, Pennsylvania. He had met her two years earlier, when he boarded in her father's home. In December 1827, three months after receiving the plates, Joseph was invited to move into the Hale home once again; deciding that Harmony could be an ideal place to complete the arduous task of translating the plates into English, Joseph happily accepted.

Joseph began copying onto paper several of the strange characters of the plates. Some he translated by means of the Urim and Thummim, the "interpreters" he had received with the plates. Joseph knew no "reformed Egyptian," but the task of translation did not daunt him, and by June 1829, later with the assistance of Oliver Cowdery, a schoolteacher who had become a close friend, the work was at last completed.

The following, from *The Restored Church*, first written in 1836 as a text for Mormon seminaries and schools, is essentially the story told by the Book of Mormon:

About 600 years before Christ, a small group of Israelites, warned of an impending destruction of their native city, Jerusalem, left their homeland and journeyed southward. Eventually they crossed the ocean in a ship of their own construction and landed somewhere on the American continent. Here they proceeded to develop a civilization, but soon divided into two groups. The most advanced group were white of skin and were firm believers in the God of Israel, and the Hebrew Scriptures, a copy of which had been carried to America. The group was called, "Nephites," after their leader. The less advanced group, called after their first leader, "Lamanites," became darker skinned, due to a curse of God upon them for their rebellious spirit. The two people were often at war with each other, the Nephites being at times forced to abandon their homes and seek new ones.

Some four hundred years after the arrival in America, the Nephites, in seeking a new place for settlement, encountered another people, the Mule-kites, who, like themselves, were Israelites who had left Jerusalem because of the political disturbances at the time of King Zedekiah (about 587 B.C.). The two people united under the Nephite ruler, King Mosiah.

During the reign of this king, an exploring expedition encountered extensive ruins of an earlier civilization and discovered a writing in very ancient characters upon 24 gold plates. These were read by aid of the power of God, and found to contain a history of a race called Jaredites, who had formerly occupied the land as a numerous people. These former inhabitants, according to the account, had left the vicinity of the Tower of Babel at the time of the Confusion of Tongues, and finally crossed the ocean in eight peculiar barges, to America. Here their civilization had flourished for better than two thousand years, finally destroying itself by internal wars.

The warfare between the dark-skinned Lamanites and the now enlarged group of Nephites continued, with some long periods of peace, during which trade and commerce flourished between the nations. A rather remarkable civilization was developed, which involved the mining, smelting and casting of metals, the weaving of fine cloths and fabrics, the use of coins, the domestica-tion of animals, the building of ships, and the erection of great cities of stone, and cement.

The Nephites developed two forms of written language, a revised Hebrew and a reformed or revised Egyptian. Art reached a high stage, even the exteriors of buildings being highly decorated with artistic designs. The sci-ences of astronomy and mathematics were unsurpassed in their day, and the accomplishments of their engineers incite the wonder of the present world.

These people became especially advanced in their religious concepts. Temples were erected to God, comparable to the Temple of Solomon. They had prophets who communed with the Most High and taught their people a wholesome philosophy of life. These prophets labored without salary, per-formed miracles like unto those of the prophets of Israel, and kept sacred records of their people. Great personalities were developed. Nephi, the first of that name, is one of the finest characters of all time. King Benjamin, one of the most beloved monarchs, and Moroni, one of the most skilled commanders of men.

The Nephites firmly believed in a Messiah who was to come to Jerusalem and, through signs which had been given by their prophets, knew the day of his birth on the old continent, and of his subsequent death.

At the time of the crucifixion a terrible storm broke over the cities of the Nephites and Lamanites. This, with disturbances of the earth and volcanic eruptions, destroyed a large part of the population, and buried many of their cities.

Following His resurrection, Christ appeared to the remnant of the Nephites on the American continent, preached great sermons to them, and ministered unto them. Having chosen twelve disciples among them and provided for the organization of His Church, with the proper ordinances, He departed from them into the heavens.

So great was the effect of the destruction and the visitation, that all wars ceased between peoples and a Golden Era of prosperity began. There were no rich or poor, but all lived in a happy brotherhood. This era lasted nearly two hundred years before dissension broke out again. A series of wars followed. In the last of these, the victorious Lamanites annihilated the Nephites as a separate people. Prior to this great destruction, Mormon, a great Nephite general and prophet, compiled the records of his people, and made an abridgement of them. His son, Moroni, survived the greater part of the destructions and prior to his death hid the completed records (about 420 A.D.). It is the abridgment by Mormon, and some of the writings of his son Moroni, which came into Joseph Smith's hands. The translation thereof constitutes the Book of Mormon.

Joseph had little money. Finding a way to get the startling book printed seemed at first a problem. But, through a friend, Martin Harris, who raised the necesssary three thousand dollars by borrowing against his farm, he managed to get the first five thousand copies published by a printing firm in Palmyra. The volume contained more than five hundred pages, and Joseph named it the Book of Mormon.

A letter preserved at Yale University suggests the kind of feverish excitement the book was about to generate along the frontier of nineteenth-century America. In the letter, written on February 12, 1830—a full month before the five thousand copies were placed on sale—Lucius Fenn, of Covert, in upstate New York, wrote a Connecticut neighbor about the curious volume being published fifty miles away, in Palmyra. Fenn briefly reviewed how the book had come to exist, that it was a bible concealed in a hillside for fourteen centuries and which an angel had only now revealed to a man named Joseph who could not read English, let alone Egyptian, but who had translated the book's gold leaves nevertheless, and predicted the gold book would soon become the news of the day.

"It speaks of the Milleniam [sic] day and tells when it is going to take place. . . . Some people think that it is all a speculation and some think that something is going to take place different from what has been. For my part, I do not know how it will be but it is something singular to me." He could only conclude, Fenn added, that as the book reached the public, there would be ". . . a greater outpouring of the spirit than ever."

When five thousand copies of the Book of Mormon reached virtually every hamlet along the American frontier, the outpouring was lively indeed, but scarcely was it complimentary. One newspaper, the Palmyra *Freeman*, immediately labeled it "the greatest piece of superstition that has ever come within our knowledge." Others called it a "fraud" and a "hoax," words that to many equally described the "Prophet of Palmyra," an unknown farm boy only a decade before who now had suddenly become one of the most famous personages in American religion.

Although the book attracted converts to Joseph's beliefs—Parley P. Pratt, Orson Pratt, Brigham Young, Heber C. Kimball, and Sidney Rigdon, later all to become leaders in the church—it stirred instant anger in other quarters. It seemed to invite either faith or antagonism; there was no middle ground.

Formal organization of the Church of Jesus Christ of Latter-day Saints soon followed (later changed, its name at first was shorter: the Church of Christ.) Six men participated formally on founding day, April 6, 1830, in the home of Peter Whitmer, in Fayette Township, Seneca, New York: Joseph and his brothers Hyrum and Samuel H., Oliver Cowdery, and the brothers David and Peter Whitmer, Jr. Joseph had been "divinely chosen" to lead the church; while the meeting was in session, he claimed he had had a revelation in which he had been designated as "a seer, a prophet and apostle of Jesus Christ." Since then he has been referred to in church parlance as "the Prophet."

The harassment that was to hound Joseph Smith to his grave began almost immediately. No sooner was the LDS church organized than he was arrested in Colesville, New York, while conducting a service. The charge was that Joseph was a "disorderly person setting the country in an uproar by preaching from the Book of Mormon." Obviously flimsy, it did not stick, and Joseph was acquitted by a court. But immediately after he was exonerated, he was arrested a second time on the same charge, of which he was acquitted again.

Jackson County, Missouri, and Kirtland, Ohio, became the two major centers of Mormonism in 1831, but less than a decade passed before Joseph and the Saints were driven from both. The pressures against the Mormons developed simultaneously in those two states.

Mormon missionaries had enjoyed considerable success in Ohio, and the state seemed a logical place where Joseph might establish a new branch of the LDS church. There was another good reason: Ohio, being closer to the western frontier of America than New York, offered a greater degree of freedom from Mormon antagonists than eastern states did. Joseph never intended Kirtland to be the Mormons' permanent Zion; that was to be established farther to the west, "by the borders of the Lamanites," its exact site unannounced in 1831. Yet the church's early years in the Ohio community were fruitful ones. It was a time of organization, a time of charting the future course of the Saints, and a time to construct the Mormons' first temple to God.

Modest by today's standards, the Kirtland temple was an imposing structure in its day, representing three years of diligent labor by the city's Mormons and a healthy slice of their tithed dollars. Dedicated in 1836, it measured 59 by 80 feet in area, and rose 110 feet to its spire. Its walls were of quarried stone covered with plaster, its interior beautifully finished with painted native woods.

As the Kirtland church grew in membership and spiritual strength, internal problems began to work against the Mormons. In January 1837, the Kirtland Safety Society Anti-banking Company was organized, among whose officers were authorities of the church. It was a bad year for business. Only a few months after the company opened its doors, a financial depression swept the country; business failures in New York alone exceeded one hundred million dollars. The Kirtland institution was swept under. Many church members who had invested their life savings in it blamed not the national condition but management of the church company; disgruntled, they began bolting church ranks. Increasing hostility from the Kirtland apostates and growing opposition to the "peculiar Mormons" among their Gentile neighbors shaped the doom of Mormonism in Kirtland.

By December 1837, Brigham Young had had enough; he left the city, never to return. Joseph Smith, accompanied by Sidney Rigdon, fled to Missouri the following month, never again to return to the community where so large and important a part of the Prophet's work was done.

In 1831, another important branch of the church had been established, in Jackson County, Missouri, a site that had been revealed to Joseph as the New Jerusalem, a gathering place for the Saints. Within a short time, it became a focal point of Mormon activities. In June 1832, the church established its first newspaper, a monthly, *The Evening and Morning Star*, with William W. Phelps appointed as editor. By the end of the year, nearly twelve hundred Mormons—most of them recent converts through the church's vigorous missionary program—had gathered in Missouri, and while the church's leaders could bask in the growing acceptance of the new religious doctrine, the embers of antagonism were already beginning to glow.

Ohio had at least been a "northern" state in the political division of the country over the increasingly volatile issue of slavery. Missouri was definitely "southern." The Mormons, who had originated in New York and settled in Ohio, were regarded as invading "Yankees" with views on slavery to match. The church had taken no stand for slavery or against it, but that made little difference to the Mormons' Missouri neighbors. In 1832, a mob broke windows in Mormon homes in Jackson County and fired Mormon haystacks. In the following year they destroyed the Mormons' printing press.

The opposition grew more organized. In the spring of 1832, the Reverend

Finis Ewing whipped up Gentile antagonism by publishing a document that charged, among other things, that "the Mormons are the common enemies of mankind and ought to be destroyed." Mass meetings followed. Edward Patridge, the bishop of the church in the new Missouri Zion, was taken from his home and tarred and feathered in a public square. (The same thing had already happened that year to Joseph Smith in Hiram, Ohio.)

Joseph had clung to his belief that the Jackson County troubles were temporary and that Zion would remain there; as late as October 19, 1833, he had the written assurance of the statehouse that Mormon grievances would receive a sympathetic hearing in state courts. The mob wanted it otherwise. On October 31, an unidentified gang armed with guns unroofed and demolished ten Mormon dwellings west of the Big Blue River; the following day, another attacked a Mormon prairie settlement, and a third drove a group of Saints from their homes in Independence.

By mid-November 1833, the Mormons were ready to leave. They fled to the countryside from Independence, an estimated 233 of their homes destroyed behind them. Many took temporary refuge in Clay County, across the Missouri River from Jackson County. To sustain themselves and their families, they worked for local settlers. The log houses they built for shelter were only temporary, and they longed for the peace and solitude that had eluded them elsewhere in the state.

Northeast of Clay County lay a large, wild, untamed expanse of prairie; the Mormons saw this as a place where perhaps they could at last be by themselves. Caldwell County therefore became yet another refuge, but only a fleeting one, for the hounded Saints.

Still believing that the original Zion could be saved, Joseph Smith, in 1834, sent help in the form of two hundred volunteers from Kirtland. Organized in companies of tens, fifties, and hundreds with officers directing each, the column became known as "Zion's Camp," and its thousand-mile march from Kirtland to Jackson County is a stirring chapter in Mormon history. The Prophet had counted on support from the Missouri state militia, however, and when it failed to materialize, Zion's Camp lost its potential muscle. The experiment was a psychological success, but it had no real influence.

Soon the "Mormon problem" was no longer a local issue in Missouri; it had inflamed the entire state, and as the decade approached its conclusion, violence had reached a critical stage. The Saints still had high hopes for solace in Caldwell County. It had been declared official "Mormon Country" by the Missouri Legislature in 1836. Assuming that official blessing offered them some measure of relief, the population of Far West—the main community in Caldwell County—had reached five thousand by 1838, and the community itself expanded to include two hotels, a printing plant, blacksmith shops, stores and one hundred fifty houses and farms.

On July 4, 1838, Far West's Mormons laid the cornerstone for a temple even larger than their first one, at Kirtland. It was to measure 110 by 80 feet. The conditions of peace and progress that they celebrated on that Independence Day were short-lived, however.

On August 6, barely a month later, anti-Mormonism exploded into a full-fledged civil war.

As if the Mormons hadn't enough troubles, Missouri had elected a new governor, an admitted Mormon-hater named Lilburn W. Boggs. Before Boggs's inauguration, the political leaders of Missouri's counties behaved as if their jurisdictions were sovereign mini-states as far as the "Mormon question" was concerned, and one inflammatory border incident led to another. Boggs galvanized the entire state into action and, after two more months of bloody skirmishes between Mormons and non-Mormons, issued what some historians have called the "extermination order."

"Your orders," Boggs instructed his statewide militia after a particularly noisy battle that resulted in at least one fatality and several injuries, "are . . . to hasten your operations with all possible speed. The Mormons must be treated as enemies, and must be exterminated or driven from the state if necessary for the public peace—their outrages are beyond all description."

The Saints' last hopes for peace in Missouri were at an end. Although Boggs's militia had officially been ordered to disperse the anti-Mormon mobs, the "extermination order" had effectively contermanded that purpose. Three days following the order, a company of marauding militia under the command of Colonel William O. Jennings descended upon thirty Mormon families who had fled to the comparative safety of Haun's Mill, a small settlement on Shoal Creek.

Nineteen Mormon men and boys were slain and at least a dozen wounded. The attackers looted the village, hauling off precious goods and wagons as well as a dozen horses. The survivors, fearing a return of the vigilantes, hastily threw their dead into a well and fled to Far West.

In Mormon history, the Haun's Mill Massacre is a black page of sorrow, shame, and simmering anger. Joseph Young, who had arrived at Haun's Mill from Kirtland only two days before, recalled the grim details of the incident in an affidavit published by the church in 1902:

After daylight appeared, some four or five men, who with myself, had escaped with our lives from the horrid massacre, and who repaired as soon as possible to the mills, to learn the condition of our friends, whose fate we had but too truly anticipated. When we arrived at the house of Mr. Haun, we found Mr. Merrick's body lying in the rear of the house, Mr. McBride's body in front, literally mangled from head to foot. We were informed by Mrs. Rebecca Judd, who was an eye witness, that he was shot with his own gun, after he had given it up, and then was cut to pieces with a corn cutter by a Mr. Rogers of Daviess

County . . . who has since boasted of this act of savage barbarity. . . . The place of burial was a vault in the ground, formerly intended for a well, into which we threw the bodies of our friends promiscuously. Among those slain I will mention Sardius Smith, son of Warren Smith, about nine years old, who, through fear, had crawled under the bellows in the shop, where he remained till the massacre was over, when he was discovered by a Mr. Glaze, of Carroll county, who presented the rifle near the boy's head, and literally blowed off the upper part of it.

Clearly, the time had come for the Mormons to flee from Missouri as they had fled Ohio. By early 1839, most of them were gone.

But there was a postscript to the Mormons' Missouri troubles. Joseph Smith, his brother Hyrum, Sidney Rigdon, and four other leaders were sentenced to be shot the morning after a summary court-martial found them guilty of treason. General A. W. Doniphan of the militia, Joseph's attorney, denounced the sentence as "cold-blooded murder," refused to carry it out, and threatened to remove his troops if the mob opposed him on the matter. Relenting, General S. D. Lucas of Jackson County had the prisoners taken to Independence instead. The militia there paraded them through the streets, where they were heaped with abuse, before turning them over to civil authorities in Richmond, where fifty-nine other Mormons were already under arrest. The charges varied from "treason, murder, arson, larceny, theft and stealing" to "having fought the State of Missouri; murder, for the death of several militiamen; and arson, larceny, theft, and stealing, for their counter-depradations."

In his Liberty jail cell, Joseph seethed with anger. "The murders at Haun's Mill, the exterminating order of Governor Boggs, and the one-sided rascally proceedings of the Legislature," the Prophet wrote, "have damned the State of Missouri to all eternity."

Despite its outrages against Joseph and his followers, Missouri did not seem to know what to do with him. The prisoners languished in the Liberty jail for a full half year, until April 1839, when the governor issued an order for their transfer to Boone County.

Meanwhile, under the leadership of Brigham Young, the evacuation of the Mormons from Missouri was organized, in January 1839. Thousands of Saints crossed the frozen Mississippi during the winter and early spring. Most of them converged in the countryside near Quincy, south of the swamp that was to become Nauvoo.

The "Missouri War" had cost both Mormon and non-Mormon dearly: In their haste to flee the state, the Saints left nearly everything behind except their faith. Missouri had spent more than two hundred thousand—a princely sum in those days—on the militia; at one time, fully three thousand Missourians were under arms, not counting the unofficial vigilantes who roamed at will without interference from the official home guard.

Many Mormons died from exposure or illness in their flight to Illinois; the loss of Missouri property has been estimated at more than one and a half million dollars.

Along the banks of the Mississippi, in both Iowa and Illinois, the Saints erected crude tents and dug cave-like dwellings from the riverbank as protection from the cold. Their food was mainly corn, and there was precious little of that. They petitioned both Governor Boggs and the Missouri legislature for redress of wrongs, but although the legislature voted to reimburse the expenses of its militia, it ignored the request of refugees it had persecuted.

In perhaps the darkest hour of the church up to that time, a few bitter and disappointed bolted its ranks. Already in 1837, Oliver Cowdery, who had been Joseph Smith's closest confidant in the earliest days of the church, had been excommunicated; David Whitmer, another close associate, was likewise banished after the Missouri exodus. Some of the dissidents formed splinter groups of Mormonism; others drifted out of the new religion entirely.

But in Liberty, despite the ugly scars of the Missouri war, Joseph Smith remained remarkably tolerant of his enemies. "We ought always to be aware of those prejudices which sometimes so strangely present themselves," he wrote in a letter from his cell on March 25, 1839, "and are so congenial to human nature, against our friends, neighbors, and brethren of the world, who choose to differ from us in opinion and in matters of faith. Our religion is between us and our God. Their religion is between them and their God."

By April 1839, though Governor Boggs persisted in his efforts to prosecute Joseph and his fellow prisoners in Liberty, Missouri had wearied of the eight-month war. When the transfer to Boone County was under way, Joseph's Liberty jailers deliberately got drunk, allowed the prisoners to buy two horses, and dozed in a drunken stupor while the Mormons escaped. Joseph and the other freed Saints headed directly for the Illinos border, crossing the Mississippi in April.

By then, the Saints who had already left Missouri were recovering from the bitter winter of 1838–39. Within a month, Joseph purchased two sites at Commerce, on the eastern bank of the Mississippi, fifty miles north of Quincy. There were far more attractive townsites available, some said; the location was deserted swampland infested by mosquitoes. But, with the help of God, the Mormons would attempt to build there, once again, a new Zion. And they would soon rename the community. It would become Nauvoo.

"These persecuted people," the Cleveland *Herald* wrote of them in December 1839, "are going ahead." While Missouri's Governor Boggs repeatedly tried to get Illinois to extradite the escaped Joseph Smith, the Prophet himself was leading the construction of a community that would soon be the pride of the state. Two months after the *Herald*'s editorial, Nauvoo was formerly incorporated and granted an extraordinary municipal charter with privileges that made it virtually an autonomous city-state. One of those voting for the generous charter was a young Springfield lawyer named Abraham Lincoln.

The losses in Missouri had been heavy. Joseph was determined that, one way or another, the Saints would be repaid. If Missouri refused to make restitution, would the federal government do so? In company with Judge Elias Higbee, Joseph went to Washington, D.C., in October 1839 and laid his case before President Martin Van Buren. The President was sympathetic but replied that, constitutionally, his hands were tied, especially by the separation of powers between national and state governments. "Gentlemen, your cause is just," he is reported to have said, "but I can do nothing for you."

On his return to Nauvoo the following March, Joseph was astonished to hear unsettling news in the young city. A crime wave of considerable proportions had developed along the river during his absence; since the Mormons had settled there during the same period, said old-time residents, were they not to blame? Once again, the Saints found themselves at the bottom of a spiral that eventually prodded them into another flight.

The first hint of serious trouble occurred on July 7, 1840, when a party from Tully, Missouri, found a large cache of stolen goods near the Mississippi in Nauvoo. Four Mormons in the vicinity were kidnaped and returned to Tully for questioning. Using pressure––the "persuasion" certainly included some vigorous arm-twisting if not downright beatings—they produced confessions from the four men.

Nauvoo's Mormons claimed the incident was a frame-up. They appealed to Illinois Governor Carlin, who in turn lodged a formal protest with the Mormons' most ardent antagonist across the river, Lilburn Boggs. Boggs, however, convinced Carlin that there may have been some truth in the accusation. At any rate, the Mormons suddenly lost another sympathizer, and not taking any chances, Joseph went into hiding. Boggs furiously demanded his extradition once again.

Just as it had in Missouri, a cycle of predictable events was unfolding along the bank of the Mississippi in Illinois, and Nauvoo's downfall was irrevocably sealed. Only, this time, there were more than religious, political, and social differences driving a wedge between the Mormons and their Gentile neighbors.

As citizens of the second-largest city in Illinois, Nauvoo's Mormons represented a solid voting bloc that raised suspicious eyebrows throughout the state. The Nauvoo charter, its critics claimed, had made the community a virtual small kingdom practically exempt from outside control, even though that charter specifically maintained state laws. Under authorization of the charter, Joseph, returned from self-imposed exile, had created the Nauvoo Legion, a civil militia complete with uniforms that was the largest military body in the nation except for the United States Army. Rumors about the growing military flew about the state of Illinois; did Joseph Smith, many wondered aloud, intend to use it to take over the country, perhaps in righteous indignation over having his pleas for justice ignored?

Adding further fuel to the fires of suspicion and resentment was the Nauvoo temple. Even more extravagant than the completed edifice at Kirtland and the planned but never finished one at Far West, its towering position on the Nauvoo hillside became to many a symbol of impending Mormon dominance.

Nevertheless, to many scholars and historians, the most divisive issue between the Mormon and Gentile worlds was a social practice that was to cause the Mormons trouble until late in the nineteenth century. Even today, many non-Mormons think of it first whenever the word "Mormon" is mentioned. That issue was, of course, polygamy, or what the church called plural marriage.

There were persistent rumors that some Mormons were engaging in polygamy, but even after Joseph Smith put into writing his revelation on "Eternity of the Marriage Covenant and Plural Marriage" and read it to the Nauvoo High Council on July 12, 1843, the practice was not preached or acknowledged by the church, and Joseph himself denied that it existed.

There was nothing illegal about polygamy at the time. Not until many years had passed, and the issue had created such divisiveness and hatred between the Mormon and Gentile worlds, did a pressured Congress finally outlaw it, in 1862. The Anti-Bigamy Act, not enforced until the mid-1870s, was the subject of several court challenges, which led to a Supreme Court decision in 1879 sustaining its constitutionality. An amendment, the Edmunds Bill of 1882, strengthened the law and led to a new and sustained campaign against polygamists. Several other court decisions and laws affected the church and its members' practice of plural marriage. In 1887, the Edmunds-Tucker Act formally disincorporated the church after it had moved to Utah. This was the final straw, which broke Mormon resistance to the practice and led to its abandonment by church edict in 1890.

All of this came much later, of course. In the 1840s, polygamy was not a legal matter to its opponents. It was a policy diametrically opposed to the long-cherished concept of monogamous marriage in America.

"The sexual mores of the frontier were exceedingly free," historian Bernard DeVoto points out in his *Year of Decision: 1846*, "but, as in all the rest of America, the monogamous family was at the core of its institutions. In Putney, Vermont, a much less turbulent society than the Mormons found in Missouri and Illinois, the mere rumor that John Humphrey Noyes's handful of followers were talking beyond monogamy sufficed to expel them to the New York forest. On the frontier polygamy was dynamite with the fuse burning."

Three facts, too seldom discussed in sensationalized reports of the time, should be understood about nineteenth-century Mormon polygamy. First, the Mormons regarded the plural marriage as an act sanctified by God. Mormonism claims to be a restoration of God's work in all previous dispensations; as the Mormon Church correctly points out, the Old Testament teaches that the patriarchs—men favored by God in ancient times—had more than one wife, under divine sanction. To the Mormon, then, the plural marriage was something that God not merely permitted but *directed*.

Further, the practice was carefully controlled by the church so that abuses of the system would be avoided if possible. In theory, the first wife's permission was required before her husband could take a second wife (although this was not universally observed), and the man had to have the approval of church leaders. This approval meant the candidate had demonstrated his worthiness by faithfully observing strict Mormon standards of morality and faithfulness to religious obligations. Polygamy was not "popular" among Mormons, and it was left to local and general church leaders to set the example. Two thirds of the polygamists studied in one survey, for instance, married only one additional wife.

Lastly, if claims of the Mormon Church are correct, polygamy was *not* the widespread practice many believed it to be. Only 5 per cent of Mormons were involved before plural marriages officially ended, in the late-nineteenth century, and those who refused to desist at that time were excommunicated.

Sanctioned by God or not, reports of "legalized" polygamy gave Mormon foes in Illinois a new reason for increasing their pressure. Two years before Joseph announced his revelation on plural marriage, an anti-Mormon party was organized by Thomas Sharp to counter the Mormons' majority in Hancock County. Nauvoo's *Times and Seasons* had begun publication in 1839; Sharp's vitriolic Warsaw *Signal* became the anti-Mormon newspaper, a rallying cry of the county's unrelenting foes of Mormonism and all it stood for.

To Sharp and the *Signal*, Joseph Smith's announcement that he intended to run for the national presidency in 1844 was a confirmation of the anti-Mormons' worst fears: the Mormons, not content to gather and multiply only in Illinois, the reasoning went, now sought a national stage from which to impose their "peculiar" religious doctrine, and social and economic programs. (Joseph was nominated by Illinois's new "Reform Party" in 1844, but his assassination in June of that year occurred before the national campaign began. Illinois lay north of the Mason-Dixon Line, and the fact that abolition of slavery was the fifth plank in his presidential platform—he proposed that the slaves' freedom be paid for by selling public lands—was not as volatile an anti-Mormon issue in that state as it had been in Missouri. Yet the other issues—Mormon economics, the rapidly growing ranks of the church, and the increasing political strength of the Mormons—burned as hotly. It is doubtful that Joseph ever believed he could win the nation's highest office, but his candidacy offered a chance to lay the Mormons' cause before the American people.)

By mid-1842, the anti-Mormon war in Illinois was gathering steam.

On the evening of May 6, 1842, Lilburn W. Boggs, now retired from the Missouri governor's office, was shot and wounded while sitting in his home.

Although the pistol was found on the grounds, the assailant himself escaped. Boggs lingered near death for several days but recovered to launch a new assault against his old enemies, who now lay across the Mississippi.

Since their anti-Boggs feelings were well known, the Mormons were the obvious prime suspects in the murder attempt. Boggs filed an affadavit accusing Orrin Porter Rockwell, a member of the LDS, of the crime. Joseph was named as an accessory before the fact, and Boggs demanded that Illinois extradite the two men to stand trial. A warrant was issued and the accused pair were arrested but released on writs of habeas corpus.

Like Joseph, Lilburn Boggs was a determined man. The fact that a court had freed the men he accused made little difference. Moreover, he now had an ally within Nauvoo who was, of all things, a Mormon himself. Dr. John C. Bennett had joined the Mormon movement as early as 1840. Bennett was a gifted man, dapper, well educated, energetic in his Mormonism, with a valuable background as a college professor, physician, and shrewd politician. Within nine months after his arrival in Nauvoo, Bennett began ascending to a position of power second perhaps only to that of Joseph himself. Among other accomplishments, as head of the Nauvoo Legion he built that force to its prominent status, and he did much to upgrade Nauvoo University. Joseph later discovered to his horror, however, that Bennett had been unstable in the past and had been involved in a number of moral offenses.

Publicly denounced by Joseph, formally cut off from the church, Bennett struck back by publishing a series of newspaper articles which he later expanded into a book. They discussed polygamy well before Joseph's revelation before the Nauvoo High Council. He suggested that Nauvoo had become a depot for stolen goods. He charged that the Mormons hoped to dominate not only the United States but the world. And after the attempted murder of Boggs, he joined the former Missouri governor in a series of harassing attempts to bring Joseph back to Missouri once again for trial.

Joseph went into hiding. He spent his time writing a number of epistles further defining the doctrine of the church. He also took a number of wives, including the poet Eliza R. Snow.

Through the latter half of 1842 and the first part of 1843, Boggs intensified his vendetta against the exiled prophet. At the urging of Illinois Governor Thomas Ford, elected with the support of the state's Mormon vote in 1842, Joseph eventually agreed to go to Springfield, Illinois—the state capital—where he hoped the Illinois Supreme Court would decide his innocence once and for all. The high court did clear Joseph, but Boggs was far from through.

Porter Rockwell had returned to Missouri where he was arrested on March 4, 1843, and charged with shooting Boggs. Boggs wanted Joseph jailed too. He evidently decided that if a direct approach would not work, deception might. Even the Illinois Supreme Court's decision in Joseph's favor did not seem to daunt the enraged Missourian. Posing as Mormon missionaries, the Jackson County sheriff and an Illinois constable managed to reach Joseph while the Prophet was visiting relatives in northern Illinois. Joseph was arrested. He may not have known that a boat was waiting at Rock Island, with a head of steam already up, in which he would be spirited down the Mississippi to a crossing into Missouri, but he managed to elude the trap through a series of deft maneuvers, including a change of venue, and a bit of political arm twisting in which he arranged to be tried not in Missouri but in Nauvoo. Once there, Joseph reasoned, he would be released on another writ of habeas corpus.

Instead of returning to Nauvoo as an accused man, however, Joseph rode home—with a troop of Mormon horsemen as escort—as a hero. It was July 4, 1843, and with the double occasion of Joseph's triumphant return and the nation's Independence Day, the Saints turned out for the noisiest celebration in the city's history. A notable absentee was Porter Rockwell; not until many more months passed did Missouri, apparently accepting the fact it had no real case against Rockwell, finally free him for good.

But Nauvoo's respite from the mob was only a fleeting one. Fanned by the flames of Joseph's revelation on plural marriage on July 12, resentment against the Mormons increased among Nauvoo's Gentile neighbors. Furthermore, Lilburn Boggs had stepped up his campaign with Illinois Governor Ford to have Joseph extradited. Elected largely by the Mormon vote, Ford had been regarded as a friend of the church, but it was election time again, and public sentiment was rising against him; Ford sent word to Joseph that the time had come for the Saints to leave the state.

Joseph and his fellow Mormons at first ignored the dictum, and even though he was still ill from a poisoning months before, he continued to lead Nauvoo in one of its busiest periods of growth. Both Nauvoo and Joseph had attracted hundreds of travelers and visitors, who were warmly welcomed and entertained at huge dinner parties. Construction of the temple continued at a steady pace, and life in Nauvoo settled down for a time.

But it could not be for long. Spurred by ringing denunciations of Mormonism by Tom Sharp's Warsaw *Signal*, the anti-Mormon forces of Hancock County, though outnumbered, gathered to launch a "wolf hunt" of military-like brilliance. They were abetted by growing dissension within the church.

The spark that exploded the power keg was ignited on June 10, 1844. Three days earlier, on June 7, William Law, who had broken with Joseph to organize a rival church in Nauvoo, published the first issue of the Nauvoo *Expositor*. The newspaper's sole purpose was clearly the abolition of Joseph Smith and the Mormon Church in Nauvoo. Its single issue accused the Mormons of "tyranny and oppression," called polygamy "an abomination" not far removed from prostitution, and accused Joseph and the apostles of criminal acts.

By the almost unlimited authority granted it under Nauvoo's city charter, the Nauvoo Council declared the *Expositor* a public nuisance and an incensed Joseph ordered the paper's presses destroyed.

The powder keg exploded.

Joseph and other members of the Nauvoo City Council were charged with riot. Justice of the Peace Robert Smith, in nearby Carthage, set bail at five hundred dollars, which was quickly posted. Sniffing blood, the Hancock County "mobocrats," as the Mormons termed them, were not content to wait for the law to take its course. From various corners of the county, they began converging on Nauvoo, and their mood was anything but conciliatory. Worried, Joseph declared martial law and quickly mobilized the city's militia. Governor Ford, concerned that he might soon have a full-fledged civil war on his hands, called out the state militia.

Meanwhile, for declaring martial law, an apparent overreaching of his authority even under the generous terms of Nauvoo's charter, Joseph and his brother Hyrum were now slapped with a second and far more grave charge: treason. In Illinois, that was a capital offense. Fearing the consequences for himself and his people, Joseph fled in the night across the Mississippi River. Stung by accusations that his flight was an act of cowardice, however, and that he was a deserter, he returned to Nauvoo and agreed to submit to arrest.

No bond was set at this time; since Joseph was charged with a capital offense, the law denied bond without an appearance before a circuit court. And the nearest circuit court was a full day's ride away. The justice of the peace who arraigned Joseph and Hyrum adjourned the arraignment without a hearing, ordering the prisoners held until June 29. By all standards of law, given the bloodthirsty, lynch-crazy mood of Hancock County's anti-Mormons, that act was outrageously unfair.

On the morning of June 24, the Prophet, his plea for an armed posse to protect him denied by Governor Ford, set out on horseback under guard, with several Mormon associates riding nearby just in case, for Carthage, the Hancock County seat. There he was placed in the city jail.

Joseph's final days were at hand. "I prophesy in the name of the Lord," he had told members of Governor Ford's militia in Nauvoo, "that you shall witness scenes of blood and sorrow to your entire satisfaction. Your souls shall be perfectly satiated with blood, and many of you now present shall have an opportunity to face the cannon's mouth from sources you think not of, and those people that desire this great evil upon men and my brethren shall be filled with sorrow because of the scenes of desolation and distress that await them."

On the fateful day of June 27, Ford dispatched a contingent of the "Carthage

Greys" to Nauvoo, leaving fifty others to guard Joseph and his fellow prisoners at the jail. At 4 P.M., when the jail guard was changed, all but eight left the scene.

Upstairs, in a room on the second floor of the jail, John Taylor began to sing "A Poor Wayfaring Man of Grief," a song about Christ that had been popular in Nauvoo, at the request of Joseph. As Taylor finished the song, "a little rustling" was heard at the door, followed by the barks of "four or five" firearms.

Dr. Willard Richards, who with Joseph, his brother Hyrum, and Taylor completed the foursome in the room, peeked outside from behind a curtain and saw a mob of about one hundred men gathering below.

The Saints next heard footsteps on the jail stairway, followed by sounds of a scuffle. There was a loud hammering on the wooden door, then a volley of shots and a crash as it burst open.

Hyrum was struck first. Then Taylor was hit, falling to the floor seriously wounded, a watch in a breast pocket apparently saved him from death. With bullets bursting through the door, Joseph dashed for a window, but three musketballs—two from the door, the third from the window—struck him almost simultaneously, and fatally. Dr. Richards escaped without injury.

The church had lost its Prophet and his brother. To an eight-year list of other indignities—arson, theft, assault, denial of human and religious rights—had now been added assassination.

For two years, under the leadership of Brigham Young, Joseph's followers continued to resist. Joseph's martyrdom had only galvanized the Mormons' spirit, and Nauvoo experienced one of the most prosperous periods in its history. But the city was doomed.

The Illinois legislature repealed Nauvoo's charter in January 1845; its power stripped away and its once-fine legion reduced to a single justice of the peace, even internal law and order began to disintegrate. During the summer of that year, outside violence increased; homes and haystacks were burned, and the satellite Mormon towns of Morley's Settlement and Green Plains were leveled. On September 24, their city dying, Nauvoo's authorities signed a formal agreement to leave the following spring, "when the water runs and the grass grows."

But the mob would not wait. In February, with the water still frozen and the grass still unsprouted, the Great Trek began.

3

Iowa

At Sugar Creek, the temperature plunged to freezing or below nearly every night during February. On the nineteenth, a blizzard dumped seven inches of snow on the huddled Saints while fierce winds blew down tents and made life miserable in general. It was an anxious time for the Mormons, those final days of the month before the trek west would officially begin.

In the face of snow, ice, and bitter cold, the Sugar Creek Saints found solace in both prayer and music. They danced almost every night. They sang camp songs and religious hymns. They tapped their feet to the rhythm of Captain William Pitt's brass band, consisting entirely of converts from England.

Sugar Creek was the staging point for the most important westward pioneer migration to date. The site had been wisely chosen. Not only did it lie west of the mighty Mississippi, a watery barrier between the Saints and their enemies, but it was just far enough away from Nauvoo that the Illinois mob seemed satisfied the Mormons were leaving their riverside Zion as they had promised they would.

In 1846, Iowa was sparsely settled, a gently rolling region of small farms, dense woods and verdant pastures. It was also Indian country. At least it had been before the United States purchased most of the territory from the Sac, Fox and Black Hawk tribes in a series of treaties that had begun in 1837.

By 1838, when the final pact was signed by white man and red man, more than fifteen million acres had become federal territory. James Clark had been appointed territorial governor by the President. Although Iowa achieved statehood the December after the Saints left Nauvoo, it was still very much "wilderness country."

Few of the Mormons knew their destination precisely. There is good evidence that Brigham Young and the Twelve had decided upon a location "over the mountains" somewhere between Bear River Valley and the Great Salt Lake Valley along the western slopes of the Wasatch Mountains, in present-day Utah. If this is true, they did not publicize their plans, even among their followers, probably in order to prevent some prior claimant from settling the area.

At any rate, those waiting in Sugar Creek knew only that a long and arduous migration ending "somewhere in the West, in Mexican Territory," awaited them.

In his diary, for instance, Orson Pratt, noting the songs sung each evening, wrote that the Saints "all were cheerful and happy in the anticipation of finding a resting place from persecution in some of the lonely, solitary valleys of the great interior Basin of Upper California, then a Mexican province, or whithersoever we might be led." "Upper California" in those days covered a lot of territory, including the present state of Utah.*

Unlike the relative handful of pioneers who had preceded them west, the Mormons were not a single body of migrants who would cut all ties with the land behind them. Many Saints were, of course, still in Nauvoo, winding up their affairs. Thousands more, especially converts from England and elsewhere in Europe, would soon arrive from the Eastern Seaboard and follow the path west blazed by the Pioneer Company. Brigham Young had planned well for this eventuality. Not only would the main body of Saints be self-contained, it would build a series of semipermanent camps between Iowa and "Upper California" so the lot of those following would be easier. Someone later would call the pioneers "an industrial column on the march," and indeed it was. Blacksmiths, rail-splitters, doctors, gunsmiths, carpenters—Brigham wisely had included each of these occupations and more in his military-like division of the Saints into companies. His list of recommended provisions and supplies for each group of five had been as specific:

> One good strong wagon well covered with a light box; two or three good yoke of oxen between the age of four and ten years; two or more milch cows; one or more good beefs; three sheep if they can be obtained; one thousand pounds of flour or other bread stuffs in good sacks; one good musket or rifle to each male over the age of twelve years; one pound powder; four pounds lead; one pound tea; five pounds coffee; one hundred pounds sugar; one pound cayenne pepper; two pounds black pepper; one-half pound mustard; ten pounds rice for each family; one pound cinnamon; one-half pound cloves; one dozen nutmegs; twenty-five pounds salt; five pounds saleratus; ten pounds dried apples; one bushel of beans; a few pounds of dried beef or bacon; five pounds dried peaches; twenty pounds dried pumpkin; twenty-five pounds of seed grain; one gallon alcohol; twenty pounds of soap for each family; four or five fish hooks

*In 1846–47, the period covered by this book, "California" designated a large area of the West, including present-day Utah. Except where otherwise specifically noted, however, "California" refers only to the area of the present-day state; the destination of the Mormon Battalion is one example.

and lines; fifteen pounds of iron and steel; a few pounds of wrought nails; one
or more sets of saw or grist mill irons to a company of one hundred families;
one good seine and hook for each company; two sets of pulley blocks and ropes
to each company for crossing rivers; from twenty-five to one hundred pounds
of farming and mechanical tools; cooking utensils to consist of bake kettle,
frying pan . . . plates, knives, forks, spoons and pans as [few] as will do; a good
tent and furniture to each two families; clothing and bedding to each family,
not to exceed five hundred pounds; ten extra teams for each company of one
hundred families.

The second major concern was money. The trek west was woefully under-
financed. Brigham had a solution for that problem too. While they were short on
cash, the pioneers were long on manpower. Wherever possible, the Mormon men,
while their women kept the camps going, would hire out to do whatever jobs were
available in the communities along the way. They would fell trees, split rails, dig
wells, husk corn, grade roads, clear fields, feed cattle—anything that would put a
few more vital coins into the camp treasury. And if that was not enough, they
would—and they did—sell off nonessential personal items, including many price-
less family heirlooms, for whatever price they would bring.

Lastly, there was William Pitt's brass band. Its stirring music proved a
welcome change from the sameness of frontier life, and Pitt's Gentile audiences
were more than willing to donate small amounts of money for the privilege of
attending concerts.

None of this, of course, guaranteed the Saints a free and safe passage through
Iowa Territory. After being hounded out of four states—New York, Ohio, Missouri
and Illinois—they wanted assurance that they could at least pass through a fifth.
And if indeed other Mormons were to follow the trail west, they would require
some assurance that they also could pass unmolested. The Mormon pioneers would
have to plant crops for their followers to harvest, build homes to shelter them.
Shortly before moving out of Sugar Creek, the Saints decided to lay the matter
before Iowa Governor Clark in a formal petition.

[We] humbly ask your excellency to shield and protect us in our constitutional
rights, while we are passing through the territory over which you have
jurisdiction. And should any of the exiles be under the necessity of stopping in
this territory for a time, either in settled or unsettled parts, for the purpose of
raising crops, by renting farms or upon public lands, or to make the necessary
preparations for their exile, in any lawful way, we humbly petition your
excellency to use an influence and power in our behalf, and thus preserve
thousands of American citizens, together with their wives and children, from
intense sufferings, starvation and death.

The petition was approved by the Sugar Creek camp council on February 28. There was no immediate reply from Governor Clark, and the silence was one that unnerved many of the Saints. Actually, Clark's failure to act on the petition may be blamed on plain old bureaucracy; he did finally approve the request the following September, but, by then, the main body of Saints had crossed Iowa and entered Nebraska. While the act did not help the Saints in early 1846, it did help those who followed later.

By February 17, when Brigham Young finally reached Sugar Creek from Nauvoo, he found morale beginning to tatter, the well-organized "march plan" weakening, and open dissension growing in the ranks of the half-frozen waiting pioneers. With the bluntness for which he would increasingly become known and respected, he called the camp together, climbed aboard a wagon and gave them a half-hour pep talk. The beginning of the trek had been delayed, he explained, because key leaders—Heber C. Kimball, William Clayton, and Bishop Newel K. Whitney, to name three—were still putting the church's affairs in order in Nauvoo. And if the migration was to succeed (he convinced them it would) there must be no loose ends east, across the Mississippi.

"I wish the brethren to stop . . . hunting, fishing, roasting their shins, idling away their time," he thundered, "and instead to fix nose buckets for their horses, and save their corn, and fix comfortable places for their wives and children to ride, and never borrow without asking leave, and to be sure and return what was borrowed lest your brother be vexed with you."

Brigham continued: "All dogs in camp should be killed if the owners will not tie them up. . . . We will have no law we cannot keep, but we will have order in the camp. If any want to live in peace after we have left this place they must toe their mark."

The next day, before returning to Nauvoo a final time to lead the last of the Mormons out of the city, Brigham completed his organization of the pioneers into four companies with captains and subcaptains.

On the night of the twenty-second, Brigham, Heber Kimball, and apostle John Taylor, who had survived his wounds in the assassination of Joseph and Hyrum two years before, recrossed the Mississippi in a skiff, dodging ice floes as they went. Two days later, on February 24, Brigham instructed Bishop George Miller to take sixteen wagons and forty pioneers to make a preliminary investigation of the best direction to take across Iowa. Specifically, Miller was to suggest how best the Saints could move their wagons between the two principal rivers they would have to cross before reaching Nebraska: the Des Moines, which lay sixty miles west, and the Missouri.

On March 1—close to a month since Charles Shumway took the first wagon across the Mississippi from Nauvoo—the camp began to roll.

The trail they followed, and that thousands of Saints followed after them in years to come, by the 1850s became an important highway across the state of Iowa. Later, as they spanned the breadth of Nebraska, forged through southern Wyoming over the Rocky Mountains, and entered the "promised land" of Utah through its northeastern corner, they largely followed trails cut by earlier pioneer parties — explorers, soldiers, fur traders, missionaries — whose westward trek had been pioneered by Lewis and Clark (though, by traveling along the north bank of the Platte River instead of the south bank, as was customary, they deviated a bit from that). But, across Iowa, a quagmire of one mudhole after another, they made history. On contemporary topographical maps of Iowa one may easily trace the route. It is the one frequently flanked by the map designation "cem." The abbreviation stands for "cemetery."

In a very real sense, the Mormons were one of the most significant forces in the settlement of Iowa. The cabins they constructed at three permanent camps were not temporary shelters but buildings intended to endure. Before the Mormons, the trail across Iowa was but a faint trace marked by mud and ruts. Afterward, it was a permanent route, with bridges flung across rivers and roads improved. Several thousand European Saints, gathering first in Mississippi, chose Iowa as a means of reaching the staging area of Council Bluffs rather than setting off from the more commonly used cities of Independence, Westport, or St. Joseph, Missouri. Later Mormons as well as non-Mormons bound for California's gold fields after 1848 "straightened" the Iowa trail here and there, but until the western movement began to tail off, two decades later, it used essentially the route forged by the Mormons in 1846–47.

For the Mormons, the period of February to July 1846 was a time of trial for humans, animals and equipment. It was tough going, especially when spring thaws turned the trail into gooey gumbo that stuck like glue to wagon wheels and the feet of horses and oxen. Food and fodder ran short, and this, as well as adverse weather, necessitated their laying over much longer than anticipated at many points. On some days, four or five miles was all the distance the Saints could manage.

On the first day, March 1, five hundred wagons lumbered out of Sugar Creek early in the morning, although Brigham Young's were delayed until nearly sundown because he had to await the return of some men and horses he had dispatched on final errands to Nauvoo. In his journal, Orson Pratt recalls the end of that memorable day:

> . . . after scraping away the snow, we pitched our tents upon the hard, frozen ground [he wrote] and after building up large fires in front, we found ourselves as comfortable as circumstances would permit. Our beds were placed upon the frozen earth, and after bowing before our great Creator, and offering up praise and thanksgiving to him, and imploring his protection, we resigned ourselves to the slumbers of the night.

Pratt took a sighting on Polaris, the North Star, to determine the latitude of the camp for future records. He found it to be 40 degrees, 34 minutes, 52 seconds north latitude, a computation that was amazingly accurate. There were other diarists in the Iowa portion of the journey west; William Clayton, the official clerk of the Saints, managed to keep a diary even when he was seriously ill months later. Orson Pratt's, however, provided infinite detail about dates, times, places and other specifics along the way. He managed to convey much of the feeling of the "Mormon experience" as well, and it thus has become one of the most important documents of those first trying months.

On the second day, March 2, the Saints slogged eight miles to the east bank of the Des Moines River, four miles south of the community of Farmington. As was the custom, the day began with the sound of a trumpet and the peal of a bell carried in one of the forward wagons. It was a Monday. Joyous that they were at last on their way, the pioneers gathered around bonfires to hear Pitt's band that evening. Several residents of Farmington had come to listen at the invitation of the Saints.

The Mormon wagons rolled through Farmington the next day, March 3. The food supply was already running low. "We had to send a wagon and team to fetch the eight bushels of corn which some of the band earned by playing last night," Clayton jotted in his journal; ". . . the roads were bad and when we had traveled about three miles it began to thunder and rain. The clouds gathered fast and it soon showed signs for heavy rain the whole day."

About noon, the Saints reached a camp established by their scout, George Miller. The value of sending someone in advance was immediately clear. Miller and his group had already cleared a field and fenced it, readying it for a planting of corn when the ground thawed later.

Thus, in the first few days of travel, the Saints had established a daily routine that would work well for them in the months ahead. As described by historian Hubert Howe Bancroft:

> Without attempting long distances in a single day, they made camp rather early, and after the usual manner of emigrants, the wagons in a circle or semicircle round the camp-fire, placed so as best to shield them from the wind and wild beasts and Indians, with the animals at a convenient distance, some staked, and some running loose, but all carefully guarded. The country through which they passed was much of it well wooded; the land was fertile and afforded abundant pastures, the grass in summer being from one to ten feet high. Provisions were cheap; corn twelve cents and wheat twenty-five to thirty cents a bushel, beef two cents a pound, and all payable in labor at what was then considered good wages, say forty to fifty cents a day.

Within only a couple of days, news of Pitt's band had spread from the Mormon

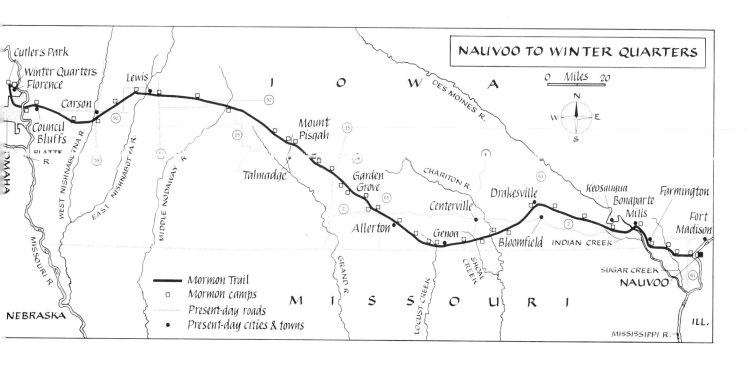

NAUVOO TO WINTER QUARTERS

0 Miles 20

Cutler's Park

Winter Quarters
Florence

Lewis

I O W A

DES MOINES R.

Carson

Council
Bluffs

PLATTE
R.

92

92

25

59

31

WEST NISHNABOTNA R.

EAST NISHNABOTNA R.

MIDDLE NODAWAY R.

OMAHA

MISSOURI R.

NEBRASKA

Mount
Pisgah

35

Talmadge

Garden
Grove

65

Allerton

2

Genoa

Centerville

CHARITON R.

63

Drakesville

Bloomfield

INDIAN CREEK

2

Keosauqua

Bonaparte
Mills

Farmington

Fort
Madison

SUGAR CREEK

NAUVOO

61

MISSISSIPPI R.

ILL.

GRAND R.

LOCUST CREEK

SHOAL
CREEK

M I S S O U R I

Mormon Trail
Mormon camps
Present-day roads
Present-day cities & towns

Photographer's Notes

In 1846, when the Mormons left Nauvoo on their historic trek to the Valley of the Great Salt Lake, the Mississippi River was virtually the western boundary of the United States. While it is true that there were communities and farms throughout much of the length of the Mississippi Valley, most were concentrated close to the river and its major tributaries. The Mormon pioneers would find few people and even fewer roads once they left the west bank of the Mississippi River.

If one were not concerned with painting a picture of the way things were, the way the country looked and what the pioneers saw on their arduous journey, it would have been a relatively simple matter to follow the charted route, recording on film scene after scene over the fifteen hundred mile journey. However, it was my desire to try to find and photograph if possible vistas along the route that would accurately portray the appearance of the countryside during the period from 1846 to 1847 when Brigham Young led the Pioneer Company from Sugar Creek to Winter Quarters and then from Winter Quarters to the Valley of the Great Salt Lake. In view of the fact that once the Pioneer Company had blazed the trail, successive waves of Mormon pioneers followed and kept the Mormon trail busy for all but the worst winter months, I decided not to attempt to match my movements day by day with the pioneers but, rather, to make my photographs in every season but winter.

While the trail starts at Nauvoo, I started at the jailhouse in Carthage, Illinois, where Joseph Smith and his brother Hyrum were murdered. The building has been restored by the church and furnished as closely as possible to the way it was in 1844. Church members conduct tours through the old jail at regular intervals during the summer months. An ambitious restoration program has been underway at Nauvoo since 1960. Many of the homes have been restored to their original condition and furnished with appropriate period furniture. However, the Mississippi River has been drastically altered by the dam at Keokuk. It is much wider today than it was in 1846 when it was navigable by shallow-draft boats only during high water. A ferry operated between Nauvoo and Montrose. The ferry landing (one of perhaps three) can be found a few hundred yards west of the Seventies Hall.

The Mormon Trail through Iowa has been reasonably well marked by the State Highway Department and the Mormon Pioneer Trail Foundation. Well-designed signs have been placed on most major thoroughfares, which indicate where the trail crosses a particular highway. Unfortunately, in attempting to follow the trail closely it is necessary from time to time to leave the major roadways that parallel the trail and strike out a right angles along some lesser routes to the points where they intersect the trail. Very seldom will a marker be found on the location of a crossing when a farm-to-market road is involved, or even some improved secondary roads. I found it necessary when pursuing this course to attempt to estimate just where the trail would cross by scaling from the available maps. Since celestial navigation involving a sextant (the instrument used by Elder Orson Pratt in charting the trail for the Pioneer Company) was and is seldom more accurate than plus or minus one-half mile, even when a good clear horizon is available, as it is at sea, I felt that my location of the trail crossing was probably as good as can be expected. Furthermore, the trail as used by successive parties of pioneers was inclined to meander. When the ruts got too deep and an easier way presented itself, adjustments were made. And in crossing the prairie, the wagons often fanned out, rather than proceeding in single file.

Iowa presented a severe photographic problem. Virtually all of southern Iowa is now farmland. The original trail lies for the most part under great fields of hybrid corn and soybeans. The land has been plowed and cultivated for so long that trail ruts have long since been obliterated. Throughout my travels from east to west I found it necessary from time to time to photograph a vista that looked as though it might be similar to that which the early pioneers saw, even though it might lie a short distance from the marked location of the trial. In every instance where I have taken this liberty it is noted in the caption.

Carthage, the old jailhouse.

Carthage jailhouse, the room in which Joseph Smith and his brother Hyrum were murdered.

Bullet holes in the door. The bullet through one of these struck and killed Hyrum Smith as he attempted to hold the door shut against the mob.

The Joseph Smith homestead in
Nauvoo.

Brigham Young's home.

The view of the Mississippi River from a window of the Joseph Smith homestead.

Unrestored house in Nauvoo.

The Browning home.

The stone quarry. Stone for the Nauvoo temple was quarried here.

The Mormon Cemetery, Nauvoo.

Sunset over the Mississippi River from the ferry landing.

Driving south on U. S. Highway 61 from Fort Madison, one crosses the trail a short distance from Montrose. Trail markers appear on both sides of the highway. Since the land in this area was being farmed when the pioneers passed through, I felt a photograph over a cornfield would be appropriate. In this vista you are looking west toward the Sugar Creek campsite. It is approximately five miles, as the crow flies, from the point where the photograph was made to the Sugar Creek staging area.

The Sugar Creek campsite. "The distance from Nauvoo to this place is called seven and a half miles." (From Clayton's *Journal,* as are the other quotations in these notes.) This important site is now marked, but it is not an easy place to find since only a gravel farm-to-market road leads to the site. I found that the easiest way to locate it was to proceed northwest on Iowa 218 from its junction with US 61 a mile or two south of Montrose. After passing Iowa J-72 (a good blacktop road), proceed another four or five miles to an unmarked gravel road leading west. This is a country road—do not get confused by the three or four dead-end roads leading to farmhouses. Once you are on this road it will wander a bit but finally take you to Sugar Creek and signs announcing the location of the campsite. It is not necessary to backtrack, since this road will eventually bear south and meet Iowa J-72.

River bottom near the Des Moines River east of Croton.

For several miles, from Farmington to Bonaparte, the trail paralleled the Des Moines River. There is a gravel road leading south along the north bank of the river at Bonaparte on which one can backtrack for several miles. It is on or very close to the original trail.

Between Genoa and Sewal on the banks of Locust Creek. At a campsite near here William Clayton wrote "Come, Come Ye Saints."

Garden Grove Cemetery. The Pioneer Company arrived and made camp at Garden Grove on April 25, 1846. It became an important stopover for subsequent pioneer wagon trains as well as handcart companies.

"This place is called Mt. Pisgah and is a very beautiful situation, the prairies rolling and rich, skirted with beautiful groves of timber on the main fork of the Grand River." To get to Mount Pisgah, take State Highway 34 west from the intersection of I-35. Turn right (north) on US 169 and proceed 2.4 miles. A gravel road leads west directly beyond a cemetery. Take this gravel road and bear left at each intersection. The Mount Pisgah Cemetery will be found 1.7 miles from Highway 169. From 1846 until 1852 Mount Pisgah was a major Mormon way station. The cemetery, west of the gravel road, is well marked with a monument erected in 1888 and a descriptive marker. The town was situated east of the road.

Mormon Trail Conservation Area (above and right, top). This park, which is on the trail, can be reached by traveling west on State Highway 92 roughly seven miles from Fontanelle. A sign on a gravel road points south to the Mormon Trail Conservation Area. Some several miles west of the Mormon Trail park there is a trail marker in the Reno Cemetery. To reach the cemetery, it is necessary to continue south on the same gravel road until it intersects County Road G61. This county road is not well marked, and the cemetery is several miles west of the intersection. I stopped and asked my way twice before locating this marker.

Approximate location of the East
Nishnabotna River ford one mile
west of Lewis.

Prairie and woods on the trail west of the East Nishnabotna River ford.

On the west bank of the West Nishnabotna River a trail leads through the woods
to the river.

Council Bluffs.

camp to the countryside around Farmington. On March 4, Pitt accepted an invitation to take his musicians to the community for a concert. The music began in Farmington's main hotel, then moved to a school and continued until darkness drew near, when the musicians accepted an offer of dinner. They also received five dollars, after John Kay sang a number of songs. According to William Clayton, the townsfolk gave the Saints three cheers as they left, at 8 P.M. But as they neared their camp, they met a guard of thirty Mormons, which had started for Farmington. Even in the midst of such hospitality, Brigham Young was cautious.

"The President," Clayton confided in his journal, "felt uneasy at staying so long and was sending the men to protect us." All through Iowa, in fact, the Mormons maintained an armed guard, headed by former Nauvoo police captain Hosea Stout, not so much for protection from Indians, who so far had indicated no hostile intentions, but against any possible attack from white neighbors in the territory. The precaution may have been unnecessary, but the Saints were taking no chances.

The wagons moved again on Thursday, March 5, reaching the town of Bonaparte about noon (it was called Bonaparte Mills in those days). There the Saints crossed their first important river after the Mississippi—the Des Moines—and then struggled with their wagons along "a very bad road up the bluff for several miles afterward." But, in terms of mileage, it was the best day so far: sixteen miles. Two days later, on the seventh they reached the first rest camp of the journey, a place called Richardson's Point. They stayed there longer than they had intended, partly because the warmer weather had turned the ground to mud and partly because Pitt's band was busy raising another important thirty-two dollars through donations at its concerts.

Two important events were recorded between the crossing of the Des Moines and the departure from Richardson's Point. At a place called Indian Creek, a horse reportedly turned sick and was unable to move. Meeting in counsel, the camp elders decided to pray for the animal's recovery and lay their hands upon its flanks. This they did and, as Mormon history tells it, the beast snorted, stirred and got up.

The second incident occurred at Richardson's Point itself. Perhaps less fearful than they had been and anxious to unburden the wagons when they could, the Saints reportedly buried a ton of ball and shot, marking the hiding place in relationship to a clump of trees. Today, the trees are gone and the exact location of the cache remains a mystery.

They remained at Richardson's Point twelve days. The respite gave the Saints time to regroup, to take inventory of their supplies and to count noses—all parts of the routine of their westward movement. Rest was critically needed, both for human and beast, but Brigham Young often reminded the Saints there was no time to dawdle; if the pioneers were to reach "Upper California" by the first snows of the following winter, every day's journey was critical. Occasionally, even in the first few weeks of travel, some Saints would be instructed to return east, to Nauvoo, to assist the few still left there who were themselves preparing to move out. Thus it was at Richardson's Point that about thirty-one of Hosea Stout's one-hundred eighty guards were released to return to their families in Illinois.

The pioneer wagons finally moved out again on March 19, delayed from a scheduled departure on the seventeenth due to the death of Brigham's nephew Edwin Little "from being over done on the road." Each day's journey west took them into territory less and less inhabited, territory where money-making opportunities became scarcer and scarcer. They bartered for corn and fodder with Pitt's music and their possessions; Clayton's journal is peppered with references to family china for which he was seeking the best price. But even this was not enough; many times, the Saints had but twigs and bark from felled cottonwood and elm trees to feed their stock.

On the twentieth, it was 10 degrees below freezing at 6:30 A.M., according to Orson Pratt, and it had dropped another degree by the following morning. But at least the cold snap froze the mud solid and made going easier for the wagons and their teams. March 21 was a twenty-mile day, in which the main party reached the east bank of the Chariton River. Crossing the Chariton was difficult because of the steep slopes on both banks; only by using long ropes as brakes to lower the wagons and to help the stock negotiate the uphill side did they manage to get across. Even at that, the job took all afternoon. "Our company got over in good season," Clayton remembered later in his journal, "but we concluded to camp after getting up the bluff as it would take all night for the whole to get up. I spent the day helping the teams till I was so sore I could scarcely walk."

The next day, the pioneers encountered more rain and thick mud until they reached a campsite on the west branch of Shoal Creek, about one hundred miles from Nauvoo. The line of wagons and pioneers took several days to congeal into one.

Orson Pratt noted:

The heavy rains had rendered the prairies impassable; and our several camps were very much separated from each other. We were compelled to remain as we were for some two or three weeks, during which time our animals were fed upon the limbs and bark of trees, for the grass had not yet started, and we were a number of miles from any inhabited country, and therefore, it was very inconvenient to send for grain. The heavy rains and snows, together with frosty nights, rendered our situation very uncomfortable. Our camps were now more perfectly organized, and captains were appointed over hundreds, over fifties, and over tens, and over these all, a president and counsellors, together with other necessary officers. Game is now quite plentiful. Other hunters bring into camp more or less deer, wild turkeys and praire [sic] hens every day.

Not all the Saints were as "perfectly organized" as Pratt described. Although it was necessary to stop occasionally, as they did, to regroup, to replenish their supplies, or merely to rest, some clearly did not want to wait. On March 23, Brigham instructed Camp Clerk Clayton to write Bishop George Miller, who had moved ahead with his group, telling him if he did not return to join the reorganization, the camp would reorganize on its own, and Miller and his group would be disfellowshipped. Three days later, on March 26, a repentant Miller returned.

By now, nearly a month of hard travel had begun to take its toll on all. Few children escaped colds, and chilblains—itching, ulcerous skin sores—were common among young and old alike. It was difficult to keep anything dry. Blustery winds often blew tent after tent down, exposing their occupants to the constant downpour. Lamented Lorenzo Young, Brigham's brother and a chronically ill man, in his journal, on March 23:

> We camped on the hill. It began to rain about noon. and raind the rest of the day. About nine oclock P.M. it began to roar in the west, and the wind began to bloe. I steped to the doare of my tent and took hold to hold it, but in A moment there came A gust of wind and blue the tent flat to the ground. My nex care was to hold my carage, which was under the tent, from blowing a way. The rain came down in torants so fast that it put out the fire. In a few minuts it was all darkness, and it was so cold that it seemed as though I must perish. I stood and held the . . . end of the carage about one hour. The rain wet me through and through, and I never felt in my life as though I must perish with the col more than I did then.

For Henry B. Jacobs' wife, Zina D. Huntington Jacobs, however, the weather that day was inconsequential. Crossing the Chariton, she gave birth to a baby boy, and "no harm happened to her not withstanding the inclement weather." Wet or no, Mrs. Jacobs named her son Chariton in honor of the occasion.

Before breaking camp at the Chariton, on April 1, Brigham polished his reorganization of the Saints. Strict rules were handed down: "No man to set fire to prairies. No man to shoot off a gun in camp without orders. No man to go hunting unless he is sent and to keep guns, swords and pistols out of sight." The spiraling price of corn worried Brigham; he stressed that part of the reason for a strict organization of the Saints was to avoid having too many people bidding against one another for food; in just a few days, such competition had pushed the price of corn from a mere fifteen cents per bushel to more than twenty-five cents. He also decided to send one company of pioneers ahead to Nebraska's Platte River country to seek jobs, begin some kind of settlement, and to store grain for the rest of the camp that was to follow.

By April 4 the pioneers had established their fourth temporary camp, at Locust

Creek. Torrential rains lasting three days turned the place into a quagmire; precious days were lost when members of the advance party had to retrace their steps to help pull the wagons of their followers out of the mud. On the sixth—the sixteenth anniversary of the church's founding—the heavens resounded with a thundershower, hail and strong winds. "Most of the tents which were pitched upon high ground were blown down," Orson Pratt recorded, "and the intimates exposed to the fury of the storm. The water in Shoal Creek, arose in a very few minutes several feet in height, and threatened to overflow its banks, and disturb our tents."

It was cold, too; even in the spring of early April, the temperature plunged below freezing at night, and when the morning sun eased the chill, it also melted the frozen mud. Inside the tents, beds began to sink into the mud underneath; only by building a supporting foundation of twigs and branches did the Saints manage to stay above the mire. Under such conditions, it was all the pioneers could do to keep themselves comfortable; the animals were turned loose to fend for themselves. Iowa was a terrible discouragement; a people less driven doubtless would have given up. But the Mormons had something few others had. They had their deep and abiding faith, and in their time of severe trial, it sustained them above all else. On April 11, Pratt summarized it well in his diary:

> . . . To any but Saints, our circumstances would have been very discouraging, for it seemed to be with the greatest difficulty that we could preserve our animals from actual starvation, and we were obliged to send off several days' journey to the Missouri settlements on the south, to procure grain. Many of the people were nearly destitute of food, and many women and children suffered much from exposure due to the inclemency of the weather, and from the lack of the necessaries of life, such as they were in former times accustomed to enjoy. But in the midst of all these temporal afflictions, the Saints were comforted in anticipation of better days; they looked forward to the time when these light afflictions would cease, and when they should have the privilege of sitting under their own vine and fig trees, with none to molest them or make them afraid. They were willing to endure hardships and privations, for the sake of escaping the unrelenting persecutions of Gentile Christians, from whom they had received for many years nothing but cruelty and the most heart-rending oppression. Their desire was to establish themselves in some lonely valley of the mountains—in some sequestered spot, where they and their children could worship God, and obey his voice, and prepare themselves for the glory which is to be revealed at the revelation of Jesus Christ. With these glorious anticipations, cheerfulness and joy seemed to animate every countenance, and sufferings were endured without murmuring. The twelve apostles of the church and other of the authorities, met in council, and determined to leave the settlements still further on our left, and launch

forth upon the broad prairies on the north-west, which were for hundreds of miles entirely uninhabited.

On the same day, Brigham convened a council of church leaders at Heber C. Kimball's camp, three miles east of Locust Creek. Brigham reiterated that the course he had chosen for the Saints—a major move to a destination somewhere in the West—he still considered justified. Despite the hardships all had endured, he was generally pleased with the conduct in the camps, but he could not condone some stealing and passing counterfeit money; even stealing from one's enemies, he reminded the camp leaders, ". . . tends to destroy the kingdom of God." The Mormons' "march plan" was going well, he added, although there was an increasing need for permanent camps, for planted crops and solid cabins, to feed and house Saints who would be coming west later. Specifically, he proposed fencing in a field of two square miles on the Grand River. Getting there, however, would not be easy. After leaving Locust Creek, on April 13, the Saints traveled a scant six miles in the following three days.

Occasionally, there was a cheering note. On April 15, William Clayton, after a brief illness, was told by Heber C. Kimball's wife, Ellen, that Clayton's wife Diantha had given birth to a son March 30. Diantha was still in Nauvoo, and two weeks was not an unusual length of time for a message to reach one hundred fifty miles across Iowa Territory. Clayton confessed in his journal that at first he did not believe the news ". . . but she [Ellen Kimball] said Brother Pond had received a letter. I went over to Pond's and he read that she had a fine fat boy on the 30th ult., but she was very sick with ague and mumps."

Clayton was ecstatic. "Truly I rejoice at this intelligence," he wrote, "but feel sorry to hear of the sickness." Later, Clayton would awake suddenly at night after a dream in which he envisioned his newborn son—whom he named William Adriel Benoni Clayton—lying down in its crib with its eyes closed and Diantha "bent over it apparently in sorrow." But the dream proved without foundation; the infant survived.

In honor of the occasion, a happy William Clayton composed a new song, "All Is Well," known today as "Come, Come Ye Saints." Set to an old English air, it today remains a popular tune among the world's more than four million Mormons and a stirring indication of their faith in the most trying months of church history:

> Come, come ye Saints, no toil nor labor
> fear,
> But with joy wend your way;
> Tho' hard to you this journey may appear,
> Grace shall be as your day.
> 'Tis better far for us to strive

Our useless cares from us to drive;
Do this, and joy your hearts will swell—
all is well! all is well!

On the following day, April 19, an advance party led by Colonel Stephen Markham arrived at a place on the east fork of the Grand River, about 145 miles west of Nauvoo. Markham had been assigned the task of leading about one hundred pioneers ahead of the main group to build and repair roads, make bridges, select campsites, establish temporary places of shelter, and scout around for sites where permanent camps could be built for Mormons who would follow in the months ahead.

The site near the Grand River seemed ideal for the last assignment. There the pioneers established their first permanent "base" since crossing the Mississippi, almost two months before. They named it Garden Grove, and a small town of that name still stands there today.

Within two days, nearly four hundred Saints trudged into the camp. They found the soil rich and the timber plentiful. Work parties were chosen to turn the barren site into a livable community. Some dug wells, while others strung fences; one hundred were designated as tree cutters, while still others set to work erecting permanent dwellings, plowing fields and planting crops.

After nearly two months on the trail, Garden Grove was a welcome respite. Although some scanty feed had begun to make its appearance on the wettest part of the prairie, food for the stock was still scarce. Worse, rattlesnakes had emerged from their winter hibernation. In his journal, William Clayton mentions them frequently. "A number of horses have been bitten by rattlesnakes and one is dead," he wrote on April 23. And on April 25; "About nine o'clock Kendall one of my teamsters, brought one of the horses he drives into camp which had been bitten by a rattlesnake. His nose had begun to swell badly. We got some spirits of turpentine and bathed the wound, washed his face in salt and water and give him some snakes master root boiled in milk. He yet seems very sick." (The animal died the following day, but Clayton suggested the cause of death may have been the cure. "Evening, Kennedy came to look at our horse and says that have given sufficient of the master root to kill four well horses.")

About the same time, the Mormons received word that an offer of two hundred thousand dollars had been made for the still-unfinished Nauvoo temple. Times were growing increasingly tough on the Illinois riverbank. The camp council later decided to sell the temple, but stipulated that twenty-five thousand dollars of the proceeds must be forwarded for use in Garden Grove; "the balance," Clayton noted after a camp meeting on April 27, "to be left at the disposal of elder Hyde, Woodruff and the trustees and to be appropriated to help away those who have labored hard to build the temple and the faithful poor of the Saints."

Garden Grove became an instant haven in the wilderness. Arriving after days of slogging through ankle-deep mud, William Huntington called it "as butiful a site as ever was seen in this region of cuntry a city of tents and waggons inhabited by the saints of the last days." Huntington may be forgiven an understandable exaggeration, but in its 750 acres the Saints had built their town of solid log houses almost overnight and had broken the rich soil around it to plant crops. In his memoirs, John R. Young later described the construction of the community:

All were . . . employed, and the camp became presently like a hive of bees. There being no room for idlers, all seemed happy. . . . Samuel Bent, Aaron Johnson, and David Fullmer were chosen to preside over those that should remain. They were instructed to divide the lands among the poor without charge; but to give to no man more than he could thoroughly cultivate. There must be no waste and no speculation. Moreover, the settlement was not regarded as more than temporary; for as soon as our leaders should find the "place," all energies were to be centered in gathering to that place. As yet, however, no one, not even Brigham Young, knew where the "place" would be; but it was talked at the campfires that President Young had seen, in vision, a wonderful valley, so large that all our people could be gathered into it, and yet so far from civilization, the mobs could not come at night to burn and whip and kidnap. Strange as it may seem, this vision formed the most entrancing theme of our conversations, and the national song of Switzerland became our favorite hymn: "For the strength of the hills we bless thee, our God, our fathers' God."

But the strain, toil and privation of the trail since Nauvoo had begun to show. Many of the Saints suffered from exposure and malnutrition; undernourished children whimpered in the night. Hosea Stout's son, Hyrum, died of whooping cough, and Stout himself was ill. The dead were buried in a small wooded cemetery at Garden Grove; the funeral ceremonies were brief, because the pioneers worked long days in preparing their wagons for the continued march ahead. All the while, those still arriving from Nauvoo and the temporary camps across half of Iowa brought news—bad news—of what was happening in Nauvoo. The temple had been dedicated and that was enough to raise spirits some, but the Illinois mob had not ceased its pressure and it was only a matter of time, most felt, before the city would fall. Dwindling supplies of food were constantly divided among the Garden Grove pioneers, usually without complaint. But there were times when conditions simply became too strained to avoid grumbling. A succinct summary of life in Garden Grove is found in these abstracts from the diary of William Clayton:

Wednesday, 6th. . . . In the afternoon a storm arose emitting very violent wind, thunder, lightning, rain and hail. Many tents blew over. One of mine blew over and most of our articles were wet and some nearly spiled. I have been informed that Esther Kay has been offering bitter complaints because they do not fare as well as some others. The hint was thrown at Margaret and she understood that it was for me. I have today let Miss Kay a pair of shoes and took down a large bag of biscuits and divided it amongst those who are needy. I have all the time let them have flour, sugar, bacon and other things as I had them and to hear of dissatisfaction because I will not let them have the last I have grieves me. I have given the band as near as I can estimate, twelve hundred pounds of flour, about four or five hundred pounds of bacon besides much of other things. . . .

Friday, 8th. . . . Andrew Cahoon arrived from Nauvoo with the mail but no letter from Diantha or father. He says the troops arrested O. P. Rockwell last Thursday evening and took him to Carthage and thence to Quincy jail. It is doubtful whether he will now escape their cruel vengeance. . . .

Wednesday, 13th. . . . Still loading my wagons and preparing to move. President Young and Heber's companies have gone and left me. I asked Jones and Terry what provisions I should have to leave them while they put in the crops. They concluded that 25 lbs. of corn meal each, and from 25 to 50 lbs. of bacon for three of them would be enough for twenty days. I think so, for we do not use as much meat in the same time in my whole family and as to 25 lbs. of corn meal each for so long a time, it is far more than my family can have. . . .

Brigham had led an advance party out of Garden Grove after a nine-day stay in the new community. Parley P. Pratt was sent ahead as a scout to find a location for the second permanent camp in Iowa. More difficult to locate today than Garden Grove, it lay near the Grand River in what Hosea Stout later described as "a beautiful grove of hickory." In his autobiography, Parley Pratt describes how he felt at seeing the place for the first time, and how he gave it its name:

I came suddenly to some round and sloping hills, grassy and crowded with beautiful groves of timber; while alternate open groves and forests seemed blended in all the beauty and harmony of an English park. While beneath and beyond, on the west, rolled a main branch of the Grand River, with its rich bottoms of alternate forest and prairie. As I approached this lovely scenery, several deer and wolves, being startled at the sight of me, abandoned the place and bounded away till lost from my sight amid the groves. Being pleased and excited at the varied beauty before me, I cried out, "This is Mount Pisgah."

At Mount Pisgah, the Mormons cleared three thousand acres of land, built permanent homes as they had at Garden Grove, and once again planted crops. William Huntington was made president of the encampment, with Ezra T. Benson and Charles C. Rich designated as counselors. Despite Parley Pratt's encounter with deer and wolves, the area generally had been thinned of game by a local tribe of Indians, the Potawatomis, "whose trails and old campgrounds could be seen in every direction," as Orson Pratt described it. Yet the richness of the soil more than made up for lack of animals. Mount Pisgah became an even more important way-stop than Garden Grove.

A look at the travel schedules of the pioneers who left Nauvoo after February is a good indication of how the bitter Iowa winter had affected the advance party of Saints. It is also a barometer of their endurance and indomitable will. Wilford Woodruff, for instance, a member of the Council of Twelve and later fourth president of the LDS, did not leave Illinois until May 26, after the advance party had hacked a community out of the woods at Mount Pisgah. Yet he arrived at the Mormons' second permanent community on June 15. Hosea Stout, William Clayton, Brigham Young and the others had trudged for three months to reach the site; Woodruff made it in three weeks.

Mount Pisgah was 172 miles west of Nauvoo, 125 east of the Missouri River. From the day Brigham Young had reluctantly agreed to abandon Nauvoo and lead his Saints west, he had envisioned a march that would be continuous from beginning to end. Temporary camps like Sugar Creek and permanent communities like Garden Grove and Mount Pisgah would be cleared along the way, but the march to Zion would be uninterrupted. The long weeks of late-winter 1846 had dictated otherwise. "Terror, winter, rain and malnutrition now assessed their tax," historian Bernard DeVoto later wrote, "and the Saints sickened. Frostbitten feet could become gangrenous, knees and shoulders stiffened with rheumatism, last autumn's agues were renewed." As summer approached in 1846, the Saints were far behind schedule if they were to reach their Rocky Mountain Zion before the winter's first snows. Further, clouds of war were gathering; a formal declaration by Congress against Mexico seemed imminent, and although the Mormons were traveling in frontier country, beyond the borders of the United States, the degree of their involvement in a coming war seemed uncertain.

Elder Jesse C. Little, meanwhile, had been appointed to preside over Mormon activities on the Eastern Seaboard. His appointment instructed him, among other things, to "take every honorable advantage of the times. . . . If our government shall offer any facilities for emigrating to the western coast," Little had been told, "embrace those facilities if possible." An enterprising people, the Mormons had hoped for some kind of commission—perhaps as builders of forts or bridges or as provisioners of federal troops traveling through the frontier country—which would help them raise sorely needed camp funds. In May, as the advance party was settling Mount Pisgah and preparing to move out to the Missouri, Elder Little went to Washington to see if there was any hope for such work.

He found it, but in an unexpected way. Congress had just declared war on

Mexico. An army of troops was being formed to march from Fort Leavenworth, Kansas, to present-day California, where they would join up with other troops already in place. President Polk did not want fort builders or army provisioners; he wanted Mormon troops to volunteer for federal service.

On June 26, Captain James Allen arrived at Mount Pisgah to sketch out the details. Polk, he said, asked for five hundred men, a full battalion, of Mormon volunteers. Enlistment would mean a year's advance clothing allowance of forty-two dollars per man. In his head, Brigham Young multiplied forty-two dollars times five hundred men. It came to twenty-one thousand dollars. That would buy a lot of stores and supplies. But the five hundred men would have to be the most able-bodied members of the party. Many of the Camp of Israel's young unmarried men had already scattered into adjoining states, seeking work whose wages would be contributed to the Saints' treasury. Five hundred Mormon teamsters, most of them with families, could hardly be spared if Young's plan for a straightforward march to the Rocky Mountains was kept. Brigham fretted about Polk's timing. "I would rather have undertaken to raise two thousand men a year ago in twenty-four hours than one hundred in a week now."

Yet, despite their open irritation at the United States for having ignored their request for help when they needed it most, the Mormons, by official commandment of the church, had vowed to respect the United States Constitution.

Complicating Brigham Young's dilemma were nasty rumors that seemed to grow each day. One insisted that the Saints' old enemies, the Missourians, not knowing what the Saints were up to, were organizing raids against the permanent camps at Garden Grove and Mount Pisgah. The day after Allen's arrival, June 27, was the second anniversary of Joseph Smith's murder, and that brought back to many Mormon minds the hatreds and animosities from which they were escaping.

Brigham Young was also a realist. Already behind schedule, he realized it would be difficult to reach the Rocky Mountains even *with* the help of the five hundred men the United States now sought to remove from him. He thought again of the twenty-one thousand dollars and what it would buy. And he thought too of the Potawatomis, whose land on the Missouri River seemed the only suitable place to camp if the Mormons stayed over for the winter. A nomadic people who themselves had been driven from their territory, the Potawatomis were sympathetic with the Saints. The Indians were looked after by federal Indian agents. Perhaps in exchange for the battalion Polk asked for, the United States would also protect the Mormon families who must remain behind, camped for another winter, this time on the Missouri River.

Brigham called a meeting of the Council of Twelve. They agreed that Polk should have his five hundred volunteers. "The United States wants our friendship," Brigham said in a letter explaining the situation to the Saints still at Garden Grove; "the President wants to do us good and secure our confidence. The outfit of this five hundred men costs us nothing, and their pay will be sufficient to take their families over the mountains. There is war between Mexico and the United States, to whom California must fall a prey, and if we are the first settlers the old citizens cannot have a Hancock or Missouri pretext to mob the Saints. The thing is from above for our own good."

The Mormons were normally not combatant men, and Brigham anticipated objections. "We feel confident," he wrote in another letter, this one to Saints remaining in Nauvoo, "they will have little or no fighting."

It took Brigham three weeks of coaxing, pleading, thundering and wheedling to convince all that the plan was just, that it was the wisest course under the circumstances. It's hard to blame those who were at first reluctant; most would be leaving their families behind, and after nearly three months of toil across Iowa, three months of incredible suffering and illness, the scheduled forced march to California in the service of an ungrateful government was, after all, something that stretched the limits of even their faith and tolerance.

Orson Pratt summarized their feelings.

. . . Another obstacle soon made its appearance [he wrote in his diary dated July 7], which seemd to completely hedge up our way from going any further this season; it was a call from the general government of the United States, upon the poor, persecuted, exiled Saints, to send 500 men into the service of the army against Mexico. The United States had the barefaced injustice and inhumanity to require of the Saints to go and fight their battles in their invasion of Mexico, after having suffered us to be driven from state to state unlawfully and unconstitutionally, with a loss of hundreds of thousands of dollars worth of property; and after the martyrdom and cold blooded butchery of scores of our men, women and innocent children. Yes, after having seen us year after year deprived of the inheritances of our own lands for which we had paid them our money, and after suffering some 30,000 men, women and children, to be driven from their own firesides, to wander houseless and unprotected upon the wild uninhabited prairies of the west—they call upon that same people to leave their wives and children in an Indian country, without food, without house, without friends, and without, to all human appearance, the least prospect of surviving the coming winter. Here, then, under these aggravating circumstances, what kind of a spirit do we find manifested by the Saints? We find a willingness on their part, to obey the call of that government who had treated them so cruelly. We find them enlisting, and immediately torn from their weeping families, when hunger, starvation and death seemed to be staring them full in the face. But why, it may be asked, did the Saints volunteer under such heartrending circumstances? It was, because it was intimated in case of refusal, that the United States would treat us as enemies, and send an army and cut us off in our journeyings; it was that we might show our loyalty to the laws and constitution of our country which we had ever held dear to our hearts, notwithstanding we had been exiled from all the privileges of American citizenship. It was that we might prove to all the world that we were willing to render good for evil. But humanity blushes while we still further relate the injustice of our nation. For, at the very time when 500 of our men were marching for Mexico, in the United States service, the same United States were suffering an organized army of several thousand strong, to march into the city of Nauvoo, and drive the aged fathers and mothers of these soldiers who were too poor to remove with the main body of the Saints. Yes, to put some of them to death, and force the last remaining remnant to wander over the plains of the west, where many of them perished without house or friends. This is but a faint sketch of the injustice and cruelty inflicted upon an unoffending people—a people who have ever held sacred the laws of their country, and who, rather than violate them would be willing to sacrifice their lives.

The final muster of troops took place on July 13. An American flag was broken out for the occasion and hoisted to a tree mast. Just before the troops left, the Saints held a dance. Colonel Thomas L. Kane later wrote this description:

> . . . a more merry dancing rout I have never seen, though the company went without refreshments, and their ball-room was of the most primitive. It was the custom, whenever the larger camp rested for a few days together, to make great arbors or boweries, as they called them, of poles and brush, and wattling, as places of shelter for their meetings of devotion or conference. In one of these, where the ground had been trodden firm and hard by the worshipers of the popular Father Taylor's precinct, was gathered now the myrth and beauty of the Mormon Israel.

Kane was as impressed by the appearance of the Mormon women at the dance. "If anything told the Mormons had been bred to other lives," his description continued, "it was the appearance of the Mormon women, as they assembled here. Before their flight, they had sold their watches and trinkets as the most available resources for raising ready money; and, hence, like their partners, who wore waistcoats cut with useless watch pockets, they, although their ears were pierced and bore the loopmarks of rejected pendants, were without earrings, fingerrings, chains or brooches. Except such ornaments, however, they lacked nothing most becoming the attire of decorous maidens."

Thomas Kane was an unusual man and one in a unique position to help the Saints. The brother of Arctic explorer Elisha Kane and the son of Pennsylvania's attorney general, who had the ear of President Polk, he had become aware of the Mormons and their plight when he attended one of Elder Jesse Little's conferences in Philadelphia in May. When he heard of the wrongs committed against the Saints, he vowed he would help the migrants if he could. And he could indeed. A frequent visitor to Mormon camps in following years, he also interceded in their behalf in official Washington, acting as an informal intermediary, and out of gratitude and respect, the Mormons named a town after him, though Kane never converted to their church. That was a singular honor, for the community of Kanesville, on the banks of the Missouri River, where the Saints spent the winter of 1846–47, became another monument to their endurance and courage. On official maps, the community was and is today Council Bluffs, 125 miles from Mount Pisgah. The pioneers reached it on July 14 after a march of only twelve days, an astonishing time, since, in the earliest days of the trek, six or eight miles was a good day's travel. All told, from Nauvoo to the Missouri, the Saints moved about three hundred miles in one hundred twenty days, making an average of only two and one half miles per day.

By Monday, July 22, about five hundred wagons had arrived at the Missouri, and nine of the church's twelve apostles were there. The council had planned to send a vanguard of perhaps four hundred men on to the Rocky Mountains, establishing the framework of their new Zion, but the march of the Mormon Battalion prevented that. The biggest hurdle at the moment was the Missouri itself; there were no ready-made ferries to take the pioneers across, as there had been on the Mississippi at Nauvoo. In his journal, Hosea Stout mentioned some of the hazards in crossing a river. The Nishnabotna River, where he was camped, was a piker compared to the Missouri, but its crossing loomed no less hazardous.

As Elder Pratt & Hancock came here this morning [he wrote] they came to creek about one mile the other side of the Indian village the bridge of which was also gone & our hands now building it as well as this one. In an attempt to cross it by swimming his mule Br Pratt & the mule came very near being drownd. He floted to shore and was so much exhausted that he could not get out. After resting awhile he attempted it again and came near being drowned the second time. I believe he was finally assisted over by some indian boys, not however untill they were satisfied that they were "Good Mormonee" as they call us. He left Br Hancock & went on but he came on and followed us soon as he could. Br Pratt was in such a hurry that he could not wait an hour or so for Br Bancock such was the emergency of his mission.

There was no chance now to forge on to Utah until spring's thaw. "The lateness of the season, the poverty of the people and, above all, the taking away of five hundred of our best men," wrote Parley P. Pratt, "compelled us to abandon any further progress westward till the return of another spring. The camps, therefore, began to prepare for winter."

"West in the spring" became a rallying cry, a shout of hope. Crossing the Missouri in increasing numbers in July and August, the Saints dug in for the long winter that lay ahead. "The Mormons took the young and hopeful side," Kane wrote. "They could make sport and frolic of their trials, and often turn the sharp suffering into right sound laughter against themselves. I certainly heard more jests while in this camp than I am likely to hear again in all the remainder of my days."

To Thomas Kane, that may have been the case. But to the Mormons, at Winter Quarters, as they called it, the winter of 1846–47 was a desperate struggle for survival.

4

Winter

In his memoirs, John R. Young called Winter Quarters "the Valley Forge of Mormondom." Other Saints nicknamed it "Misery Bottom." Historian Bernard DeVoto felt that nothing in American history—"not the ephemeral towns of mining rushes nor the hardier ones of real-estate booms"—was quite like it. An entire population had paused there, on the banks of the Missouri River, in Indian country, to put down temporary roots and to chart the journey to the Rocky Mountains. But Winter Quarters became far more than a mere rest stop. During the winter of 1846–47, it was a busy supply station. It was the nerve center of all Mormon church operations, including its far-flung missionary programs. It was a work center whose income was badly needed to finance the rest of the trek.

There are many historical high points in Mormon history; with ample evidence, Winter Quarters, miserable and tragic though it was, with its six hundred graves, its suffering, hunger, privation and disease, may be judged as the place where sagging Mormon fortunes at last turned upward.

Called Florence today, a suburb of the Nebraska city of Omaha, Winter Quarters was chosen partly because it provided an excellent natural defense against mobs. It was one of several places where the Saints wintered that year. Smaller outposts were strewn north and south in Nebraska, as well as across the Missouri in Iowa. And of course many Mormons—perhaps fifteen thousand altogether along with their belongings and thirty thousand head of livestock—were scattered across Iowa in the camps established earlier at Mt. Pisgah, Garden Grove and Sugar Creek, and on the trail in between. But no amount of activity in the satellite communities could begin to rival that in Winter Quarters, and it will forever be accorded a hallowed niche in Mormon history.

As he watched the Mormon Battalion depart, Brigham Young had not entirely abandoned the idea of sending a vanguard on to Oregon or California in 1846. There, he hoped, a permanent location for the church could be found, the first houses built, and crops planted early in the spring of 1847, which would be nearing harvest when the main body arrived. On Monday, July 20,—Brigham called for volunteers to form the advance party. His pioneer companies already had crossed the Missouri into Nebraska Territory and were camped four miles west, near some springs called Cold Springs. Brigham was in a hurry; he wanted the volunteers on their way the next morning, and within twenty-four hours, seventy-five men with their families had responded to the call. By the evening of the following day, July 22, they had arrived at the Elkhorn River. Fourteen wagons crossed over before dark and busily organized into military-like companies with captains and a "march plan" that specified the number of Saints, wagons and oxen and other livestock that each would include. By July 28, the first company had moved to a spot on the main Platte River nearly one hundred miles west and a bit north of where Winter Quarters was later established. Within another week, leaders of three companies made up of two hundred wagons decided to group at an encampment on the South Fork of the Loup River. There, two days later, on August 7, the plan to move west ended. Returning from the main camp, Newel Knight and John Hay delivered a letter from the Council of the Twelve that suggested they not "cross the mountains this fall." Instead the Council had agreed, after considering a host of problems connected with the plan, as many Saints as possible should winter at a Pawnee Indian village on the Loup River, and the remainder at Grand Island. The following spring, all would join up and march west together.

Wherever the camps were situated, of course, they were on Indian lands, and the Indians were in turn under the jurisdiction of the United States Government. Thus, some kind of agreement with both the Indians and the government was necessary. On August 9, the Saints met with a delegation of the Ponca tribe, who had been at war with the Pawnees of the region. The Saints did not intend to stay forever, the Poncas were told, and because the Mormons offered to intercede as peacemakers with the Pawnees, the Ponca chief invited the Saints not only to remain in the area but to spend the winter at the main Ponca camp itself, "only three sleeps away." Instead, twenty-nine families among the advance party were delegated to winter at the Pawnee Mission, not far from Winter Quarters, while the balance—in one hundred sixty wagons—would travel the ninety miles to the main Ponca community on the Niobrara River. The rest of the main body remained behind.

It was a tough, hard, eleven-day trip over rocky country, and by winter's end, the Mormons learned they had made a bad mistake. At Running Water, as the Mormons called the Niobrara, they were too far from supply centers, and at one point during the winter, the Saints there were subsisting on bread and water alone.

Twenty-three of their number died before spring, and many of the deaths were attributed simply to exposure, overwork or pure exhaustion. To make matters worse, a prairie fire of unknown origin swept toward the village on Christmas Day 1846, destroying five stacks of precious hay needed for livestock, as well as a wagon. Only the fact that the village fort had been made of green logs saved it from total destruction. At the end of March 1847, the survivors returned to the Missouri to rejoin the main Saints party.

Winter Quarters was selected as the main wintering site on September 11, when the surveying of it began; Brigham Young moved there from Cutler's Park on September 23 to supervise its laying out and the construction of its buildings. At first, Winter Quarters was divided into thirteen wards, but by midwinter, when its population had mushroomed to more than thirty-four hundred—the majority women and children—the wards were increased to twenty-one.

Winter Quarters was enclosed by a stockade, mainly to ward off the Omaha Indians, whom the Saints found to be constant thieves. A few rough fortifications and a blockhouse were built. Protected by these were a meeting house for council and worship, workshops of many kinds, houses, and a gristmill on the bank of the Missouri. The latter greatly eased the need for constant hand grinding of coffee and grain.

The houses were built chiefly of logs covered with clapboards or with willows laid across poles and covered with dirt. Some Saints lived in caves dug out of hillsides, or "dugouts." By January, the houses numbered more than seven hundred, and by the following spring they had been increased to more than one thousand.

As the buildings went up and winter's first snows drifted down on the encamped pioneers, it was time to organize the community and to begin thinking and planning for the spring trek to the mountains. With great sickness already upon them, with the hillside cemetery beginning to fill, and with Indian troubles impending, anything the Saints could do to occupy their time proved a blessing. Church historian B. H. Roberts described the Saints' government:

The community had no laws save such as were self-imposed; no officers save those provided in the church organization, and their special appointees to exercise functions of a semicivic nature such as a marshal of a camp and his aides to enforce order and prevent people from trespassing upon each other in regard to stock running at large, destroying gardens, or intruding into camp grounds; also to hold in check the thoughtless buoyancy of youth which had not yet learned the lessons of self-restraint, and ever grows somewhat impatient of discipline; also to guard the camps from the intrusion of strangers who would spy out their liberties and impose upon the unwary, and likewise to check by punishing promptly, the thieving propensities of the Indians by whom they were surrounded. Their laws were edicts or regulations issued from the councils of their wisest men. It was literally the rule of Carlyle's "*can*-ning, or able-men," voluntarily submitted to by the people with right willing loyalty and nothing doubting, because they recognized in the edicts promulgated "precisely the wisest, fittest" thing which in all ways it behooved them to do.

With so much against them, the Saints tried to relieve the monotony with some fun. Parties were frequent, and Captain Pitt's Quadrille Band played every day. Games, mock trials, singing classes, spelling bees, quiltings—all went on despite the harshness of the season and the toll of sickness and disease which kept Mormon gravediggers increasingly busy on the hill.

Sometimes during that winter, disease wiped out entire families. Others suffered bitter losses. Hosea Stout, captain of the guard, saw his wife Marinda die in childbirth, along with her baby, on September 26. His son Hyrum had already died on the trail in Garden Grove. A second son, William Hosea, was buried between Mount Pisgah and the Missouri.

Charles Shumway lost his wife at Winter Quarters. Before the main party reached the Missouri, Shumway and a companion, George Langly, had been dispatched from Mount Pisgah by Brigham to carry messages and letters to various outlying Mormon camps, one of them two hundred miles south, in Missouri. A talented linguist, Charles had also been assigned as an interpreter among the Indians. The trail already had been hard on the Shumways, and the special mission told on Charles even further. By the time he returned to Mount Pisgah, he had "been out nine days, mostly without food." Only a few kernels of corn had stood between him and starvation.

Shumway remained in bed for several days, suffering from a severe chill. But his skills as an interpreter were badly needed by Brigham on the Missouri. A war was brewing between the Sioux and Pawnee tribes, and Charles was summoned as a peacemaker.

On the journey to Council Bluffs, Shumway's wife, Julia Ann, became so ill with black canker she could hardly leave her wagon. Food was running scarce; for the entire trip, she had nothing to eat but corn meal and bits of dried buffalo meat. Finally reaching Winter Quarters, Charles fashioned a log house for his family, but Julia Ann's condition only worsened.

By November, she was seriously ill. She could hardly breathe, and her throat was so badly swollen that eating a single bite was painful. On the morning of November 14, she asked Charles to summon their children. Struggling to hide the pain, she gently embraced each. In midafternoon, she died.

In one satellite camp west of the Missouri, as early as August, Thomas Kane reported 37 per cent of its population ailing with a sort of "scorbutic disease, frequently fatal, which the Saints named the black canker." The disease was also called "blackleg," a form of scurvy, caused by the lack of vegetables in the Saints' poor diet. So serious did the outbreak of black canker become at one point during the winter that Brigham dispatched a party of men to Missouri to bring back some potatoes and horseradish, considered a good cure. The dampness of the Missouri marshes did not help either; in late summer, fed by smaller, sluggish streams, the great river became "impure as open sewers," which accounted for the disdainful nickname of "Misery Bottom." Indians living along the river were reported to have lost half their population the previous winter.

Colonel Kane knew firsthand the conditions in "Misery Bottom." He himself fell so ill with a "nervous, billious fever" that he could barely put pen to paper. He described that winter in a lecture delivered in Pennsylvania in 1850.

They [the Mormons] were collected a little distance above the Pottawatamie Agency. The hills of the "High Prairie" crowding in upon the river at this point, and overhanging it, appear of an unusual and commanding elevation. They are called the Council Bluffs, a name given them with another meaning, but well illustrated by the picturesque congress of their high and mighty summit. To the south of them, a rich alluvial flat of considerable width follows down the Missouri some eight miles, to where it is lost from view at a turn, which forms the site of the Indian town of Point aux Poules. Across the river from this spot the hills recur again, but are skirted at their base by as much low ground as suffices for a landing.

This landing, and the large flat or bottom on the east side of the river, where crowded with covered carts and wagons; and each one of the Council Bluff hills opposite, was crowned with its own great camp, gay with bright white canvas, and alive with the busy stir of swarming occupants. In the clear blue morning air the smoke streamed up from more than a thousand cooking fires. Countless roads and by-paths checkered all manner of geometric figures on the hill sides. Herd boys were dozing upon the slopes; sheep and horses, cows and oxen, were feeding around them, and other herds in the luxuriant meadow of the then swollen river. From a single point I counted four thousand head of cattle in view at one time. As I approached the camps, it seemed to me the children there were to prove still more numerous. Along a little creek I had to cross were women in greater force than blanchisseuses upon the Seine, washing and rinsing all manner of white muslins, red flannels, and parti-colored calicoes, and hanging them to bleach upon a greater area of gress and bushes than we can display in all our Washington Square. . . .

There was something joyous for me in my free rambles about this vast body of pilgrims. I could range the wild country wherever I listed, under safeguard of their moving host. Not only in the main camps was all stir and life, but in every direction, it seemed to me I could follow "Mormon Roads," and find them beaten hard, and even dusty, by the tread and wear of the cattle and vehicles of emigrants laboring over them. By day, I would overtake and pass, one after another, what amounted to an army train of them; and at night, if I encamped at the places where the timber and running water were found together, I was almost sure to be within call of some camp or other, or at least within sight of its watch-fires. Wherever I was compelled to tarry, I was certain to find shelter and hospitality, scant, indeed, but never stinted, and always honest and kind. After a recent unavoidable association with the border inhabitants of Western Missouri and Iowa, the vile scum which our own society, to apply the words of an admirable gentleman and eminent divine, 'like the great ocean washes upon its frontier shores,' I can scarcely describe the gratification I felt in associating again with persons who were almost all of Eastern American origin—persons of refined and cleanly habits and decent language—and in observing their peculiar and interesting mode of life; while every day seemed to bring with it its own especial incidents, fruitful in the illustration of habits and character. . . .

The most striking feature . . . of the Mormon emigration was undoubtedly their formation of the Tabernacle Camps and temporary Stakes or Settlements, which renewed, in the sleeping solitudes everywhere along their road, the cheering signs of intelligent and hopeful life.

I will make this remark plainer by describing to you one of these camps, with the daily routine of its inhabitants. I select at random, for my purpose, a large camp upon the delta between the Nebraska and Missouri, in the territory disputed between the Omaha and Otto and Missouri Indians. It remained pitched here for nearly two months, during which period I resided in it.

It was situated near the Petit Papillon, or Little Butterfly River, and upon some finely rounded hills, that encircle a favorite cool spring. On each of these a square was marked out; and the wagons as they arrived took their positions along its four sides in double rows, so as to leave a roomy street or passage-way between them. The tents were disposed also in rows, at intervals, between the wagons. The cattle were folded in high-fenced yards outside. The quadrangle inside was left vacant for the sake of ventilation, and the streets, covered in with leafy arbor work, and kept scrupulously clean, formed a shaded cloister walk. This was the place of exercise for slowly recovering invalids, the day-home of the infants, and the evening promenade of all.

From the first formation of the camp all its inhabitants were constantly and laboriously occupied. Many of them were highly educated mechanics and seemed only to need a day's anticipated rest to engage at the forge, loom, or turning-lathe, upon some needed chore of work. A Mormon gunsmith is the inventor of the excellent repeating rifle, that loads by slides instead of cylinders, and one of the neatest finished fire-arms I have ever seen was of this kind, wrought from scraps of old iron, and inlaid with the silver of a couple of half-dollars, under a hot July sun, in a spot where the average height of the grass was above the workman's shoulders. I have seen a cobbler, after the halt of his party on the march, hunting along the river bank for a lapstone in the twilight, that he might finish a famous boot-sole by the camp fire; and I have had a piece of cloth, the wool of which was sheared, and dyed, and spun, and woven, during a progress of over three hundred miles.

Their more interesting occupations, however, were those growing out of their peculiar circumstances and position. The chiefs were seldom without some curious affair on hand to settle with the restless Indians; while the immense labor and responsibility of the conduct of their unwieldy moving army, and the commissariat of its hundreds of famishing poor, also devolved upon them. They had good men they called Bishops, whose special office it was to look up the cases of extremest suffering; and their relief parties were out night and day to scour over every trail.

At this time, say two months before the final expulsion from Nauvoo, there were already, along three hundred miles of the road between the city and our Papillon camp, over two thousand emigrating wagons, besides a large number of nondescript turn-outs, the motley make-shifts of poverty, from the unsuitably heavy cart, that lumbered on mysteriously, with its sick driver hidden under its counterpane cover, to the crazy, two-wheeled trundle, such as our own poor employ for the conveyance of their slop-barrels, this pulled along, it may be, by a little dry-dugged heifer, and rigged up only to drag some such light weight as a baby, a sack of meal, or a pack if clothes and bedding.

Some of them were in distress from losses upon the way. A strong trait of the Mormons was their kindness to their brute dependents, and particularly to their beasts of draught. They gave them the holiday of the Sabbath whenever it came round: I believe they would have washed them with old wine, after the example of the emigrant Carthaginians, had they had any. Still, in the Slave-coast heats under which the animals had to move, they sometimes foundered. Sometimes, too, they strayed off in the night, or were mired in morasses; or oftener were stolen by Indians, who found market covert for such plunder among the horse-thief whites of the frontier. But the great mass of these pilgrims of the desert was made up of poor folks, who had fled in destitution from Nauvoo, and been refused a resting-place by the people of Iowa.

It is difficult fully to understand the state of helplessness in which some of these would arrive, after accomplishing a journey of such extent, under circumstances of so much privation and peril. The fact was, they seemed to believe that all their trouble would be at an end if they could only come up with heir comrads at the Great Camp. For this they calculated their resources, among which their power of endurance was by much the largest and most reliable item, and they were not disappointed if they arrived with these utterly exhausted. . . .

Beside the common duty of guiding and assisting these unfortunates, the companies in the van united in providing the highway for the entire body of emigrants. The Mormons had laid out for themselves a road through the Indian Territory, over four hundred leagues in length, with substantial, well-built bridges, fit for the passage of heavy artillery, over all the streams, except a few great rivers where they have established permanent ferries. The nearest unfinished bridging to the Papillon Camp was that of the Corne à Cerf, or Elk Horn, a tributary of the Platte, distant may be a couple of hours' march. Here, in what seemed to be an incredibly short space of time, there rose the seven great piers and abutments of a bridge, such as might challenge honors for the entire public-spirited population of Lower Virginia. The party detailed to the task worked in the broiling sun, in water beyond depth, and up to their necks, as if engaged in the perpetration of some pointed and delightful practical joke. The chief sport lay in floating along with the logs, cut from the overhanging timber up the stream, guiding them till they reached their destination, and then plunging them under water in the precise spot where they were to be secured. This, the laughing engineers would execute with the agility of happy, diving ducks.

Our nearest ferry was that over the Missouri. Nearly opposite the Pull Point, or Point aux Poules, a trading post of the American Fur Company, and village of the Pottawatamies, they had gained a favorable crossing, by making a deep cut for the road through the steep right bank. And here, without intermission, their flat-bottomed scows plied, crowded with the wagons, and cows, and sheep, and children, and furniture of the emigrants, who, in waiting their turn, made the woods around smoke with their crowding camp fires. But no such good fortune as a gratuitous passage awaited the heavy cattle, of whom, with the others, no less than 30,000 were at this time on their way westward; these were made to earn it by swimming. . . .

After the sorrowful word was given out to halt, and make preparation for winter, a chief labor became making hay; and with every day dawn brigades of mowers would take up the march to their positions in chosen meadows, a prettier sight than a charge of cavalry, as they laid their swaths, whole companies of scythes abreast. Before this time the manliest, as well as the most general daily labor, was the herding of the cattle; the only wealth of the Mormons, and more and more cherished by them, with the increasing pastoral character of their lives. A camp could not be pitched in any spot without soon exhausting the freshness of the pasture around it; and it became an ever recurring task to guide the cattle, in unbroken droves, to the nearest place where it was still fresh and fattening. Sometimes it was necessary to go farther, to distant ranges which were known as feeding grounds of the buffalo. And there were sure to prowl parties of thievish Indians; and each drove therefore had its escort of mounted men and boys, who learned self-reliance and heroism, while on night guard alone, among the silent hills. But generally the cattle were driven from the camp at the dawn of the morning, and brought back thousands together in the evening, to be picketed in the great corral or enclosure, where beeves, bulls, cows and oxen, with the horses, mules, hogs, calves, sheep and human beings, could all look together upon the red watch-fires, with the feeling of security when aroused by the Indian stampede, or the howlings of the prairie wolves at moonrise.

When they set about building their winter houses, too, the Mormons went into quite considerable timbering operations, and performed desperate feats of carpentry. They did not come ornamental gentlemen or raw apprentices, to extemporize new versions of Robinson Crusoe. It was a comfort to notice the readiness with which they turned their hands to woodcraft; some of them, though I believe these had generally been bred carpenters, wheelwrights, or more particularly boat-builders, quite outdoing the most notable voyageurs in the use of the ax. One of these would fell a tree, strip off its bark, cut and split up the trunk in piles of plank, scantling, or shingles, make posts, and pins, and pales—everything wanted almost of the branches; and treat his toil from first to last with more sportive flourish than a schoolboy whittling his shingle.

Inside the camp, the chief labors were assigned to the women. From the moment, when after the halt, the lines had been laid, the spring-wells dug out, and the ovens and fireplaces built, though the men still assumed to set the guards and enforce the regulations of police, the Empire of the Tented Town was with the better sex. They were the chief comforters of the severest sufferers, the kind nurses who gave them in their sickness those dear attentions with which pauperism is hardly poor, and which the greatest wealth often fails to buy. And they were a nation of wonderful managers. They could hardly be called housewives in etymological strictness; but it was plain that they had once been such, and most distinguished ones. Their art availed them in their changed affairs. With almost their entire culinary material limited to the milk of their cows, some store of meal or flour, and a very few condiments, they brought their thousand and one receipts into play with a success that outdid for their families the miracle of the Hebrew widow's cruse. They learned to make butter on a march by the dashing of the wagon, and so nicely to calculate the working of barm in the jolting heats that, as soon after the halt as an oven could be dug in the hill-side and heated, their well-kneaded loaf was ready for baking, and produced good leavened bread for supper. . . .

Every day closed as every day began, with an invocation of the divine favor; without which, indeed, no Mormon seemed to dare to lay him down to rest. With the first shining of the stars, laughter and loud talking hushed, the neighbor went his way, you heard the last hymn sung, and then the thousand-voiced murmur of prayer was heard, like bubbling water falling down the hills. . . .

In the camp nearest us on the west, which was that of the bridging party near the Corne, the number of its inhabitants being small enough to invite computation, I found as early as the 31st of July, that 37 per cent of its inhabitants were down with the fever, and a sort of strange scorbutic disease, frequently fatal, which they named the Black Canker. The camps to the east of us, which were all on the eastern side of the Missouri, were yet worse fated.

The climate of the entire upper "Misery Bottom," as they term it, is, during a considerable part of summer and autumn, singularly pestiferous. . . . The Mormons were scourged severely. . . . The fever prevailed to such an extent that hardly any escaped it. They let their cows go unmilked. They wanted for voices to raise the psalm of Sundays. The few who were able to keep their feet, went about among the tents and wagons when food and water, like nurses through the wards of an infirmary. Here at one time the digging got behind hand; burials were slow; and you might see women sit in the open tents keeping the flies off their dead children, some time after decomposition had set in.

In our own camp, for a part of August and September things wore an unpleasant aspect enough. Its situation was one much praised for its comparative salubrity; but, perhaps, on this account, the number of cases of fever among us was increased by the hurrying arrival from other localities of parties in whom the virus leaven of disease was fermented by forced travel.

But I am excused sufficiently the attempt to get up for your entertainment here any circumstantial picture of horrors, by the fact, that at the most interesting season, I was incapacitated for nice observation by an attack of fever—mine was what they call the congestive—that it required the utmost use of all my faculties to recover from. I still kept my tent in the camp line; but, for as much as a month, had very small notion of what went on among my neighbors. I recollect over-hearing a lamentation over some dear baby, that its mother no doubt thought the destroying angel should have been specially instructed to spare.

I wish, too, for my own sake, I could forget how imperfectly one day I mourned the decease of a poor Saint, who, by clamor, rendered his vicinity troublesome. He, no doubt, endured great pain; for he groaned shockingly till death came to his relief. He interfered with my own hard-gained slumbers, and I was glad when death did relieve him.

Back in Nauvoo, as the Saints prepared for winter on the Missouri, the city's death was near.

Although most of its Mormons had managed to get out before the first of May, when the advance party of Saints approached the Missouri, some had not been so fortunate. By August about one thousand still remained, many of them aged and sick. They were not ready for evacuation into unknown territory to the west. May 1 had been the date the mob had set for the city to be emptied of its population; considering the condition of the stragglers, few would have believed the city would continue to be under pressure after that deadline. Even Major W. B. Warren, ordered to Hancock County by Governor Ford earlier in the year to keep the peace, was ordered to disband his troops in mid-April, "when the last of the Mormons have left." But Ford quickly countermanded the order when dark rumors reached his office that many Hancock County residents were gathering to demand that the last remnants of the "Mormon plague" be driven from Illinois, even at the cost of "extermination."

Returning to Nauvoo, Warren set up headquarters in the Nauvoo Mansion—formerly the residence of Joseph Smith—and sent the Warsaw *Signal* a placating dispatch that "the Mormons are leaving with all possible speed." The ferry taking them across the Mississippi, he wrote, was working as fast as possible, and new settlers—non-Mormons—were taking their place in the city. Warren's "evacuation report," however, was insufficient evidence for the mob, and on May 11, his anger rising at events transpiring in and around the city, Warren issued a proclamation that read in part, "[I] can say to you with perfect assurance, that the demonstrations made by the Mormon population, are unequivocal. They are leaving the state, and preparing to leave, with every means that God and nature have placed in their hands . . . this ought to be satisfactory."

Satisfactory, it was not. "A man near sixty years of age, living about seven miles from this place," Warren fumed, "was taken from his house a few nights since, stripped of his clothing, and his back cut to pieces with a whip, for no other reason than he was a Mormon, and too old to make successful resistance. Conduct of this kind would disgrace a horde of savages."

Warren's outrage, printed a week later in the Quincy *Whig*, did little to quiet the mob; if anything, it only whetted its anger, and by midsummer, anti-Mormon feelings were reaching the boiling point. As the Fourth of July approached, one group of Carthage citizens, meeting to draft plans for an Independence Day celebration, paid the Mormons the supreme insult. Since there were still Mormons in the county, the mob argued, the people of the county really could not be considered "free." Therefore, should they celebrate the national holiday at all? By coincidence, the day of that meeting—June 6—happened to be the first date fixed by Ford on which volunteers would be accepted to fight in the Mexican War. Throughout the United States, war fever was rampant; President Polk was having no trouble at all raising troops to defend national honor in the West. Since it was too early to engage the faraway enemy, the mob turned its fury on one closer at hand. In a wheat field just outside the city one day late that summer, the spirit of patriotism boiled over. A small party consisting of both Mormons and non-Mormon new residents of Nauvoo were surrounded by a mob and captured. Their arms were taken away, and they were beaten with hickory goads. When the perpetrators of the outrage returned to Nauvoo and were arrested for the crime, they argued that the Mormons had not been idly harvesting grain but boisterously shooting up the surrounding fields and farm buildings and using an old stable for target practice. The excuse didn't stick well with Nauvoo's newer townsfolk, however, and the attackers were ordered held for trial. In retaliation, five Mormons—Phineas H. Young, his son, Brigham Young, Richard Ballantyne, James Standing and a Mr. Herring—were kidnaped from their homes, whisked away to a nearby woods and held, as virtual "hostages," for fourteen days. Although the prisoners finally escaped and returned to Nauvoo, the kidnaping had made its point. Transferred to Quincy on a change of venue that placed them in far friendlier hands, the assault suspects were soon released, with all charges formally dropped.

Even Major Warren, no Mormon sympathizer but apparently a staunch believer in law and order, was fed up. In mid-August, he resigned in disgust, but his replacement, Major James R. Parker, assigned to Nauvoo on August 24, was scarcely more patient. Sent to the city with only ten men as a defense force, his pleas to the mob were met with open contempt. He joined Major Warren in early retirement.

Like Warren, Parker was replaced a few days later, by a Major Clifford, but Nauvoo's third military defense command proved to be a phantom. Now it really was the mob's turn. In early September, a civilian, Thomas S. Brockman, marched an armed posse of seven hundred men against the beleaguered defenders of Nauvoo. Though historians disagree on the exact number, there were fewer than three hundred older residents—Mormons and non-Mormons alike—left in the city (in his *History of Illinois*, Ford placed the total at one hundred fifty). Though they had the advantage of entrenchment in a familiar place, they were hardly a match for the crazed mob that, on the days of September 10, 11 and 12, 1846, closed the books on the Mormons' Illinois Zion in the Battle of Nauvoo. Many accounts have been published of that three days of terror. One of them, written with some forgivable exaggeration by a participant, Curtis Edwin Bolton, follows:

> A couple of steamboat shafts, long useless at the river, were cut and three temporary cannons were formed for they were hollow. Finally after many false alarms the mob was seen coming toward Nauvoo—about 2,000 men with banners flying. The temple bell was rung and shortly our companies formed and marched out to meet the enemy. The mob had five pieces of cannon.

Finally the mob encamped for the night just beyond Joseph Smith's farm, and at dark we returned to Nauvoo to get food. I lay and slept under a gourd vine.

By 7 a.m. Friday, September 11th, I was picked as one of 50 sharpshooters. Just as the Temple bell was rung giving notice that the mob was in action, we started out Parley Street where we had been the night before. One of our spies reported the mob had gone back to the prairie and was coming in on Young Street. We started toward the norwest and reorganized in a pretty ravine. Our group took the name of the Spartan band.

Off we started on the run and soon came in view of the mob. We concealed ourselves in a cornfield intending to let the artillery pass, then rush in and separate it. They discovered us and detached 300 men to march in behind and surround us. We retreated into an open space, formed line and received their fire which wounded one man in the heel. We returned fire and they retreated, we following.

Capt. Anderson ordered us to leap the fences and form a line in the road in front of their cannon. I and about nine others did so. They opened with their cannon but miraculously only hit our clothing. We choose to retreat to where we had a quantity of gunpowder buried and a musket lock put to it. We retreated slowly hoping to draw them to the plot, but some treacherous wretch had given them the information on those plots.

We retreated into town and as a last forlorn hope threw ourselves into some log houses, determined to do or die. Breckman,* a Campbelle preacher of the enemy shoved in all his moves for he was a good tactician and first rate officer. He saw the advantage of our position in a moment but did not know we were already there. He ordered his horses and men to move down and take possession of this valuable point. The men numbered about 120. They charged gallantly down the gentle slope and then charged ungallantly back again for we were there with our repeating rifles, which could be fired 7 and 8 times without reloading.

William Greene came to our aid with a small piece of steamboat shaft and fired lead balls which were insinuating for they went through the air without noise and hit without warning which was not to their taste. It was then 4 p.m. Several fell and were carried away. The mob then retreated to the brow of the hill and prepared to camp near Law's field. Anderson led us to a timber. After dark we returned to town and were quartered in a new house minus doors, windows, plaster and without any supper.

At 6:30 a.m. the next day we were back on Temple block. We marched Indian file, to the square in front of Anderson's home where his wife served us sandwiches. Anderson had seen his wife for the last time. At 11 a.m. the mob marched into town, banners flying, cannons roaring. We were ordered to

* Brockman.

crouch low, trailing our rifles. Anderson gave his last order: Boys follow me, and do as I do!

The mob had considerable loss and retreated with horrible oaths. The officers succeeded in returning them to the fray. We, having rested a bit, were able to fire incessantly and they broke up again. Anderson had been shot dead, his only son also, and an elderly man named Morris. Some eight or nine were wounded in this inhuman, unholy war.

I had been shot in the stomach and after Anderson's death, his command was offered to me, but I could not accept. I kept getting weaker and more feverish and decided to ambush myself in front of the mob, lie and shoot as long as I could. Decided on a spot in a garden, pulled weeds over to build a screen and lay behind it—but the mob did not stir. About 11 a.m. I started home but fainted. Dr. Bernhisel came. I was delirious but recovered. Hearing a treaty was planned and the mob was to march in, I and my wife, Ellen, started for the river. We took a steamboat to Burlington, Iowa, stayed three days, then took a stagecoach to Montrose, Iowa. My father having sent me $100 recently, we hired a boat. We crossed the river in a heavy rain.

The west bank of the Missouri quickly became an evacuation center. Its "Mormon days" nearly done, the city was a shambles when Kane arrived, in late September. After a quick inspection trip through the community, a trip he later said shocked his senses, he, too, crossed the river to locate the Battle of Nauvoo's survivors:

It was after nightfall, when I was ready to cross the river on my return. The wind had freshened since the sunset, and, the water beating roughly into my little boat, I headed higher up the stream than the point I had left in the morning, and landed where a faint glimmering light invited me to steer.

Here, among the dock and rushes, sheltered only by the darkness, without roof between them and the sky, I came upon a crowd of several hundred human creatures, whom my movements roused from uneasy slumber upon the ground.

Passing these on my way to the light, I found it came from a tallow candle, in a paper funnel shade, such as is used by street venders of apples and peanuts, and which, flaring and guttering away in the bleak air off the water, shone flickeringly on the emaciated features of a man in the last stage of a bilious, remittent fever. They had done their best for him. Over his head was something like a tent, made of a sheet or two, and he rested on a but partially ripped open old straw mattress, with a hair sofa cushion under his head for a pillow. His gaping jaw and glazing eye told how short a time he would monopolize these luxuries; though a seemingly bewildered and excited person, who might have been his wife, seemed to find hope in occasionally forcing him to swallow awkwardly measured sips of the tepid river water, from a burned and battered bitter-smelling tin coffee-pot. Those who knew better had furnished the apothecary he needed; a toothless old bald-head, whose manner had the repulsive dullness of a man familiar with death scenes. He, so long as I remained, mumbled in his patient's ear a monotonous and melancholy prayer, between the pauses of which I heard the hiccup and sobbing of two little girls who were sitting upon a piece of drift-wood outside.

Dreadful, indeed, was the suffering of these forsaken beings; bowed and cramped by cold and sunburn, alternating as each weary day and night dragged on, they were, almost all of them, the crippled victims of disease. They were there because they had no homes, nor hospital, nor poor house, nor friends to offer them any. They could not satisfy the feeble cravings of their sick; they had not bread to quiet the fractious hunger-cries of their children. Mothers and babes, daughters and grand-parents, all of them alike, were bivouacked in tatters, wanting even covering to comfort those whom the sick shivers of fever were searching to the marrow.

These were Mormons, famishing in Lee County, Iowa, in the fourth week of the month of September, in the year of our Lord 1846. The city—is Nauvoo, Illinois. The Mormons were the owners of that city, and the smiling country around. And those who had stopped their ploughs, who had silenced their hammers, their axes, their shutles, and their workshop wheels; those who had put out their fires, who had eaten their food, spoiled their orchards, and trampled under foot their thousands of acres of unharvested bread; these were the keepers of their dwellings, the carousers in their temple, whose drunken riot insulted the ears of their dying. . . .

They were, all told, not more than six hundred and forty persons who were thus lying on the river flats. But the Mormons in Nauvoo and its dependencies had been numbered the year before at over twenty thousand. Where were they? They had last been seen, carrying in mournful train their sick and wounded, halt and blind, to disappear behind the western horizon, pursuing the phantom of another home.

On September 17, five days after the echo of the last shots died away, Nauvoo formally surrendered. Though the community never completely went out of business, Nauvoo never again regained the prominence it held in its brief shining moment of 1839–46—seven short, turbulent, but abundant years. Until The Church of Jesus Christ of Latter-day Saints decided to restore a part of the community, more than a century later, Nauvoo dwindled into relative obscurity on the rolling plains of mid-America, all but forgotton. Forgotten, that is, by all except those who remembered Zion.

The march of the Mormon Battalion from Council Bluffs through the Southwest to California was not directly a part of the Saints' trek from Nauvoo to Utah's Great Basin, and technically, perhaps, is not properly within the scope of this book. However, it was such an important contributor to the success of the pioneers' westward migration, perhaps the greatest single factor in the financing of that success, that it deserves a retelling here. It was mentioned earlier that the financial contribution of the Mormon troops not only enabled the pioneers to survive the bitter winter of 1846–47 at Winter Quarters, but helped pay the bills the rest of the way to Utah. The battalion's importance, however, was far more than economic. To the surprise of many, especially some in Congress who had been clearly anti-Mormon when the Saints were in Ohio and Illinois, it underscored the Saints' steadfast loyalty to a country that had repeatedly ignored their pleas for help. The march of the battalion was of major importance in the development of the Southwest and Far West; in community after community through which they passed, especially at trail's end in San Diego, weary, haggard Mormon soldiers extended helping hands to local citizens, digging wells, repairing buildings, widening roads, tending livestock, keeping busy in any way they could. And as important for the growing Church of Jesus Christ of Latter-day Saints, the battalion's march offered a serendipitous opportunity for unofficial missionary work, for gathering new converts to a religion then but sixteen years old.

The Saints' 2,200-mile march was the longest single sustained movement of infantry in the history of the United States Army. Despite its many hardships, despite the fact that many of its participants were worn both physically and mentally from the rigorous crossing of Iowa in midwinter, there were surprisingly few casualties along the way.

As outlined by Captain James Allen at Mount Pisgah in July 1846, the mission of the battalion was twofold. First, it would reinforce General Stephen Kearney's "Army of the West," which was scheduled to depart for California from Santa Fe, New Mexico, in September, after the declaration of war with Mexico. Second, the soldier-Saints were asked to build a wagon road along the route. Whether or not the Mexican War ended early, which it did, the Army felt that a permanent road between the two points would be vitally necessary for any future resupply operations. Even when the war was over, the westward movement was about to get up full steam, and deployment of army troops throughout the West was a foregone conclusion. In the years to follow, as it turned out, the wagon road carved out of the southwestern desert was used by the famed Butterfield Stage Lines, and when railroads displaced the stagecoach, the route of the Southern Pacific was chosen and the land for the Gadsden Purchase selected by using maps drawn up by the Mormon Battalion.

The nondescript Mormon troops looked like perhaps no other soldiers in the United States Army. Since they had elected to contribute the forty-two dollar-per-man uniform allowance to their brethren along the Mormon Trail, none except company officers wore standard army uniforms, and after their travel across Iowa, even their everyday clothes were literally coming apart at the seams. (One account of the battalion mentions that at least one enlisted trooper wore a gaudily festooned hat carried over from Nauvoo Legion days, a sight that must have caused curious stares from passersby along the route.)

Few of the troops carried any kind of shelter, since they had left almost everything they owned with their destitute families now preparing for the winter at Council Bluffs. As pay, each had been offered seven dollars per month, but most agreed to send at least a part of this allowance, as well as the clothing allowance, back to the Saints' winter camp. Twenty women were allowed to accompany the battalion as laundresses (four for each of the battalion's five companies), and an additional thirty-three women and fifty-one children, families of the officers and sergeants, went along. The battalion itself consisted of 549 soldiers when it marched out of Council Bluffs, on July 20.

It took the battalion, singing "The Girl I Left Behind Me" in roaring unison, ten hard days to march the first, three hundred-mile leg from Council Bluffs to Fort Leavenworth, where they received their rifles and other equipment. It was a grueling introduction to military life. The route generally followed the steaming lowlands of the Missouri River, buzzing with swarms of malaria-carrying mosquitoes and constantly drenched with torrential summer rains. There is no evidence that any of the volunteers had been given a physical examination prior to leaving Council Bluffs, or that any physical standards were required of the troops. Even the age requirements were overlooked; although Captain Allen had specified that the volunteers must be at least eighteen and not over thirty-five, records indicate that the youngest was D. W. Hendricks, a boy barely sixteen, and the oldest was David Pettigrew, fifty-five. Most were in their mid-twenties or early thirties, however.

Only three days out of Council Bluffs, the battalion suffered its first fatality. The incident is described by Sergeant Daniel Tyler, thirty-six, an early convert to Mormonism who maintained a journal of the march to California and whose book, *A Concise History of the Mormon Battalion in the Mexican War*, later written at the request of the church, remains one of the best detailed histories of the march.†

He [Elder Jesse C. Little] spent that night with us [Tyler wrote] and the next day, at the request of the officers, he delivered a short and encouraging address to the command while formed in a hollow square. He spoke in high terms of the integrity and energy of Brother Samuel Boley, who was danger-

---

†Various histories of the march of the Mormon Battalion disagree slightly on the number of soldiers, servant women, wives, and children who participated. Even official LDS Church archival records are in disagreement, although attempts are currently being made by the church, from diaries and other data, to reconcile the numbers. The figures used here are taken mostly from Sergeant Tyler's book, and if discrepancies are noted, the conflicting records are at least partly at fault.

ously ill. The invalid was very kindly nursed and doctored by our assistant surgeon, Dr. Wm. L. McIntyre. The 5th company, having been previously filled up and organized, overtook the command on Mosquito Creek.

On the morning of July 23rd, we had to perform the painful duty of burying brother Samuel Boley, who died between the hours of 12 and 1 o'clock the previous night. This was the first death that occurred in our ranks. He was wrapped in his blanket and buried in a rough lumber coffin, which was the best we could get.

Although malaria was the most frequent cause of illness along the route of the march, Tyler did not mention the cause of Boley's death. It was malaria, however, that took the life of the battalion's commander, James Allen, a non-Mormon the Saints respected highly. He died of fever in Fort Leavenworth, after the Saints had left that city on August 12 on the second leg, a grueling nine hundred-mile march to Santa Fe.

Allen's temporary replacement, Lieutenant A. J. Smith, caused considerable grumbling among the Saints because in his overpowering desire to get the battalion to Santa Fe he apparently failed to take account of the soldiers' debilitated condition. To make matters worse, the battalion had been assigned a doctor of questionable medical experience, Dr. George B. Sanderson, whose favorite cure for almost any ailment—a white, tasteless powder (actually mercurous chloride and arsenic), administered by force, if necessary—proved more devastating than no medicine at all.

The Mormons resented Sanderson's medicine not only because it only made them sicker but for religious reasons as well. Smith, however, was required to be committed to the surgeon. And when the sick Saints flatly refused to attend Sanderson's sick call, Smith lost his patience. As Tyler, himself among the ill, remembered later in his book:

Lieutenant Smith . . . pulled several of the sick out of the wagons because they had neglected to report themselves to Dr. Sanderson. When he learned that some of them did not deign being drugged, he used some horrid oaths and threats. Sergeant Thomas S. Williams, who had purchased a team to haul a portion of our knapsacks, had some of the sick in his wagon. Smith approached the wagon with the intention of hauling the sick out, when the Sergeant ordered him to stop. At this Smith became furious and drew his sword and threatened to run Williams through if he attempted to allow any more sick to ride in the wagon without his permission. Williams braced himself, grasped the small end of his loaded whip and told him if he dared to make one move to strike he would level him to the ground; that the team and wagon were his private property and he would haul them as he pleased. He further told him

[Smith] that these men were his brethren, that they did not believe in taking drugs and that he would never leave one lying sick on the ground while they could crowd into the wagon, or so long as his team could pull them. Smith slunk away. . . .

Faint from the blistering heat, dog-tired from the rapid pace demanded by Lieutenant Smith, their food running low, and their illnesses only aggravated by "Doctor Death's" singular "cure," the debilitated troops finally reached Santa Fe on October 12,1846, after averaging about fifteen miles a day for sixty-one days. Some of their families were missing; when it had become obvious that even the toughest men of the battalion were nearing breakdowns from exhaustion, Smith had ordered a number of women and children detached and sent up the Arkansas River to what is now Colorado, to spend the winter.

Lieutenant Colonel P. St. George Cooke took over at Santa Fe as permanent commander of the battalion. He was not encouraged by the prospects of the route ahead. "Everything conspired to discourage the extra-ordinary undertaking of marching this battalion eleven hundred miles," he later wrote, "for the much greater part through an unknown wilderness without road or trail, and with a wagon train. It was enlisted too much by families, some were too old, some feeble, and some too young; it was embarrassed by many women; it was undisciplined; it was much worn by traveling on foot, and marching from Nauvoo, Illinois; their clothing was very scant; there was no money to pay them or clothing to issue; their mules were utterly broken down; . . . and mules were scarce. . . . Those produced were very inferior, and were deteriorating every hour for lack of forage or grazing. I have brought road tools and have determined to taken through my wagons; but the experience is not a fair one, as the mules are nearly broken down at the outset."

With that gloomy prediction, Cooke decided that he could at least rectify a part of it; before leaving Santa Fe, he screened the battalion and sent all the women but five [some records say four], all the children, and almost one hundred fifty of the weakest and sickest men to Fort Pueblo. If they were still needed by the following spring, Cooke told them, they could come on to California when they were rested. By their firm opposition to Dr. Sanderson, the Saints had meanwhile managed one important concession from Cooke; Dr. William L. McIntyre, a Mormon who had been appointed assistant battalion surgeon by Lieutenant Allen before he died, not Dr. Sanderson, would decide which soldiers were unable to proceed west. With Captain James Brown in command, about eighty-six enlisted men and many women and children left Santa Fe on October 18, replenished their supplies at Fort Bent, and arrived in Pueblo on November 17.

On October 19, the main battalion left Santa Fe on the third leg of its march. The column comprised three hundred fifty men, a handful of women, twenty-five wagons and six cannons. Ahead lay eleven hundred miles of sparse southwest country, with few roads and which no wagon train had ever penetrated. The odds against success were staggering; not only were food rations by necessity reduced week after week, they were now formally entering enemy territory—land claimed by Mexico and protected by pockets of armed Mexican troops—as well as that of Indian tribes whose degree of tolerance to intruders was unknown. Worse, perhaps, the battalion was led by guides who could only guess at what they might encounter; none had ever traveled the route before.

The initial route from Santa Fe led southward along the Rio Grande, to a point near the present city of El Paso. From there it took a large loop southwest and then northward toward the Mexican village of Tucson, now in Arizona. It was raw, rugged, hostile territory—hostile not only because of the Indians and Mexicans but because it offered so little in the way of food and shelter and protection from a broiling sun. By November 10, less than a month after leaving Santa Fe, Saints were dropping exhausted by the wayside. Colonel Cooke weeded out fifty-five more men from his ranks and ordered them detached to Santa Fe before moving on to rest quarters at Pueblo. They were to be given twenty-six days' worth of reduced rations to make the whole journey but only five days' worth to reach Santa Fe, a distance of three hundred miles over which it had taken the main battalion ten days coming west. The detachment reached Santa Fe in fifteen days, arriving on November 25, but the toll was high: three Saints died along the way. After a few days' recuperation, they were reprovisioned, given fresh teams, and sent on their way to Pueblo, which they reached on December 10, with another death en route.

By mid-December, Pueblo was becoming a substantial Mormon settlement. Due to the battalion's sick, who had arrived in three detachments, the Saint population now numbered one hundred fifty, along with perhaps eighty women and children. In addition, there were about forty-seven Mormon pioneers there from Mississippi, known as the Mississippi Saints. Intending to join Brigham Young's party, they had arrived at Fort Laramie (now in Wyoming) in the summer of 1846, only to learn too late that the main body of Saints had elected to remain on the Missouri River, in Winter Quarters, until spring. Fort Laramie was even then an important way-stop on the major east-west pioneer route, but there was not enough food to sustain forty-seven unexpected arrivals. Rather than travel all the way east to Winter Quarters, the Mississippians marched instead to Santa Fe, where, in the winter of 1846–47, the total Mormon population reached nearly three hundred. It was in Pueblo that the first Anglo-Saxon children born in Colorado were born, to Latter-day Saint women that winter. But even in the dead of a Colorado winter, the Mormons found it vital to keep lines of communication open with Winter Quarters. On December 23, two soldiers, John H. Tippets and Thomas Woolsey, set out for the Missouri River encampment with battalion paychecks in their saddlebags. It was a tough, fifty-one day journey, the last three days of which they were out of food, but the Army money was a godsend for the

Saints, then enduring their own share of sickness, destitution and hunger.

While the Iowa Saints were shivering in the freezing cold, inundated almost every day by winter rains, the rest of Colonel Cooke's Saint-soldiers were thirsting for water. The supply ran so short, in fact, that on November 10 the commander found it necessary to order two wagons and some equipment left behind.

As they slogged along day by day, many began to wonder why their path continued south, instead of west, in the direction of California. What if their one-year enlistment should end before they reached the shores of the Pacific, what if they found themselves marooned in the middle of the arid Southwest?

Perhaps Colonel Cooke had been reading their thoughts, or perhaps he was growing tired himself of continuously moving south. At any rate, on the morning of November 21, he rose suddenly in his saddle, ordered a halt, and said, "This is not my course. I was ordered to California; and . . . I will go there or die in the attempt." Turning to the battalion bugler, he shouted the order, "Blow the right!"

Turning northward, the battalion passed over the Continental Divide on November 28. Tyler found the scenery at America's backbone "beautiful, with mountain precipices and rocks in all shapes and sizes heaped upon each other."

The mountain area also offered a welcome change in diet. For the previous week or so, the Saints had subsisted largely on the carcasses of pack animals. They had been devoured completely, "even to the hides, tripe and entrails, in many cases without water to wash them in." The soldiers considered the marrow bones a special luxury, and they "were issued in turns to various messes." But in the Rockies, deer, bear, antelope and small game were plentiful. A guide named Charboneaux, marching slightly ahead of the battalion, was confronted by three grizzly bears on November 25 — three days before the troops reached the summit — and managed to shoot one while evading the charge of the other two by climbing a rock. That night, the grizzly made a mouth-watering supper.

On November 29, Colonel Cooke began making preparations for descending the Rockies into a valley on the western side. He had estimated that the task would require five to ten days, but by laboriously lowering the pack animals on long ropes, it required only two. "One of [the animals] by accident, got loose," Tyler noted, "and ran down with such force that it became badly damaged, and was abandoned as worthless. One or two others were slightly injured, but were soon repaired."

On December 2 the battalion reached the ruins of San Bernardino, in present-day New Mexico, where the troops saw their first wild cattle. "They were of Mexican stock," Tyler recalled later, "having been brought here by a Mexican, who was driven out by the Apache Indians and forced to leave his stock behind. One of the guides killed a wild bull and was found drying his meat upon our arrival. A few hunters were immediately sent out, and more went out on their own responsibility,

[I] being among the latter. Every now and then, a bull bounded past . . . having been routed by the hunters. After following one and another, in the hope of getting a shot, [I] discovered one standing under a lone tree, at a distance of perhaps half a mile. [I] crouched and sneaked along from bunch to bunch of the Mozquit‡ until one half the distance was made, when the crack of a musket and a rather sharp screech or lowing of the animal proved that another hunter had found his quiet resting place . . . another shot succeeded in bringing him to the ground." Uncertain that the animal was dead, Tyler suggested to another trooper, Walter Barney, that they sneak up and slit its throat, "to save a waste of ammunition." Barney argued that was too risky, and they decided instead to throw a rock, "about the size of a man's fist, at the wounded beast."

"Quick as thought," Tyler remembered, "he bounded to his feet, and, with a wild, shrill bellow, hobbled after me on three legs." Tyler fired again; the steer dropped in its tracks, but struggled to rise, when Tyler fired a third time. "This time," he said, "a bullet from my musket ended the battle. Six bullet holes, all in fatal places, showed that these cattle could endure as much as a buffalo."

Nine days later, on December 11, the battalion was to engage in the only "battle" it would encounter in its 2,200-mile march. The enemy wasn't Mexican troops, nor hostile Indians, but a herd of wild cattle every inch as ferocious as the single animal Tyler and Barney had managed to kill after such effort.

The cattle, which the Saints encountered as they moved along a stream bordered by low-lying bluffs, numbered in the hundreds, according to Tyler. Frightened by the rumbling of the wagons, some animals ran, but "others, to gratify their curiosity, perhaps, marched toward us, as if bent upon finding out who dared to intrude upon their quiet retreat." Tyler found the cattle "terribly beautiful forms and majestic [in] appearance . . . quite impressive."

Impressive or not, the wild animals launched a frightening attack, which kept the surprised Saints busy for a while. Despite orders to the contrary, the soldiers carried loaded guns; soon "the roar of musketry was heard from one end of the line to the other."

One of the initial victims was a battalion mule, strapped in a wagon harness with a mate. The poor animal was so badly gored, according to Tyler, it was hurled atop the second animal. Other cattle rammed the wagons themselves, stoving in end gates and terrorizing helpless humans sick inside.

The Saints resorted to whatever defensive tactic seemed handiest. Some, seeing no immediate shelter, prostrated themselves on the ground, finding, perhaps, that pounding hooves are less lethal than slashing horns. Others plunged into the camouflage of mesquite bushes; "still others . . . climbed up in small trees, there being now and then one available."

Miraculously, no Saint was killed in the melee, although perhaps ten were

‡ Mesquite.

injured. Tyler pays particular note to Amos Cox, who "was thrown about ten feet into the air, while a gore from three to four inches in length and about two or three in depth was cut in the inside of his thigh near its junction with the body." A year later, Tyler was to encounter Cox in Iowa, where "he still felt the effects of his injury."

There is no accurate estimate of the number of cattle killed, but various witnesses have placed the total between twenty and eighty-one.

Two days later, on December 13, battalion scouts reported that a detachment of Mexican soldiers was stationed at Tucson, the walled village that now lay directly in the Saints' path to California. To bypass the village would mean a march of several hundred additional miles, and Cooke knew his men were in no condition to do that. On the other hand, the Mexican commander of Tucson, a Captain Comaduran, was under strict orders to allow no armed force to pass through the town. Through his guides, Cooke dispatched a letter to Tucson's civilians that the advancing Mormon Battalion sincerely wanted to avoid bloodshed, that civilians were not considered enemies.

"We came not to make a war on Sonora [Tucson was part of that Mexican province at the time] and less still to destroy an important outpost of defense against Indians," Cooke's dispatch, signed by an adjutant, read. "But shall I remind you that the American soldier ever shows justice and kindness to the unarmed and unresisting? The property of individuals you will hold sacred."

Cooke felt that the dispatch would set civilian minds at ease. But he was less certain how Comaduran would accept it. Cooke decided to bluff. Although well garrisoned, the Mexican troops were estimated to number only about two hundred. Nevertheless they held two enormous advantages. They had the best defensive position. And they had not just completed a long, wearying march that had left limbs numb, throats parched and stomachs aching for food. Cooke's bluff was to suggest to his Mexican counterpart that the Mormon Battalion was much larger than it actually was, and it worked. Taking Cooke up on his word that the Mormons' front guard alone numbered more than 360 men and that an even larger force was following, Comaduran and his troops scattered to the nearby countryside. Not a single shot was fired in anger. The Mexican civilians accepted them as peaceful visitors and accorded them respect. "The author remembers with much gratitude," Tyler later recalled in his book, "the silver-haired Mexican, of perhaps three score years and ten, who, when signs of thirst were given, ran to the brook as fast as his tottering limbs could carry him, dipped up his water, and, almost out of breath, but with cheerful countenance, delivered the refreshing and much needed draught. He has doubtless, long since, been gathered to his fathers; if so, peace to his ashes. Surely, 'I was athirst, and he gave me drink.'"

After passing through Tucson and making camp a half mile beyond, Cooke's soldiers returned to town to buy food. They were particularly interested in two thousand bushels of "public wheat," which had been ground not by the mortar-and-pestle method they had observed in Indian camps along the way, but in a donkey-powered gristmill.

With a quantity of this wheat and other foodstuffs packed away, the battalion was on its way again on December 18. It followed the Gila River until it joined the Colorado River, encountering thousands of friendly Pima and Maricopa Indians en route. But their supply of both water and food ran short once again, and this leg became one of the most arduous of the entire march. Even in midwinter, the southwestern desert was scorching, and every waterhole became more precious than a pot of gold. The battalion traveled by day, and nightfall found them scattered over several miles of the trail. "The men might be found all along the road in squads of two or three," Tyler remembered, "without blanket, fire or tent. In the evening, the Colonel gave permission to the Captains to halt their companies at discretion . . . but only for a short time at once, as the only hope for water was by traveling on, and both men and mules could travel in the cool of the night without water better than in the day time. But in no case were the halts, during the night, to exceed six hours."

They reached the Colorado River on January 9, 1847. Daniel Tyler found it ". . . quite as wide, though not as deep as the Missouri, and the water much the same color as that river," but the soldier-Saints were in poor shape to cross it, worse even than had been Brigham Young's pioneers at the Missouri the previous midsummer. As the soldiers lingered on the banks to rest and plan the crossing, a group of troops sent back to the Gila to pick up supplies left behind finally caught up; Tyler described the ragtag lot in his book:

> These men were in a pitiable plight; their clothing was torn into shreds, through having to crawl through thorny bushes to get to the [Gila] river bank to search for the provisions. They had also suffered severely for want of food. One man reported being two days without anything to eat.

The Colorado where they crossed it was nearly a half mile wide, and the current was swift. In the middle there were several channels. At one point, the water was so deep that those fording it could not touch bottom with their tent poles. Planks were laid atop wagon beds, and some of the provisions were stacked on them. Mules had been herded across the river in advance, and they hauled on the makeshift ferries with long ropes. Two mules never made it across; they drowned on the way, and several wagons were mired helplessly on thick sandbars in midstream. Once safely across with all his men, Cooke grumbled that the Colorado was "the most useless river on the face of the earth!"

But if fording the Colorado was tough, the final miles to San Diego were the cruelest. On the march now more than half a year, the battalion's survivors—and survivors they were indeed—were half naked, shoeless, weak both from hunger and the tortuous physical strain, frying by day under the desert sun, half freezing at night. "The march of the last five days," Tyler wrote, "was the most trying of any we had made, on both men and animals. We have found the heaviest sand, hottest days and coldest nights, with no water and little food." Of how the soldiers rigged makeshift shoes to protect their blistered feet, he added:

. . . the men were nearly barefooted; some used, instead of shoes, rawhide wraped around their feet, while others improvised a novel style of boots by stripping the skin from the leg of an ox. To do this, a ring was cut around the hide above and below the gambrel joint, and then the skin taken off without cutting it lengthwise. After this, the lower end was sewed up with sinews, when it was ready for the wearer, the natural crook of the hide adapting it somewhat to the shape of the foot. Others wrapped cast-off clothing around their feet, to shield them from the burning sand during the day and the cold at night.

Frequently during those final days, the Saints marched one company at a time in double file ahead of their wagons, in order to pack down the desert sand so the wagon wheels could roll. Men following tugged sometimes for hours on ropes to help their starving animals pull the wagons along. Both men and beasts had almost no food; when an animal died, guts, hide, all but the hair and hoofs, and some of the skin, was used to make clothing. When the men collapsed from thirst and hunger, their comrades rolled them under a bush or rock and marched on. On January 16, 1847, they finally staggered down the banks of Carrizo Creek and gorged themselves on fresh water; only then, selecting the strongest men and teams, did they return to the desert to rescue those left behind.

The next five days' travel, in what is presently California's San Diego County, was still rugged, although the Saints had finally left the desert and were traveling in country pocketed by flowing streams, grass for the animals and small game. On January 17, they camped between two mountains, after a decent fifteen-mile march, slaughtered some of the few remaining skinny sheep they carried, and devoured their last four ounces of flour. The eighteenth was spent resting, cleaning arms and drilling to prepare for battle. They must have been appalled at the prospect of an impending military engagement after such a body-breaking, two-thousand mile march. But their God was benevolent; the war with Mexico was over before San Diego was reached.

On January 21—exactly six months and one day after they had marched out of Council Bluffs—the Mormon Battalion reached Warner's Rancho, near the present Warner's Hot Springs, in San Diego County. There the men had their first full meal in months. They headed toward Los Angeles, where the battalion was to reinforce the troops of General Kearney in securing that city, but were reordered instead on January 25 to San Diego, and on January 29, 1847, the weary Mormons glimpsed the Pacific Ocean for the first time.

Once at San Diego, battalion soldiers functioned as an army of occupation. To pass the time, the men, well rested at last, turned earnestly to city-building. One company built Fort Stockton, atop a hill. Others "white-washed nearly every home in town," dug wells, fired about forty thousand bricks, dug a small coal mine on Point Loma. The remaining companies marched to Los Angeles as part of Kearney's command to build Fort Moore there. Some men, discharged in July 1847, continued northward up the San Joaquin Valley toward Fort Sutter (near Sacramento) and there met a messenger who told them their families had reached the Salt Lake Valley. Most of the discharged soldiers went immediately to Utah; a few remained at Sacramento under contract to build a gristmill and sawmill for John A. Sutter. They were therefore on hand to participate in Sutter's historic discovery of gold, on January 24, 1848.

Proud of what had been accomplished by the Mormons under his command, Colonel Cooke issued an official order on January 30, 1847, congratulating the battalion. "History," the order read, "may be searched in vain for an equal march of infantry."

5

Nebraska

From Omaha, the Platte River Valley reaches west across mid-America as a great natural corridor. It is a valley steeped in history, five hundred miles of dusty, sandy, flat prairie on the east and rolling bluffs on the west which someone, not intending to be complimentary, called "America's Valley of the Nile."

It is no barren, inhospitable Death Valley, the Platte, nor is it a Sahara. In the nineteenth century, when it was a major wagon highway for west-bound emigrants, buffalo by the millions roamed the prairies, providing a never-ending supply of meat. There were antelope and deer, and fish in the rivers. Except where the Indians burned off vast stretches of grassland to stimulate new growth, there was plenty of fodder for cattle and horses. Certainly, there was no scarcity of water; though muddy and shallow, the two forks of the bountiful Platte varied in width from seven hundred yards to two miles, and it was fed by tributaries all along the way.

To many pioneers of the nineteenth century, however, the Platte Valley was merely a place to endure, to pass through on their way somewhere else. Especially at its western end, it seemed as bleak and worthless as any barren area of the world. Except by Indians, it was scarcely settled; its cities and towns would come much later.

To the Mormon Saints, however, scarcely recovered from the costly winter of 1846–47, the valley was a road to hope, a path to Zion. And they were not merely passing through; they noted every waterhole and clump of cottonwood and river crossing with infinite detail, for they knew they were only an advance guard of thousands of other Saints to follow. They had learned well in the Iowa winter. No longer were they a largely disorganized lot. Their morale was high, despite the fact that their strongest men had been marched off to war, their ranks decimated by hunger, privation, illness and death, and their beautiful Zion on the Mississippi snatched from their grasp. In the winter of 1846–47, though they had suffered and buried many dead, the Saints had found time to plan with care for the final leg of the journey ahead, along the Platte, over the Rockies, and into Utah.

In the only revelation of his formally accepted into the church canon, Brigham Young on January 14, 1847, related the rules of the march as he had been given them by the Lord. To begin in the spring, the final trek would include in its ranks all of the Latter-day Saints "and those who journeyed with them." Strict military-like organization was important; the Saints were to group into companies with captains of hundreds, fifties and tens. Each was to provide itself "with all the teams, wagons, provisions, clothing and other necessities for the journey that they can." The companies would carry along teams, seeds and farming utensils, but not merely to sustain themselves. "When [they] are organized," the Lord commanded Brigham in the revelation, "let them go with their might, to prepare for those who are to tarry." As it had been in Iowa, in other words, the march across Nebraska and Wyoming and into Utah was not merely to sustain a single column of pioneers. It was also to pave the way to Zion for thousands of stragglers still scattered east across Iowa, and other thousands who would later move west from the East.

Let each company bear an equal proportion [the revelation continued] according to the dividends of their property, in taking the poor, the widows, the fatherless, and the families of those who have gone into the army, that the cries of the widow and the fatherless come not up into the ears of the Lord against this people.

Let each company prepare houses, and fields, for raising grain, for those who are to remain behind this season, and this is the will of the Lord concerning his people.

Let every man use all his influence and property to remove this people to the place where the Lord shall locate a stake of Zion.

As they prepared for the march, the Lord had said, the Saints were to have no fear of their enemies, "for they shall not have power to stop my work." They were to refrain from evil, specifically "speaking evil and drunkenness, and possessing that which did not belong to him," and each should "praise the Lord with singing, music, dancing, prayer, and thanksgiving."

That was in January 1847. The Saints were busy in Winter Quarters, making ready. Wagons were repaired, and those that could not be mended were torn apart and the parts used to build new ones. Women stitched patches on torn wagon covers and tents. They knitted socks and repaired shoes to replace those that had been worn away across Iowa. The wisdom of building a gristmill now became evident; with spring near, all its stored grain, except that allotted to feed the stock, was ground into flour and carefully parceled out among the pioneers. The women Saints not assigned these tasks kept busy weaving baskets and half-bushel measures while their men made washboards. "Hundreds of dollars' worth of these items have already been completed and there is a prospect of quite an income from this source in the spring," Brigham explained in a letter to apostles who had gone to England, dated eight days before his revelation of January 14.

The road west was hardly unknown or unexplored. Four decades earlier, the Lewis and Clark expedition, of 1804–6, into the wilderness of Oregon Territory, drew America's attention to her sprawling far-western frontier. Heeding the call first were pioneering fur traders and trappers, first as individuals and later as organized companies. They were of course after profit, but in their wanderings they also brought back the first store of knowledge concerning the mountain country they exploited; the rivers and streams became as familiar as the streets of New York, and the forts later established by the Army to protect them from hostile Indians became guideposts for following pioneers. The fur trade was on the wane by the time the Saints prepared to start west in 1847, but the legacy of information remained a valuable asset to Brigham and his followers. Missionaries followed— mostly Catholic priests who pushed northward from Mexico into California, Arizona and southern Utah—as did a retinue of non-emigrant civilians such as teamsters, laundresses, and telegraphers, who mainly served the military, and stage passengers and drivers.

By the time the Mormons moved west, they had been preceded by waves of other emigrants by a full ten years, although none of the pioneer wagon trains was of any substantial size until about 1841. In 1843, a company of about one thousand pioneers from several states rolled out of Independence, Missouri, in one hundred twenty wagons and went west as far as Fort Bridger before turning north to Oregon. The pack train included the first of a full ten thousand emigrants who had trod the Platte by the time of the Mormon exodus in 1847. Best-remembered, perhaps, was the Donner party, which took the first wagon train down Utah's Emigration Canyon in 1846 and around the south end of Great Salt Lake; the next year, the Saints' own wagons would follow in those ruts. By that spring, the Platte and the "Oregon Trail," on its south bank, had been made a great national highway.

Yet the Mormons in their trek west from Winter Quarters were unique. They alone were on the move not out of choice but because they were *forced* to go. Where others (later) sought gold in California, silver in Nevada, or mercantile profit in Oregon, the Saints primarily sought peace, isolation from their enemies, and an opportunity to enjoy a religious freedom guaranteed them by the constitution but so long denied them. Unique, too, was the social structure of the Mormon column. Years later, the National Park Service described it: "No longer were the migrations composed solely of an agrarian people, but shop keepers, artisans, mechanics, and skilled persons of all types. The economic motive, so dominant among the earlier migrants, gave way to the desire to worship in peace and to live in isolation from those who would deny this right."

The trek west from Winter Quarters was hardly the hasty exodus the wintry flight from Nauvoo had been. As recounted in at least fifteen journals meticulously maintained among the 148 members of the original Pioneer Company, there were four major problems and little hardship, and the column reached Utah's Great Salt Lake Basin without a single fatality. Though a few horses were lost along the way, though there were a few Indian scares, and though at times food and firewood were hard to find, most arrived at their destination in excellent health. There was grumbling occasionally, at times discipline tattered, and there was at least one open rebellion; church histories recall in detail the defection of Bishop George Miller, who had frequently quarreled with Brigham Young. He openly declared his opposition to the plans of the Council of Twelve, and disgustedly marched off instead to Texas with his family a few days before the Pioneer Company left for Utah. And toward the end of the first leg west, Brigham was driven to deliver a long and stern rebuke about the breakdown of order between Nauvoo and Salt Lake.

But compared to the trek across Iowa, that from Winter Quarters to Zion went off splendidly. For one thing, the Mormon Pioneer Company was expertly chosen. As Wallace Stegner succinctly described them, its members were "picked men, well-supplied, well-armed, and well-led. . . ." Forms of trouble "that afflicted some wagon trains even unto death—Indians, weather, poison water, dry *jornadas*,* lack of feed, were for them no worse than annoyances. The Mormon pioneers lost more days to the Sabbath than to any hazards of the trail." Yet although the trail had already been marked before them, the trek across Nebraska to Fort Bridger was no easy affair. The Pioneer Company once again risked the unknown by traveling not on the south side of the Platte but on the north. Still designated as the "Mormon Trail," the route was chosen over the favored one, which it generally paralleled, for reasons most histories do not make clear. The Oregon Trail, along the Platte's south bank, already existed. No new road had to be cut, no bridges had to be built, and the grass was greener and more plentiful, since it was left unmolested by the Indians with their torches.

Why, then, did the Saints choose the north bank of the Platte, where prairie fires in places had left only stubble and which was several miles longer? Perhaps the lingering memory of the church's previous turbulent years provides an adequate answer. The north bank simply was farther from Missouri—still a hotbed of anti-Mormonism in 1847 and a place from which, rumors still insisted in the spring

*A day's march on the desert, or a stretch of desert

of that year, new attacks by the mob might originate. Many of the pioneers moving west along the Platte were Missourians, and the Saints had had their fill of them. Further, blazing a brand-new trail meant that the Mormons could establish their own camps along the way, not merely inherit someone else's in which more than temporary occupancy might be questionable.

Picking a Pioneer Company was no easy task. Half a thousand of the Mormons who had left Nauvoo had been conscripted for the Mexican War. Many others were in Garden Grove and Mount Pisgah. At Winter Quarters, the long winter had left six hundred dead,† and only about thirty-five hundred of the twenty-five thousand who had been in Nauvoo only two years earlier now were on the banks of the Missouri as spring approached. And even among Winter Quarters' "permanent" population, scores of men were absent; they had been dispatched across the river into Iowa and south to Missouri to earn income for the Saints as rail-splitters, plowmen and mill workers.

On March 29, Brigham called a meeting of the officers of the two emigrating companies. The first, the Pioneer detachment, he told them, would march straight through to the Great Basin without stopping, taking only two pioneers per wagon. There, they would locate "a stake of Zion," and then return for their families, in the second body, or main company. And there would be no delay in getting under way. They would have to leave Winter Quarters even before the prairie grass turned green if they were to accomplish their goals before the next winter's snows.

On Monday, April 5, Heber C. Kimball moved six of his teams out of Winter Quarters, stopping at a point three miles west which had been selected as a rendezvous point for other members of the Pioneer Company, who would follow. Although most histories list that date as the "official" start of the trek to Utah from Winter Quarters, much had yet to be done and the actual march of the full company did not begin until mid-April. Kimball's camp was a short distance east of Little Papillon Creek, about two and one half miles northeast of the present Nebraska community of Irvington, in Douglas County. The site was not new to the Mormons; then called Cutler's Park, it had been the first campground established west of the Missouri the previous year.

Other wagons joined Kimball's as soon as they could, and they moved forward together to the Elkhorn River. Brigham Young was not among them; he had remained in Winter Quarters to conduct the annual spring conference of the church on April 6, in which the Saints unanimously sustained eleven of the twelve apostles with Brigham as their leader. Lyman Wright, who was in Texas contrary to the

---

†Thomas L. Kane's estimate of six hundred deaths at Winter Quarters is not accepted by some historians and may be overstated. The most difficult times on the Missouri River were the summer months, especially the first summer, of 1846, when a lack of vegetables caused many to contract scurvy. The number of Saints who perished that first summer is not recorded, but from mid-September 1846 to May 1848, scurvy, consumption, and chills and fever caused 359 deaths at Cutler's Park and Winter Quarters, according to a sexton's records. It is probably more correct to state that six hundred Mormons died during a two-year period at Winter Quarters, rather than during the first season alone.

wishes of his fellow apostles, was not accepted unanimously, and his case was held over for further consideration.

The day following the conference, April 7, Brigham left Winter Quarters and traveled ten miles to the site where twenty-five wagons were now waiting. Word was received the next day, however, that Parley P. Pratt had returned to the Missouri River from England; Brigham, anxious to hear his report as well as to receive equipment for the exodus that Pratt was scheduled to bring, returned to the main encampment. In Winter Quarters, Pratt reported that the Great Britain mission had gone well. As welcome to Brigham was the news that Elder John Taylor would arrive in a few days with a number of scientific instruments the pioneers planned to use to help guide them west. Though eager to move on, Brigham decided to wait for Taylor, and spent the interim days directing the movements of other members of the Pioneer Company toward the rendezvous point on the Elkhorn.

Taylor arrived at Winter Quarters on April 13. He had brought along "two sextants, one circle of reflection, two barometers, several thermometers," and a number of telescopes and other instruments the Saints had ordered months before. As important, Taylor gave Brigham two thousand dollars in gold raised among the British Saints. The gold was warmly welcomed; since the pioneers would soon be traveling through country with few signs of civilization, there would be no money-raising work available for the rest of the trip, and since the Mormon Battalion's march was over, funds to finance the trek would be in short supply. The Saints also had been furnished with maps of the route to Oregon, as well as maps of Captain John C. Frémont's route to California via the Great Salt Lake in 1843, and of his return the following year by way of southern California, the Mojave River, Las Vegas, the Virgin River, the Sevier River, Utah Lake, Spanish Fork, and Pueblo, in present-day Colorado.

It was not until the afternoon of April 16 that the Pioneer Company was completed. It consisted of 143 men, three women and two children. (Originally the number of men totaled 144, but one of them, Ellis Eames, became sick a few days later and returned to Winter Quarters; he was the only "dropout" the rest of the way to Zion.)

Originally, Brigham did not intend to include women or children in the group; the hardships and dangers that lay ahead were simply too great. But Harriet Page Wheeler Young, the wife of Lorenzo D. Young—Brigham's brother—though weakened from the long winter at "Misery Bottom," pleaded successfully with Brigham to accompany her husband to the mountains. The other women were Clara Decker Young, Brigham's wife, and Ellen Sanders Kimball, wife of Heber C. Kimball. The children were Isaac Perry Decker, Mrs. Lorenzo D. Young's son by a former husband, and Lorenzo Sobieski Young, by her present husband. The number of wagons in the party was seventy-three; there were also ninety-three horses, fifty-two mules, sixty-six oxen, nineteen cows, seventeen dogs and a few chickens.

Although church histories say that only two children were among the Pioneer Company, there was actually a third, Charles Shumway's son, Andrew, who was thirteen. The histories are not incorrect; among the Mormons, as among other pioneer groups of the mid-nineteenth century, a boy was considered a man when he did a man's work, no matter what age, and that certainly included young Andrew, who accompanied his father from beginning to end of the journey to the Salt Lake Basin. Andrew had probably felt the tragedy of his mother's death more keenly than anyone except Charles Shumway himself. Now faced with the prospect of remaining behind with a stepmother who had been in the family for just over a year, he begged to go along. Charles in turn convinced Brigham that his son was a resourceful, hard-working lad who would be an asset to the company. John D. Lee gave the Shumways a span of mules, and father and son marched off together on April 14. There was a tragic reason for the Shumways' late departure from Winter Quarters. Left behind with his wife and his daughter Louisa was another daughter, Harriet, who was extremely ill; she died two days later, on April 16.

There was a dual organization to the Pioneer Company to which the Shumways and the others now belonged. One was spiritual in character, based upon the revelation received by Brigham. The second was military. In the latter, Brigham was lieutenant general; Stephen Markham, colonel; and John Pack and Shadrack Roundy, majors. The camp carried with them one cannon, and Thomas Tanner, appointed in charge of it as a captain, was assigned eight men to assist him. The cannon was a mobile one, mounted on wheels, and usually brought up the rear. Just before leaving the Elkhorn rendezvous, Brigham announced:

After we start from this spot, every man must carry his loaded gun, or else have it in his wagon where he can seize it at a moment's notice. If the gun has a cap-lock, he should take off the cap and put on a piece of leather to exclude moisture and dirt; if a flint-lock, he must take out the priming and fill the pan with tow or cotton. The wagons must now keep together while traveling and not separate as heretofore they have separated. Every man is to keep beside his own wagon and is not to leave it except by permission.

The day after William Clayton wrote this down for the record in his *Journal*, Brigham's further orders of the march were entered:

At five o'clock in the morning the bugle is to be sounded as a signal for every man to arise and attend prayers before he leaves his wagon. Then the people will engage in cooking, eating, feeding teams, etc., until seven o'clock, at which time the train is to move at the sound of the bugle. Each teamster is to keep beside his team with loaded gun in hand or within easy reach, while the extra men, observing the same rule regarding their weapons, are to walk by the side of the particular wagons to which they belong; and no man may leave his post without the permission of his officers. In case of an attack or any hostile demonstration by Indians, the wagons will travel in double file—the order of encampment to be in a circle, with the mouth of each wagon to the outside, and the horses and cattle tied inside the circle. At half-past eight each evening the bugles are to be sounded again, upon which signal all will hold prayers in their wagons, and be retired to rest by nine o'clock.

By grouping each wagon "to the outside," Clayton meant that its forward wheel would be locked with the hind wheel of the wagon it followed; this would form a solid corral except for one open gateway on each side of the circle which the Saints placed under heavy armed guard. "Circling the wagons" became a standard defense against Indian attack in the opening of the West; it was the Mormons, however, who perfected it.

The Pioneer Company moved for the first time under these regulations on April 19. It was a good day's travel, nineteen miles. As Wilford Woodruff described it:

> . . . Prof. [Orson] Pratt took an observation and found the latitude to be 41 degrees 27 minutes and 5 seconds. The point of observation was on the north bend of the Platte, 10½ miles north of where the Saints had crossed the river. It was while camping at this place that Elder Little overtook the Saints on his return from the Eastern States mission. On the evening of that day we camped near a grove of timber on the banks of the Platte where we formed a semi-circle. The river on one side was our defense. . . . There was a hard wind during the night and the morning was fair with a strong south-west wind which covered our wagons with sand dust.

Even with the approach of summer, the Platte River Valley grass was not yet high enough for suitable feed for the horses. The column therefore had to pause during the day, Woodruff noted, so that the Saints could cut down cottonwood trees ". . . in order that the horses might gnaw off the bark and browse from the limbs, a kind of food which the horses at this season of the year seemed to enjoy. The ration of corn for each horse was two quarts per day."

The Saints were now heading west on a broad floodplain that the Indians called the Nebraska, or Shallow Water. To the east, where the Platte was joined by the Elkhorn, there was a low-lying ridge covered by cedar trees that formed a sort of barrier in that direction. Ahead, however, was a flat natural highway up to fifteen miles wide. The Platte itself at this point flowed deep, rapid, and unobstructed, and was about a mile wide. On the following day, however—April 20—the pioneers reached the first of a series of mid-river islands that still characterize the Platte. The largest, about ten acres, was covered with timber.

Food at this point was growing increasingly important, but in the valley of the Platte the Saints were in luck. One help was a novel boat which they called the *Revenue Cutter*. It was made of leather and placed on wheels like a wagon box. On land, it could be pulled like a wagon, carrying a small cargo of goods and equipment. When it was to be used as a boat, it was merely pushed into the water, and thus became a sort of early amphibian.

At one point when the Saints' food supply was running low, Luke S. Johnson was asked by Stephen Markham to backtrack a mile or two down the river and try his hand at fishing from the *Revenue Cutter*. The two drove back over their route, launched the boat and cast a small net over the side. That day the net, according to church records, contained but "one snapping turtle, four small turtles, one duck, two small catfish and two creek suckers." Later fishing would be far more productive.

As official record keeper of the march, William Clayton up to this time had, by a simple arrangement, kept a log of the daily distance traveled. First, he measured the circumference of a wheel on one of the wagons, then he tied some red flannel on a spoke. Walking constantly beside that wheel, he could count its revolutions by the passing of the flannel past a given point. At the end of each day, he simply multiplied the number of wheel revolutions by its circumference and translated the result into miles. But it was tedious work and could go wrong if Clayton was distracted from his flannel counting.

He was convinced there was an easier way. Though a bad tooth was paining him, as usual, he took Orson Pratt down to the river on April 19 to describe a new invention he had thought up. Working out its kinks helped Clayton forget his annoying toothache from April 19 onward.

By April 20, small game and fish were becoming more plentiful. The Saints crossed Shell Creek that day, a stream only about eight feet wide spanned by a poor bridge; all the wagons got over without incident. This time their luck angling from the *Revenue Cutter* was much better; the seine produced two hundred fish, mostly buffalo fish and carp.

About a mile from the crossing, they encountered a prairie-dog town that covered about six acres of ground. They also saw gopher hills from one to six feet in diameter, and from three to twelve inches high, resembling small potato patches. The hills made the traveling rough for the wagons. Three deer strolled past within sight of the place where the Saints halted for lunch, but although O. P. Rockwell and Thomas Brown rode off in pursuit on horseback, Clayton noted, they "did not succeed in taking any of them."

The Saints now were approaching the heart of Pawnee Indian country. Though the Pawnees were not considered as dangerous as the Sioux, they were given to petty thievery, and the Saints doubled their guard after circling the wagons that night. They had their first face-to-face encounter with these tribesmen the following morning. In his diary, Wilford Woodruff described the meeting:

At 12:30 [on April 21] we came in sight of seventy horses and mules, and soon in sight of a large Pawnee village on the north side of the Loup Fork, and also one on the south side of it. We drove on by the village, and soon they began to sally out to meet us. We camped in the form of a half-moon, the bank of the river forming a parallel line in front. The Indians, numbering about two hundred on the south side of the river, came down to the shore. Some waded over and about seventy five came into the camp, including the grand chief of the nation, with many war chiefs. We met them and made them presents of four pounds of tobacco, fifteen pounds of lead, powder, fishhooks, beads, flour, salt, etc., but still they were not satisfied; considering our numbers, they thought they ought to have more. When we left the ground, the Indians appeared very dissatisfied, but we harnessed up our horses and drove on to Looking-glass Creek and camped at its mouth for the night on the bank of the Loup Fork.

After turning out the horses that night, Woodruff reported later, "the whole camp volunteered to stand guard, one-half of them the fore part of the night and a half the other part." Woodruff, himself one of the guards, wrote of the discomfort that rain and a hard wind had created; he wrapped himself tightly in a buffalo robe and tried vainly to keep warm. About 1:00 A.M., when it appeared the Indians would be no further bother, the guard was released. Before retiring, however, the Saints fired off a few rounds of the cannon just to let the Pawnees know they were alert. No Indians appeared.

The wind abated later. Rolling out as customary at 5:00 A.M., when the bugle sounded, on April 22, the Saints reached and crossed Beaver Creek, eight miles west, by 2:30 P.M., and seven miles farther arrived at an old Pawnee missionary station. The station was formerly occupied by the Reverend J. Dunbar but had been deserted the previous year. A government station where an agent, James Case, had lived, was just to the south. Case, now a member of the Pioneer Party, had been dismissed from government service the previous November when he converted to the Mormon Church, and raiding Sioux had swooped down and burned most of the buildings after his departure and stolen much of the equipment. They had not touched a lot of old and new iron equipment lying around, however. The scrap could have been put to good use by the Saints, particularly the plows, but Brigham forbade the pioneers from removing any of it, although he allowed them to feed their livestock on station hay, which apparently was not being used. How to pay for it was a problem, until he learned that the government still owed Case some back pay. Young proposed that Case take the hay as part payment, give it to the Mormons, then tell the government how much this had reduced the credit owed him.

The Saints were becoming increasingly concerned about crossing the Loup Fork and avoiding its quicksand. Traveling along its north bank had already taken them more than forty miles from their intended course. And they were more than twenty miles north of the Platte.

On the morning of the twenty-fourth, they could postpone the crossing no longer. They discovered at daybreak that a favorite horse of Brigham's, driven by John Y. Greene, had fallen into a ravine and strangled to death on a chain around its neck. It seemed an ill omen for the crossing, but Heber Kimball, Lorenzo Young and Howard Egan went on up the river to find a ford. But no place seemed safe. When they returned to camp, they found the others already in the water. Woodruff describes the hazardous task the pioneers accomplished that day:

The men commenced searching out a ford and found the whole bed of the river one body of quicksand into which if a horse or wagon stopped it would begin to sink. We had two channels to cross and a sand-bar in the middle. The deepest water was from three to four feet and very rapid and about three hundred yards across. At some places the quicksand sank both man and beast instantly; and the more they struggled to get out, the more they would sink. Of course, we avoided such places as much as possible.

As I led the van with my ten, being captain of the first ten, it fell to my lot to make the first trial. Prof. O. Pratt, having a pair of strong horses, went forward and I followed him. I had two yoke of cattle and my horses on my carriage with about ten hundred on it. As soon as I started, I immediately saw that the cattle did but little good, being slow and in the way, we would begin to sink. I jumped out of my carriage into the water up to my waist. About ten men came to my assistance with a rope and hitched it to the oxen and helped me in getting across the first stream, though with great difficulty. We stopped on a sand-bar out in the water, but my horses and wagon began to sink. By treading the ground a little, it would become a perfect quagmire, and though we were sinking in it, the men had to leave the wagon where it was and go to the assistance of Orson Pratt, who, in trying to cross the second stream, had sunk into a bed of quicksand, and all the men had to go to his relief to get his horses and wagon out. The horses were unhitched from the wagon, and the load taken out and carried to shore; the wagon was drawn out by the men.

I took off most of my load in a boat and went through the second stream. I got two other wagons in the same way, but it was so difficult an undertaking that the rest of the camp would not follow us, so here we found ourselves on the opposite side of the river, six men of us, to spend the night, together with our horses and wagons to guard against the whole Pawnee band, who were then camped below us on the same side of the river, and it was supposed that they numbered six hundred warriors. We divided our company, putting three on guard at a time. Brother Pack, Orson Pratt, and myself went on guard the fore part of the night. Although I had been in the water the whole afternoon, I stood guard in my wet clothing one-half of the night and slept in them the other half.

When we had guarded our part of the night we were joined by five men from the camp who crossed in a boat. They were sent by President Young to assist us, making eleven of us in all, and we divided our force accordingly. The night, however, passed off in peace, with no disturbance from the hostile Indians.

The morning was pleasant and Prof. Pratt took an observation on the south bank of the fording place of the Loup Fork. The latitude was found to be 41 degrees, 22 minutes, and 37 seconds. The camp on the other side was now busy devising plans to cross the river. They drew together timber and rails to build two rafts and began to put them together. Some of the brethren made another trial to cross with wagons by putting on several horse and mule teams. They went a little higher up than we did and got over with much less difficulty. The more the ground was trod in the water, the smoother and harder it grew, so the whole company turned their wagons back to the ford and abandoned the raft. By unloading one-half of the baggage, they could cross in safety; and they all crossed by doubling teams and by going back and forth until all were over. Each captain with his ten assisted the others across. In this way all Israel who were present went over the Loup Fork of the Platte River in safety went over the Loup Fork of the Platte River in safety without hurt to man or beast; and we felt thankful to God for His mercies and rejoiced that we were on the south side of the river.

We all loaded up our wagons and drove four miles and camped for the Sabbath on the bank of the river; and after our wagons were arranged, the Twelve took a walk on the high table lands to make observations, through their glasses, of the surrounding country.

On the next day, the Sabbath, they rested. Brigham had issued strict orders that the column would not move on Sunday. It was to be a day of rest and prayer and reflection. Nor would there be any fishing or hunting. Some of the men of the Pioneer Company had formed a choir, and it opened the 5:00 P.M. worship service with the hymn "The Earth Was Once a Garden Place." Several of the pioneers spoke briefly. When it was the turn of George A. Smith, he chose hunting as his topic, reminding the brethren of the martyred Joseph Smith's admonition "not to kill any of the animals or birds or anything created by Almighty God merely for the sake of killing." Almost on cue, a huge black wolf appeared near the camp and strolled nonchalantly within fifty rods of the wagons. That was also the day many of the pioneers saw their first antelope.

After dark, the Twelve and some others met near Brigham's wagon to organize a party for buffalo hunting in the days ahead. The Saints were nearing buffalo country, and they had anticipated that this most magnificent of all Great Plains beasts would sustain them well during the remainder of the journey to the Great Basin.

Buffalo were plentiful on the Plains at the time of the Mormon Trek; it was not until the 1880s that they were nearly exterminated by over-hunting. During its peak migration phase, in fact, the American buffalo population was counted in the tens of millions, and the Platte River, including its two forks, was a prime habitat. Not only did the Platte run down the center of one of the world's major grasslands, it furnished the millions of gallons of water consumed daily by these beasts. The river was shallow; buffalo could cross it easily to find the best fodder. For these and other reasons, the Platte as early as 1834 was considered the true center of the buffalo's American range, and the Saints had counted heavily on its abundance.

The Saints picked a team of eight riders as hunters. More would have been better, but they had only eight spare horses. Eleven others were chosen to hunt on foot. And whenever the number had to be limited further, those among the Twelve would have first preference. Brigham warned again that there would be no promiscuous hunting; only enough animals to feed the company would be taken. And he cautioned, too, that the Saints should be wary, that a buffalo stampede could be a highly dangerous thing. Only two years earlier, John Wyeth, traveling in the region, had written after watching a herd of angry buffalo on the loose:

> We saw them in frightful droves, as far as the eye could reach, appearing at a distance as if the ground itself was moving like the sea. Such large armies of them have no fear of man. They will travel over him and make nothing of him.

Now that they had crossed the river, the Saints had entered a midwestern region whose flora and fauna and even its weather were drastically different from what they had just left. The tall grass they had known gave way to a variety of much shorter blades, called buffalo grass. Timber was scarcer. Around them, in addition to an increasing number of antelopes, they found animals—lizards, wolves and prairie dogs, to name three—more adapted to a near-desert ecosystem than the animals in the lusher region of the Loup crossing. The climate was drier too; human skin lost its moisture and wood dried up and split open.

And there were more Indians. On the morning of April 26, just before daybreak, the Saints were jolted awake by the sound of a rifle shot. A guard had fired the weapon at what he thought were some wolves in the grass near the camp. They were Indians. As Wilford Woodruff described the incident:

. . . two Indians crept upon their hands and knees, approaching the camp to steal horses. They got within three yards of the guard before they were discovered. The guard at first thought them to be wolves and snapped at them. They rose and ran. Two of the guards fired and four others rose out of the grass. The bugle was sounded and all arose to arms, but no more were seen of them.

After a day of hunting (they bagged one wild goose and an antelope) and exploring the relics of an old Indian village, the Saints returned to camp, thinking the Indian scare had been an isolated incident. Just after dusk, however, an alarm was sent through camp that Indians had stolen two horses. Another horse had been destroyed earlier in the day in a freak accident when a bullet was accidentally fired and had broken its hip. With the loss of Brigham's horse, the Saints were now four valuable animals short. The Saints took off in pursuit.

Toward evening [Woodruff wrote later] they returned and reported that they had been attacked by fifteen Indians, who were in ambush in the grass. They came upon them, determined to take their horses from them, but the brethren kept them off by their rifles and pistols. The Indians were armed with guns and bows. When they found that they could not scare the brethren, they professed friendship to get to them; but the brethren were resolute and determined not to move but to fight, though only four to fifteen. The Indians finally rushed upon them to catch the horses by the bits. The brethren drew their pistols upon them, determined to fight and do their best. The Indians, seeing the determination, broke and ran, but fired their guns at the brethren. The balls whistled around them, but no one was injured. The brethren did not return the fire, not wishing to kill any of them if they could help it.

On April 27, the pioneers were forced for the first time to dig to find water. Just after crossing San Creek and scaling a series of small ridges that William Clayton said "were very sandy and dry," they dug three shallow wells but could not drink the water, because it had a coppery taste. Hunters of the party were out scouting for buffalo, but they reported back empty-handed. Brigham and Heber Kimball discovered a prairie dog town, and in one of their holes, there was also a rattlesnake. "And around the holes were also many small owls," Clayton wrote in his *Journal*, "which seem to correspond with what travelers have said previously— that the prairie dog, rattlesnakes, and owls all live in the same hole together." The weather was becoming drier still ("Our cattle and horses were very dry," Woodruff remembered), although the skies threatened rain.

The Saints also began to encounter piles of buffalo dung, sure signs that buffalo were not far away. With timber now in scarce supply, the buffalo chips made an excellent fuel for camp cooking fires.

Heber C. Kimball devised an ingenious way to cook over a fire using the new kind of fuel. First, he dug a hole in the ground about eight inches deep, fifteen inches long and eight inches wide. At each end of the hole he dug another of roughly the same dimensions, leaving three inches of earth between the middle and two end holes. Through these partitions he made a hole about three inches in diameter to serve as a draft. The buffalo chips were placed in the bottom of the middle hole and two wagon hammers were laid across the fire pit to support the pans. Because there was a great amount of free circulation underneath, Heber's stove required very little fuel.

Luke S. Johnson invented another type of stove for buffalo dung. He cut off the tips of the horns of a buffalo skull so that they became chimneys; the hollowed-out skull itself became an oven.

On April 28, Brigham tightened security in the camp again. The pioneers had seen no Indians, but they were taking no chances. They had not yet seen any buffalo either, but orders were issued that only hunters were to leave the vicinity of the wagons; all others would maintain a ceaseless vigil.

With each passing day, the weather became more springlike. William Clayton noted on the twenty-eighth, "the wind blew strong from the northeast which makes it much cooler"; the previous night's light rain had also given some respite from the dryness. Many wolves and antelope were spotted, and Clayton mentioned wild onions, ". . . the largest . . . I have ever seen."

April 28 was also the day the pioneers came into view of the Platte's Grand Island for the first time. It is one of the world's longest mid-river islands, estimated variously at between forty-five and fifty-two miles long, with fertile soil and rich stands of timber and rushes. Grand Island was discovered in 1812 but left virtually untouched until a year or two before the Mormon Pioneer Company passed by. Once owned by the Shawnee Indians, the island was acquired from the tribe by treaty in 1883 for two thousand dollars in goods and merchandise. Wilford Woodruff took a party of hunters to the bank of the Platte adjacent to the east end of the island the following morning and bagged a wolf and a goose; although they could see herds of deer on the island itself, they gave up the idea of fording over to it when Brigham cautioned that Indians might be lurking in its cottonwoods.

The pioneers' journals mention Indians almost every day along this section of the trail. On April 30, for instance, Clayton wrote:

> . . . we passed a place where the Indians had camped no doubt during their hunt. They must have been very numerous for their camp has covered a number of acres of ground. President Young, Kimball and Lyman are gone

ahead on horseback to look out the road. We have thus far followed the Indian trail, but it is now so grown over and so old it is scarcely discernible.

After a brief wet interlude from the rain of a few days earlier, it had become dry once again; Clayton noted that one of Orson Pratt's horses had taken sick and lay down several times in its harness. "I am not astonished," he recorded, "as the wagons and everything else is shrinking up, for the wind is perfectly dry and parching; there is no moisture in it. Even my writing desk is splitting with the drought . . . the clouds of dust were almost sufficient to suffocate everyone."

On May 1, the Saints saw their first buffalo. Accounts of the Mormons' buffalo hunt differ slightly in detail (they disagree, for instance, on the exact number of animals slain), but on one fact they are in enthusiastic accord: May Day 1847 was a banner day for the meat-hungry pioneers. An ardent hunter, Wilford Woodruff was especially elated at the sight of the great beasts of the plains. It was shortly after the camp arose at 5:30 A.M. and traveled its first six miles that the first buffalo were sighted. There were three of them, grazing contentedly on bluffs north of Grand Island. They could be clearly distinguished even without a spyglass. Three hunters—Porter Rockwell, Thomas Brown and Luke S. Johnson—immediately mounted their horses and rode off in pursuit. No sooner had they left camp when other herds came into view; with their glasses, Clayton counted seventy-two, Pratt, seventy-four. It was a long morning as the main party, halting at 8:15 A.M. near Grand Island, awaited news of the hunt. The excitement was later described by Woodruff:

We had not traveled more than two miles farther before we discovered another large herd five miles before us. The hunters assembled and held a council. We determined to get some of the buffalo meat if possible. We traveled, however, with the camp until within a mile of the herd when a halt was made and fifteen hunters started together. Amasa Lyman and myself of the Twelve were with them. We went along together until we reached a bluff within a few rods of the herd and then divided. Brother Grover and Luke Johnson went on to the bluff, O. P. Rockwell and Brother Brown took the entire left, and so we divided into companies on the right, left, and center. I was with the company in the center of the herd.

We all made a charge upon them from the bluffs and rushed on to the plain. The herd ran down the rough bluff into the plain, but when we reached the plain we soon overtook them, and each company singled out its game. We made choice generally of cows, then rushed up to the side of them and fired upon them with our pistols, which we found much better to carry than the rifles, which we found much better to carry than the rifles which were very cumbersome in running. The first we gave chase to was a cow with her calf. I rode up to her side and fired two balls, both of which took effect. The other brethren with me also fired at her until she was killed. I then ran my horse to the assistance of another party who had wounded one which was soon dispatchd.

I then saw that O. P. Rockwell had three bulls at bay on the prairie. Brother Pack and myself ran with our horses to his assistance. At the same time Brother Kimball came up. We surrounded them and commenced firing. They bolted ahead. I put spurs to my horse and ran in front and was within about a rod of them when they all pitched at me and gave me a chase for a fight. It hurried me to get out of their way. Two broke for the bluff and Brother Brown followed them; but Rockwell, Kimball, Pack, and myself stayed with an old bull. I fired two balls into him, Kimball one, and Pack one. The bull fell dead. We also shot a calf that was with him. I returned to Brother Brown on the bluff and found that one of the bulls to which he had given chase was wounded and had lain down; but Brother Brown having no more powder or ball, the bull got up again and ran into the herd on the bluff before I could reach him. We now all returned to our hunting ground to gather up the buffaloes we had killed; there being three cows, three bulls, and five calves, making eleven in all.

In the morning, Brother Solomon Hancock had gone out to hunt buffaloes on foot. As he did not return in the evening, we felt greatly concerned about him; but in the morning he returned, having killed a three year old cow which he watched during the night to keep the wolves from eating her. Three wolves came upon him. He shot one and the rest ran away. This was our first day's buffalo hunt and we considered the results quite good in as much as we were all strangers to a buffalo hunt, very few of us having ever seen one before.

While Woodruff's hunting instinct influenced his description of the chase, Clayton patiently recorded the visual impression the buffalo made upon the pioneers the first time they saw them:

The appearance of the wild buffalo at a distance is somewhat singular. The color of the back and about half way down the sides is a light brown, and the rest is very dark brown. The shoulder appears slightly rounding and humped. When running, the large shaggy head hangs low down, about half way in height between the ground and the top of the shoulder. They canter like any ox or cow, but appear far more cumbersome and heavy, especially about the fore parts, which look larger than they really are on account of the long, thick matty hair. They run tolerably fast, but a good horse will gain on them. They will run a long time without diminishing their speed. Their meat is very sweet and tender as veal.

Prairie dogs also fascinated Clayton. He was as intrigued by their sprawling colonies, or towns ("in some places the town is nearly two miles broad") as their vast number (". . . thousands of the little dogs"). Clayton vainly tried to approach the holes for a better look, but "I could not get near enough to see their form distinctly, for they are so quick into their holes when anything approaches, you can only have a partial view of them." The Platte's prairie dog reminded Clayton slightly of the common gray squirrel, with a tail "resembling that of a dog" and the chirp of an English throstle. The prairie dogs apparently were quick indeed; although Clayton mentions that the Saints frequently took pot shots at the little dogs, they "failed in killing any."

May 2 was again the Sabbath, a day scheduled for rest. It was a fine morning but cold; Woodruff's journal mentions that a half inch of ice formed on the Platte. The Saints were relieved at breakfast to see Joseph Hancock strolling back into camp. They had worried, as Woodruff mentioned, that he had been lost during the previous day's hunt. After breakfast, Hancock joined the other hunters in retrieving the carcass of his slain buffalo, but to their dismay they found that hungry wolves had beaten them to it despite the fact that Hancock had carefully fenced off the dead animal with wooden stakes before returning to camp.

The hunters bagged two antelope on their way back to camp (Brigham said that because it was the Sabbath, that would be all) and then spent part of the day dressing and drying the meat of the other buffalo. They cut up the hides and tongues and stretched the former on stakes.

Because it was Sunday, the wagons normally would have been immobile all day. But Brigham was worried about a shortage of grass for the stock; increasingly as they moved west into buffalo country, they found the rangeland burned off by Indians, and except for the cottonwoods and willows near Grand Island on the Platte, even tree leaves were in short supply as a food source. After morning prayer and lunch, therefore, Brigham decided to break the Sabbath ritual and move a bit farther west. At three-fifteen the column got under way. Two miles on, across a ravine and past another huge prairie dog town, the pioneers made camp at the mouth of Elm Creek, where it emptied into the Platte. Grass there was plentiful and water was also; the site was such a fine one, in fact, that Brigham decided it would be a good place to lay over an extra day for some much-needed blacksmithing, hunting and general repairs.

The Saints now were headed in a generally southwest direction, down the eastern half of a long crescent the Platte makes at that point before turning near present-day Kearney. They were near the eastern end of Grand Island, and Orson Pratt's celestial observation placed their position at latitude 40 degrees, 51 minutes, 42 seconds. This tallied closely with that of John C. Frémont's, except that the Mormons were still traveling along the north bank of the Platte.

As the camp hummed with activity that Monday, the pioneers saw smoke from a prairie fire set by Indians to the west. Later, when Mormon hunters on the perimeter spotted an Indian party of perhaps two or three hundred, they reported back in haste. As a precaution, Brigham ordered the cannon removed from its wagon bed and thenceforth "hauled in the rear of the company for immediate use."

The following day, May 4, Brigham ordered the wagons to roll four abreast instead of two, so they could be circled faster in case of an emergency. The Indians' grass fires were more common now. Instead of trouble, however, they saw other wagons moving east on the opposite side of the Platte, and for the first time since leaving Winter Quarters, they considered crossing the river before the ford they had scheduled at Fort Laramie.

One of the other wagoners was a half-breed fur trader named Charles Beaumont. He came across the Platte to satisfy *his* curiosity about the Saints' wagons. Beaumont told Brigham that his three fur-laden wagons were sixteen days out of Fort Laramie headed eastward to deliver their cargo.

Satisfied that Beaumont was who he said he was, the Saints offered bread, water, sugar and coffee (Beaumont said in three years at Laramie he had not tasted fresh bread once) and accepted the fur trader's offer to carry letters back to Winter Quarters. Beaumont was in a hurry and did not have long to tarry, he told Brigham, but he would wait long enough for the Saints to hastily scribble their letters. As he refreshed himself, Beaumont expressed surprise to find a wagon train on the "wrong" side of the river. The trail on the other side, he said, was good and hard. It had good grass for stock, and it was devoid of Indians. It would be no great task for the Mormons to cross over at this very point, where the Platte was only knee deep and with a good hard bottom.

The Mormons considered doing what Beaumont suggested. After all, the north bank was still little traveled, and they had become increasingly apprehensive about the Indians and their grass fires. On the other hand, they remembered their main reason for choosing the north bank: it was a trail chosen not only for themselves but for thousands of Saints to follow. And while crossing the Platte in spring might be easy, they did not know what their present site would be like when the river's waters rose.

Brigham dispatched two Saints to cross the Platte and look over the situation.

We drove on three miles [Woodruff wrote] and let our teams graze until the brethren returned from the French traders. They made a report to the camp of what was said to them. A council of the whole company of the pioneers was called to determine whether we should cross the Platte, or continue along the north side of the river. We were convinced that it would be better for us to cross the river on to the old traveled road to Laramie as there was good grass on that side, while the Indians were still burning it off on the north side. . . . When, however, we took into consideration that other companies would soon follow and that we were pioneers, and had not our wives and children with us, we thought it best to keep on the north bank and face the difficulties of burning prairies. A road would thus be made which would serve as a permanent route, independent of the old immigrant trail. There was the further consideration that the river would separate us from other immigrant companies that might be disposed to quarrel with us over grass and water. Besides, by the time the next company came along, the grass would be much better than on the south side of the river. A vote was called for. . . .

The Saints were unanimous: they would proceed to Laramie on the north bank as planned.

The Mormons called the buffalo "the Lord's cattle." By the first week of May, so many were seen on the Plains that the Saints had difficulty keeping them separated from their domestic stock. "During the time of our halts," Orson Pratt wrote, "we had to watch our teams, to keep them from mingling with the buffalo." Strays frequently wandered into the pioneer camp itself. Others, isolated from the herd for one reason or another, were often sighted. "One buffalo cow we found near our road," Pratt's journal for May 6 reads, "which seemed to be sick or weak through old age, although able to stand, yet she did not feel disposed to run; we gathered around her, while some caught her by the horns, but she was too weak and feeble to do any harm. We left her quietly to live or die." The buffalo probably did the latter; packs of hungry wolves were seen wherever there were buffalo, and weakened or sick animals were easy prey. One young buffalo calf that wandered into the pioneer camp was later attacked and devoured in minutes by wolves.

The pioneers had to drive the buffalo away from the wagons every day, "judging," William Clayton explained, "that it was unsafe to risk them between the wagons and the river." Brigham joined in the buffalo roundup; on May 6, he lost a forty dollar spyglass in the process and delegated another Saint to ride back over the trail to see if he could locate it; the following day, the errant instrument was retrieved.

No entries in the journals between Winter Quarters and Fort Laramie seem as repetitive as those concerning buffalo, and the Saints' astonishment at seeing the Plains' great beasts for the first time is evident. Clayton's journal entry of May 6 is typical: "The prairie looks black with them, both on this and the other side of the river. Some think we have passed fifty, and even a hundred thousand during the day, or have seen them. It is truly a sight wonderful to behold, and can scarcely be credited by those who have not actually seen them." Pratt said that hundreds fed within a quarter mile of the Mormon trail, and "did not seem alarmed at our approach." But although the animals were an abundant source of food, the amount of grass they consumed was enormous, and more than one pioneer diarist complained about the increasing scarcity of plains grass. And what little buffalo left seemed burned off by Indians.

The pioneers neared the juncture of the north and south forks of the Platte. The valley was gradually narrowing now, and timber was scarce except for cotton-wood on the midriver islands, which the Saints felled for bark to feed their livestock.

Orson Pratt took a celestial sight on May 7 and found the latitude to be 40 degrees, 51 minutes, 18 seconds north. Ever the precise scientist, he found this to be "the meridian of the greatest cold."

. . . For if the isothermal lines, or the lines of the same annual mean temperature of the northern hemisphere are traced from the eastern parts of Asia, they will generally be found to end northwards, arriving at their greatest extremity in a northern direction in the western parts of Europe. Here they take a gradual sweep towards the south, arriving at their greatest southern extremity in the central parts of North America, in about 100 degs. west of longitude; hence, those places in the northern hemisphere, through which the lines of equal annual temperature pass, have about 14 deg. or 15 deg. difference in latitude. In the west of Europe, those places situated 1,000 miles north of the places on this meridian, will have about the same annual mean temperature; while those countries in the eastern parts of the old continent, which are situated on the meridian of greatest cold on that continent, are still some 400 or 500 miles north of the countries bordering and ranging on the meridian of greatest cold on the New continent. . . .

While Pratt dissected the weather in infinite detail, William Clayton was busy improving his "roadometer." Counting a wagon wheel's revolutions hour after hour was a dizzying and boring business, and by May 8 he had nearly finished his invention. He had enlisted the help of Appleton Harmon and Orson Pratt. Later, in his journal, Clayton gave a detailed explanation of its function:

Accordingly, this afternoon I proposed the following method: Let a wagon wheel be of such a circumference, that 360 revolutions make one mile. (It happens that one of the requisite dimensions is now in camp.) [The wheel of one of Heber C. Kimball's wagons in which William Clayton rode was this size.] Let this wheel act upon a screw in such a manner that six revolutions of the wagon wheel shall give the screw one revolution. Let the threads of this screw act upon a wheel of sixty cogs, which will evidently perform one revolution per mile. Let this wheel of sixty cogs be the head of another screw, acting upon another wheel of thirty cogs. It is evident that in the movements of this second wheel, each cog will represent one mile. Now, if the cogs were numbered from 0 to 30, the number of miles traveled would be indicated during every part of the day. Let every sixth cog of the first wheel be numbered from 0 to 10, and this division will indicate the fractional parts of a mile or tenths; while if anyone shall be desirous to ascertain still smaller divisional fractions, each cog between this division will give five and one-third rods. This machinery (which may be called the double endless screw) will be simple in its construction, and of very small bulk, requiring scarcely any sensible additional power, and the knowledge obtained respecting distances in travelling will certainly be very satisfactory to every traveller, especially in a country but little known. The weight of this machinery will not exceed three pounds.

Actually an odometer, it was used for years by later pioneers. It was simple in design, it was amazingly accurate, and no one had to watch the roadometer for it to function.

It was completed on May 12 and attached to a wagon wheel. Clayton further refined it by encasing it in a weatherproof shield. He then staked a trail guidepost stating the distance from Winter Quarters.

Signs of Indians became more frequent. On the evening of May 12, Wilford Woodruff returned from a hike to the top of a bluff near camp and reported he had sighted two hundred Sioux wickiups and that they apparently had been occupied "very recently." He found a cured buffalo skin there and parts of other hides. In his diary, Erastus Snow also mentioned seeing remains of Indian encampments. "We passed . . . the carcasses of over one hundred buffalo lately slaughtered by them. They have taken only the hides, tongues, marrow bones and here and there a choice piece of meat, leaving the buffalo to the wolves, which are by no means scarce or backward in waiting upon themselves." Buffalo bones were everywhere; in fact, the Saints nicknamed the area The Valley of Dry Bones, a name that stuck with later bands of pioneers moving west along the trail.

The Saints of course had no way of knowing how many Sioux were in the region. But, counting the number of dead buffalo and estimating how many Indian hunters it took to kill them, and counting moccasin tracks, they guessed between five hundred and one thousand. During his hike, Woodruff also found a medicine bag tied to a six-foot-long stick and stuck into the riverbank. He had seen acres of land covered with buffalo wool—clues to the fact that the Sioux had dressed their slain game there.

The waste of buffalo by the Indians must have rankled with the Saints, who had been repeatedly instructed by Brigham that they were to kill no more than necessary and that every usable part of a slain animal was to be put to use; on one occasion, Brigham called for a vote to sustain this policy, and the verdict to support him was unanimous.

They were now well into May, and as the days passed they thought more and more often of their families. Except for the chance meeting with Charles Beaumont, the Mormons had had no Gentile company for more than three hundred miles, and their self-imposed isolation on the Platte's north bank heightened their sense of aloneness. On Sunday May 9—the Sabbath, always a good day for introspection—Clayton jotted down his thoughts this way:

After washing and putting on clean clothing, I sat down on the bank of the river and gave way to a long train of solemn reflections respecting many things, especially in regard to my family and their welfare for time and eternity. I shall not write my thoughts here, inasmuch as I expect this journal will have to pass through other hands besides my own or that of my family but if I can carry my plans into operation, they will be written in a manner that my family will each get their portion before my death or after, it matters not.

The compelling sense of loneliness haunted Clayton. As if to escape its monotony, he confessed in his journal of May 10, he had created a wild adventure in his dreams. Brigham, Heber Kimball and a group of others had gone up the river in a flat boat, "without stating their object," when a herd of buffalo charged the camp, "right amongst our horses and cattle, causing them to break their ropes and fly in every direction." Clayton's immediate concern was for Brigham's safety.

Seeing a small skiff in the river [he wrote] I sprang into it, and [with] a paddle lying in it, I commenced rowing in pursuit of the President. It seemed as though I literally flew through the water passing everything on the way like a railway carriage. In a few minutes I overtook the brethren in the flat boat, took the skiff and threw it on shore and to my astonishment I saw the skiff was made only of barks and cracked all over, and it seemed impossible to put it in the water without sinking it. The paddle with which I had rowed proved to be a very large feather and I had another feather in my left hand with which I steered the skiff. When I got to the flat boat, I made known what had passed in the camp, but the brethren seemed no ways alarmed.

Three days later, on May 13, it was Wilford Woodruff's turn to dream:

. . . we had arrived at our journey's end where we were to build up a stake of Zion. As we came to the place, an open vision of a temple was presented before me. I asked some brethren who stood by me if they saw it; they answered that they did not, but I gazed upon it and the sight was glorious. It appeared as though it were built of white and blue stone. The sight of it filled me with joy. I awoke and, behold, it was a dream.

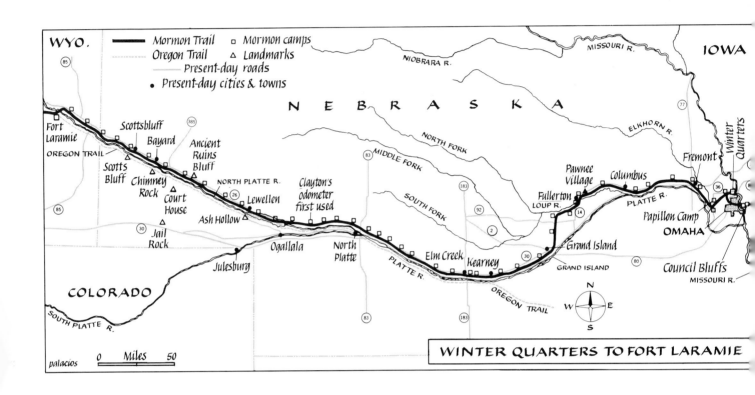

WYO.

IOWA

85

MISSOURI R.

NIOBRARA R.

NEBRASKA

Mormon Trail □ Mormon camps
Oregon Trail △ Landmarks
Present-day roads
• Present-day cities & towns

77

ELKHORN R.

NORTH FORK

Fort
Laramie

385

Scottsbluff

OREGON TRAIL

Bayard

Ancient
Ruins
Bluff

Scotts
Bluff

Chimney
Rock

Court
House

NORTH PLATTE R.

26

Lewellen

MIDDLE FORK

83

SOUTH FORK

183

92

Clayton's
odometer
first used

Pawnee
Village

Columbus

Fullerton

Fremont

Winter
Quarters

36

LOUP R.

PLATTE R.

85

Jail
Rock

30

Ash Hollow

2

14

Papillon Camp

OMAHA

Julesburg

Ogallala

North
Platte

Elm Creek

PLATTE R.

Kearney

30

Grand Island

GRAND ISLAND

80

Council Bluffs

COLORADO

N

MISSOURI R.

W   E

OREGON TRAIL

S

SOUTH PLATTE R.

83

183

palacios

0   Miles   50

WINTER QUARTERS TO FORT LARAMIE

The Missouri River shortly after sunrise. The approximate location of the ferry crossing.

At the Mormon Pioneer Cemetery at Winter Quarters (State Street and North Ridge Drive, North Omaha). Most graves were not marked.

The prairie near Schuyler.

Beyond Schuyler a trail leads through a cottonwood grove on the north bank of the Platte River. While this trail is in use today, it may have been used by the pioneers on their way to the river to water livestock. According to William Clayton's journal, for instance: "About ten miles farther—encamped near a cotton wood grove on the banks of the river."

Plumb Creek. "Its banks are lined with a little timber. There is also a steep bank on each side, and between these banks is the valley which is a few rods wide. . . . This place according to my account is 34 miles from Winter Quarters, and a lovely place to live."

Site of Loup River ford. "This is the pioneers' ford, but is considered not so good as the upper ford. River about 300 yards wide."

The Nebraska prairie near Palmer (above and overleaf).

Sunrise over the Platte River, eight miles south of Grand Island and a short distance from the Mormon Island Wayside Area.

Looking west from the bridge over the Platte River south of Gibbon.

Sandhill cranes along the Platte River. Every spring, several hundred thousand of these birds rest on the Platte for several weeks during their northward migration. The greatest concentration is between Grand Island and Kearney. Two roosts can be seen from the bridge at Gibbon. Over thirty thousand have been counted on the roost to the east of the bridge. Peak numbers generally are counted during the first weeks of March. The Pioneer Company saw mostly stragglers, although succeeding emigrants who left Winter Quarters early enough saw vast numbers.

Prairie two miles west of the city of North Platte. The "roadometer" invented by William Clayton was put into use a few days after the Saints passed this site.

Near Sutherland the sand hills on the north bank of the North Platte River parallel the river closely.

Sand Creek, looking north from the trail.

Ash Hollow. "At the farther side of this bottom is a grove of trees not yet in leaf. Brother Brown thinks they are ash and that the place is what is called Ash Hollow and on Fremont's map Ash Creek."

Wild turkeys moving up Ash Hollow.

Sunrise through the mist; cattle in the foreground.

Ancient Ruins Bluff. "We viewed the surrounding scenery which looks more like the ruins of an ancient city with its castles, towers, fortifications, etc. . . . Dr. Richards names these bluffs 'Bluff Ruins.' . . . The whole of the scenery around is one of romantic beauty which cannot be described with either pen or tongue."

Part of prairie dog town at the base of Ancient Ruins Bluff.

Court House and Jail Rocks. "Opposite the camp on the south side of the river is a very large rock very much resembling a castle of four stories high, but in a state of ruin. A little to the east a rock stands which looks like a fragment of a very thick wall."

"A few miles to the west Chimney Rock appears in full view. . . . Elder Pratt found that Chimney Rock is 260 feet high from its base to its summit."

Dome Rock. The Oregon Trail passed to the right (north) of this rock and then south of Scott's Bluff.

"To the southwest Scott's Bluff looks majestic and sublime."

The ferry crossing of the North Platte at Fort Laramie. It was also forded at low water. After crossing the North Platte here, the Mormon pioneers followed the Oregon Trail for most of the way across Wyoming.

When the Pioneer Company went through Fort Laramie, much of the fort had
not yet been built. However, when the major migration took place, many of the
buildings seen in this photo had been erected.

On the same day as Woodruff's dream, the pioneers faced a river—a tributary of the Platte—that Erastus Snow called "the most different" they had forded so far. It had a quicksand bottom fully as bad as the Loup Fork, and it was very shallow and about a mile wide. Whenever a south wind blew, the water was pushed to the north shore, almost as if a small tide were in progress. But when the wind shifted to the north, that shore was left high and dry and a man could walk across. Even though one bank was periodically dry, three wagons mired in the sand and "the men got very wet." In all streams that had quicksand bottoms—and the Platte's tributaries were famous for them—the pioneers learned to keep their wagons constantly in motion to avoid being bogged down. They safely negotiated the river and found a grassy spot to camp for the night, and Clayton noted that the day's progress had been 10¾ miles, and the distance from Winter Quarters was 341 miles.

By now, Clayton's roadometer had caught the fancy of the entire camp. He had begun also to erect daily wooden mileposts of the distance from Winter Quarters as a guide for future emigrants. Occasionally, other members of the party carved their initials on these posts. He had a right to be proud of the invention, but by May 14, he was becoming a little bothered that others in the group, Appleton Harmon specifically, were criticizing his mileage figures, and perhaps even taking more credit for the design than was theirs. "I discovered that Brother Appleton Harmon is trying to have it understood that he invented the machinery . . . which makes me think less of him than I formerly did. He is not the inventor of it by a long way, but he has made the machinery, after being told how to do it. What little souls work. . . ."

His irritation did not deter Clayton from his patient recording of other occurrences of the journey, however: the changing topography and weather, the wildlife along the trail, the availability of food, and countless other details which he would later incorporate into one of the country's first true travel guides, to be sold to others coming along the trail. First published in 1848, the year after the Saints reached the Great Basin, it is a remarkable little volume whose popularity was such that buyers were willing to pay five dollars a copy for it. Though its title was a rather ponderous one *(The Latter-day Saints' Emigrants Guide: Being a Table of Distances Showing all the Springs, Creeks, Rivers, Hills, Mountains, Camping Places, and All Other Notable Places from Council Bluffs to the Valley of the Great Salt Lake)*, its entries were a gold mine of information. As important perhaps to the Mormons was the fact that it delineated an all-*Mormon* route, passing along such details as sites of best timber, availability of water, the difficulties the reader might expect to encounter before reaching the next *Guide* entry. The *Guide* is reproduced in its entirety as an Appendix to this book. Here, however, is one typical entry:

North Bluff Fork, 6 rods wide, 2 feet deep. Swift current, muddy water, low banks, quick-sand bottom, but not bad to cross. Poor place for grass. Dist. miles [from last entry] 3½. From W. Qrs. miles 320¾. From C of GSL 710¼.

On Sunday, May 16, one of the pioneers returned to camp with the carcasses of an antelope and a buffalo. Woodruff noted that since it was the Sabbath, "it was a violation of the camp," and the fact was not lost on Brigham Young, either; he was growing increasingly displeased with infractions of camp rules. Thomas Bullock once again read the rules of camp, chastised those who had hunted wantonly, and dismissed the meeting.

The rule against needless killing applied to any animal, but not even Brigham could bring himself to enforce the edict when it came to rattlesnakes. On May 18, riding along the bank of a small creek, he heard the familiar ominous rattling only a few feet away. He managed to turn his mount away, quickly, before the snake could strike. Thomas Woolsey, following only a few feet behind, came even nearer to the danger. The snake coiled and sprang at Woolsey's horse and its rider. Brigham yelled at John S. Higbee to fire at the snake; he removed its head with a single, clean shot. The snake was four and one half feet long and had seven rattles. Brigham ordered it thrown into the creek. Since the stream at that time had no name, he called it Rattlesnake Creek, and it is so named on many maps today.

The pioneers had relied almost entirely on Frémont's topographical map, given them by Colonel Thomas Kane, for their guidance. On the evening of May 18, however, camp leaders met to decide whether the map was accurate enough to be used by other Mormon pioneers. That meeting may well have provided the impetus for William Clayton's *Emigrants' Guide,* for it was decided that when the pioneers reached the Salt Lake Basin, they should compile and cross-index all the information their many journals had recorded, and develop an all-Mormon map for future emigrants.

May 19 was one of the worst days on the trail. Woodruff's diary mentions that the Saints "encountered today the worst sand hill on the journey, and what made it worse, the rain was pouring down continuously." Clayton remarked that it was "the most uncomfortable day since Winter Quarters" and "especially tough on the teams."

But on the next day they reached one of the trail's most notable sites. The widest and deepest of the many draws, or canyons, that converge on the Platte, Ash Hollow is a picturesque oasis of greenery that in 1847 had the greatest abundance of firewood west of the Missouri. It also had flower gardens and cool springs of fresh water, all protected by a series of spectacular white cliffs rising more than two hundred fifty feet to the more arid tableland above. To many travelers on the California road, it seemed almost out of place, this four-mile-long canyon, a striking contrast to the bumpy, dusty, barren trail they had followed for miles.

It was not an easy canyon to enter, nor its river an easy one to cross. Orson Pratt said that "four of us launched our boat and crossed over, being obliged to drag it most of the way over shoals and quicksand," and the wagons had to be laboriously hauled up and down the slopes by using long ropes and extra teams of oxen. The emigrants called one of the rocky bluffs "Windlass Hill," because the wagons had to be winched down and up. But once inside Ash Hollow, which a few of the Saints visited, it was well worth the labor:

There was a good deal of rocky bluff on both sides of the river [Wilford Woodruff wrote in his journal] and some of the south side was formed into natural terraces, rotundas, squares, etc., from fifty to a hundred feet high and looked like good foundations for fortifications and strong-holds. They resemble the works of art and look something like the old castles of England and Scotland.

By the following morning, May 21, the Saints had left Ash Hollow eight miles behind. They were 409 miles from Winter Quarters. Later in the day, one of the pioneers discovered a large petrified bone. "It was a curious specimen of ancient zoology," Orson Pratt noted, ". . . belonging, probably, to the mammoth or some other species; it was the leg bone, from the knee downward—length 17½ inches, greatest width 11 inches, greatest thickness, 6 inches; its weight was 27 lbs after some had been broken from it." But there was no time to dally, or to study ancient skeletons; the Saints left it where they found it and moved on.

They saw more Indians that day and a few days later. Late in the afternoon, an Indian and his squaw were seen peeping over the edge of a hill. "The squaw fled to the bluffs as fast as her horse could go," Clayton noted, "but by signs made to them, they gathered courage and came up." The Indians signaled that they were Sioux, part of a larger party just beyond the bluffs. Through a spyglass, the pioneers could see the others and their ponies. The nearest wore a good cloth coat and was dressed in white man's clothes. The Saints were impressed; the Pawnees they had sighted earlier wore only breechcloths and were generally unkempt.

On May 22, the pioneers caught a faraway view of the trail's most impressive landmark, Chimney Rock. Credit for spotting it first goes to Porter Rockwell, who had ridden ahead of the main party to scout the trail. He was excited when he returned to camp; although Chimney Rock "appeared a long distance off," he told the Saints, it was every bit as spectacular as maps and previous accounts of Platte River road claimed it to be. He guessed the distance to be twenty miles.

Called by many "the eighth wonder of the world," Chimney Rock engendered more enthusiasm and awe in the travelers' diaries than perhaps any other natural phenomenon west of the Missouri. Now marked by the National Park Service as a national historic site, it is situated south of the Platte near the western edge of Morrill County, Nebraska, three and one half miles southwest of Bayard and twenty miles southeast of Scott's Bluff. Seen from twenty miles away or more, it is a slender column rising from a conical base or mound, standing apart from the principal ridge that bounds the North Platte Valley on the south bank. According to a geological survey made in 1895, its summit towered 4,242 feet above sea level, but wind and weather had chiseled seventeen feet off that when a later survey was completed, in 1965.

Writes former National Park Service historian Merrill J. Mattes in his *The Great Platte River Road*, a definitive history of the sprawling Platte Valley:

> The significant thing about Chimney Rock was the powerful impact of this strange and spectacular phenomenon on the mind and emotions of the traveler. Ash Hollow created some excitement with its "perpendicular descent" into its oasis-like canyon. Court House Rock has elicited admiration for its solitary grandeur and its mirage-like qualities. But Chimney Rock was the great scenic climax, a spectacle of such rarity that it seemed, like Niagara Falls, to rival the Seven Wonders of the Ancient World.

William Clayton, viewing Chimney Rock from about twenty miles away, thought it reminded him of "factory chimneys in England." He seemed as interested in bluffs closer at hand. "After gratifying my curiosity [at seeing Chimney Rock from a high vantage point] and seeing the men collecting their teams for a march, I descended on the west side of the bluff. The descent at this point looks more alarming than on the other. The side being very steep and all along huge rocks standing so critically, that to all appearance, a waft of wind would precipitate them to the prairie below with tremendous force. In one place in particular, a ponderous mass of rock appears to hang from the edge of the bluff without any visible means of being retained in its position." The Saints named one such bluff Frog's Head Bluff; a gravelly ridge was designated Cobble Hills. Still others "look more like the ruins of an ancient city, with castles, towers and fortifications on all sides." Appropriately, the Saints named them Ancient Ruins Bluffs.

The changing topography with its grandeur apparently gave new spice to the emigrants. That night, they played music, danced, and held a mock trial, one of their favorite pastimes. James Davenport was chosen as the defendant, charged with "blocking the highway and forcing ladies to detour around him." Although Clayton's journal notes the names of the presiding judge, the defense counsel and the prosecuting attorney (Jackson Redden, a Saint identified only as "Whipple" and Luke Johnson, respectively) there is no record of whether Davenport was convicted or acquitted. It really doesn't matter, for as Clayton explained, "we have many such trials in the camp which are amusing enough and tend among other things to pass away the time cheerfully during leisure moments."

There was less levity in camp the following day, Sunday, May 23. For many past days, the Saints had encountered rattlesnakes along the trail, and on this day, one struck home with vengeful fury. The victim was Nathaniel Fairbanks, a twenty-four year old New York stonecutter who had been exploring a series of bluffs near their camp. Scrambling down the hill, he heard the familiar rattling but jumped too late; the snake bit him on the calf, and in two minutes, Clayton tells us, "his tongue began to prick and feel numb." Soon afterward, Fairbanks began to feel stomach pains and he complained of dizziness. His fellow pioneers soaked a mixture of tobacco juice and turpentine, applied this to the bite, and fed Fairbanks a concoction of alcohol and water. The mixture made him retch, but he began feeling better in a few hours.

The incident had an especially sobering effect on that day's noontime Sabbath services. After remarks by Erastus Snow and Brigham, the Saints kneeled in prayer "and poured out our souls to God for ourselves, the camp and our dear families in Winter Quarters." A chill wind suddenly blew through the camp, and a gust knocked Heber Kimball's hat from his head and sent it tumbling across the prairie. It was a fine hat and Kimball did not want to lose it, but he restrained himself until the service ended and then ran a full mile to fetch it.

On Monday, May 24, after halting for a rest about ten miles from the previous night's encampment, the Saints were surprised to see two Sioux at the camp's edge, who motioned in sign language that they were hungry, and asked for food. After wolfing down a meal of bread, meats, beans and coffee, they indicated their main party was camped on the south side of the Platte and offered an informal invitation for the Saints to come over for a visit. Taking along an Indian dog that had been following the Mormon party for several days, they then disappeared.

Just before 6:00 P.M., when evening camp was made, Mormon scouts sighted the Indian party across the river. Brigham, curious to have a look, sent some men down to the riverbank carrying a white flag. The Indians responded by hoisting an American flag, and about thirty-five began fording the river toward the Saints' camp, "some of them singing."

They are all well dressed and very noble looking [Clayton wrote], some having good clean blankets, others nice robes artfully ornamented with beads and paintings. All had many ornaments on their clothing and ears, some had nice painted shells suspended from the ear. All appeared to be well armed with muskets. Their mocassins were indeed clean and beautiful. One had a pair of mocassins of a clear white, ornamented with beads, etc. They fit very tight to the foot. For cleanness and neatness, they will vie with the most tasteful whites.'

The Saints led their guests on a tour of the camp (making certain that, among other things, they saw the pioneers' repeating rifles and cannon—they even demonstrated a mock loading of the latter) and invited an elderly chief and his squaw to remain for the night. The chief was delighted with the invitation, and spent a fascinated twenty minutes viewing the moon through Clayton's telescope. "The Indians," Wilford Woodruff said, "were very good and stole nothing."

Chimney Rock was now close at hand; on May 25, the Saints estimated they came within two miles of its base. But they weren't certain; distances on the Great Plains were deceiving, and only by the judicious use of scientific instruments such as Orson Pratt's were they able to make accurate measurements. Those measurements, by the way, often were found by the Saints to be more accurate than their equivalents on the Frémont map which had been guiding them. It was that day also that the pioneers passed a formation on the south side of the Platte known as Court House Rock, so named because an earlier emigrant from St. Louis thought it resembled the courthouse in his home town.

Chimney Rock marked the approximate halfway point on the trail between Winter Quarters and the Great Salt Lake Basin. They were less than a week from Fort Laramie; soon it would be impossible to continue along the Platte's north bank any longer. The bluffs on that side of the river were growing higher and more arduous for both men and teams. Past Chimney Rock, the ridges, which Clayton called "truly delightful beyond imagination," merged into Scott's Bluff, named after an early trader. Nearby is the present town of Scottsbluff, founded in 1899, a half century after the first Mormons passed through. Today, Scottsbluff is the hub of a major agricultural region, with sugar beets as a thriving crop. In 1846, Thomas Bullock thought the ground was fertile; as an experiment, he planted three grains of white corn, "to show the next camp some Indian corn growing on the prairie."

Camp hunters were busy, as usual. They killed four antelope, which were skinned, dressed and divided among the companies. The Saints generally had heeded Brigham's oft-repeated admonition against over-hunting, but in other respects their conduct was an increasing irritant to him. On Saturday, May 29, his anger boiled over.

Camp journals vary in detail on exactly what was said that day, but they agree on one thing: Never in the days along the trail, before, or after, had Brigham unleashed such a well-defined, specific and stinging rebuke. In a printed version of his journal published years later, Clayton devotes twelve full pages to the "sermon," his longest single entry from Nauvoo to Salt Lake.

The bugle had sounded at 10:30 A.M. for the march to begin that cold, wet, cloudy morning, but Brigham passed the word the wagons would not move until he had had his say. Summoning the camp together, he mounted the leather boat as a pulpit and asked for a roll call.

He refused to travel a step farther, Brigham said, his voice rising as he went on, because of the attitude the Saints were displaying. "That as to pursuing our journey with this company with the spirit they possess," Clayton paraphrased him later, "I am about to revolt against it. This is the text I feel like preaching on this morning, consequently I am in no hurry."

Since leaving Nauvoo, he said, the Saints had left their persecutors far behind. "We are beyond their reach, we are beyond their power, we are beyond their grasp. What has the devil now to work upon?"

The Saints listened without a murmur. No one dared even cough. "Upon the spirits of the men in this camp," Brigham continued, "and if you do not open your hearts so that the spirit of God can enter . . . you are a ruined people and will be destroyed. When I wake up in the morning, the first thing I hear is some of the brethren jawing at each other and quarreling because a horse has got loose in the night. I let the brethren dance and fiddle night after night to see what they will do. But I do not love to see it." He also criticized gambling, card playing, checkers and dominoes; "the spirit of the Lord has been neglected while all this occurs. . . .

"Joking, nonsense, profane language, trifling conversation and loud laughter" were condemned, he thundered. "You don't know how to control your senses."

His sermon consumed nearly an hour. When it was over, Brigham asked each Saint "to repent of his weakness, of his follies, of his meanness, and every kind of wickedness, and stop your swearing and profane language."

Brigham paused, stepped down and let Stephen Markham say a few words. Then he climbed on the boat again, called the camp forward, according to rank in the priesthood, and asked its members to signify by raising their hands if they were willing to repent.

> Many were in tears and felt humbled. President Young returned to the boat as Brother Markham closed his remarks and said . . . the Lord will forgive us if we all turn to Him with all our hearts and cease to do evil.

The vote was called for. All hands went up.

At one-thirty, the camp began to roll once again. Brigham's rebuke had had its effect. "No loud laughter was heard, no swearing, no quarreling, no profane language, no hard speeches to man or beast," William Clayton recalled. "It truly seemed as though . . . we had emerged into a new element, a new atmosphere and a new society."

The following day, the Sabbath, May 30, Clayton noted that "I have never seen the brethren so still and sober on a Sunday since we started."

On Monday, May 31, the pioneers crossed the border between the present-day states of Nebraska and Wyoming. They estimated Fort Laramie, the first major milestone on their way to Zion, to be twenty-five to thirty miles away. The prairie at that point was bare, devoid of grass, but later in the day they encountered the first trees they had seen on their side of the river since May 10. For fifty-six days, they had trudged along the Platte's north bank. They were now thoroughly seasoned. Spurning convention, avoiding the more comfortable, more familiar, better trodden south bank of the Platte, they had been pioneers in the truest sense of the word. Now that phase of the road to Zion was nearly over.

The next day, they reached the fort.

6

Wyoming

Named for a French fur trapper who was killed by Arapahoe Indians on a stream bearing his name, Fort Laramie in 1847 was an oasis in the wilderness. For eleven years before the Mormons arrived, it had been owned by the American Fur Company. It had become a major trading center on the eastern flank of the Rocky Mountains, a place where fur traders came to barter and whose supplies they came to depend upon in times of trouble. Bands of Sioux, Cheyennes and Arapahoes camped near the fort, trading pelts and robes for dry goods, tobacco, beads and whiskey. The old fort, today partially restored, is situated about two miles from the south bank of the Platte, on the left bank of the Laramie River and about a half mile from the Laramie's confluence with the Platte.

June 1, the day of the Mormon pioneer party's arrival, was Brigham Young's forty-sixth birthday. The Saints formed a V-shaped camp, which William Clayton figured was 523½ miles from Winter Quarters, and spent an anxious night waiting to enter the fort to meet, for the first time since leaving the banks of the Missouri, another group of Mormons. Even from the distance of their campsite, they could see that the fort was nearly vacated and fast crumbling to ruin. For the record, Orson Pratt noted in his diary that the fort was 102 by 144 feet in size, 11 feet high, and was built of brick or unburnt clay. About eighteen men were stationed there, under the charge of a trader named James Bordeaux.

Advance scouts of the pioneer party had confirmed that other Mormons were already at the fort. Part of a company of Mississippi Saints who had crossed the Nebraska prairie ahead of Brigham's group the previous year, these were the Saints who had spent the winter in the settlement at what is now Pueblo, Colorado, where they were joined by the Mormon Battalion's sick detachment.

It was a happy reunion at Laramie, a fine birthday present for Brigham. "It caused us much joy to meet with brethren in this wild region of the country," Clayton noted, "and also because we should have some news from the brethren in the army." But there was sadness, too; from the Mississippians Brigham learned that some members of the Mormon Battalion had died at Pueblo, and at least one other was lingering near death at last report.

The Saints remained encamped across the Platte the following day, June 2, while Brigham and a small detachment crossed in the *Revenue Cutter* to inspect the fort personally. On the south side, they made a brief visit to old Fort Platte, which had been abandoned some years earlier, and then moved on to Fort Laramie, two miles away. Pratt measured the width of the river before crossing and found it to be 108 yards; "the water is deep in the channel and the current runs about four miles an hour." The measurements were important; Brigham knew that either here or just west of the fort he would have to cross the Platte to the south side for the first time, since the "Mormon trail," to the north, was fast becoming impassable.

They were "politely welcomed" by Bordeaux, Clayton reported; the fur trader confirmed the reports that only by crossing to the Platte's south bank could they expect to proceed west. ". . . We learned that we cannot travel over four miles further . . . before we come to bluffs which cannot be crossed with loaded wagons," said Clayton. "The road is better on this side, . . . it being hard and sandy. Feed [is] scarce mostly lying in little patches along the river." The fort had the equipment to ferry wagons across the Platte, Bordeaux told them. "They have got a flat boat which will carry two wagons easily which we can have for fifteen dollars or he will ferry us over for $18.00 or 25¢ a wagon," Clayton learned. The Saints agreed to consider the plan, then accepted the trader's offer of a tour of the fort. They were surprised by the inflation in prices of goods that had occurred since they left the Missouri, an increase that was undoubtedly also due to the fort's distance from centers of civilization. A pair of moccasins and a lariat each fetched one dollar. Tobacco cost $1.50 a pound, and a gallon of whiskey, $32.00. There were no prices posted on sugar, coffee or spices, Clayton noted, "as their spring stores have not arrived yet."

Bordeaux also had some disquieting news for the Saints.

Many of the Gentile pioneers moving westward included Missourians, he said, and one party had been led by their old nemesis, former Missouri Governor Lilburn Boggs. Boggs had obviously attempted to influence Bordeaux against the Mormons. "He told me to take care of my horses and cattle or the Mormons would steal them." But even Boggs had to admit, Bordeaux went on, that he was having as much trouble controlling his own men as he expected to have if he encountered the Mormons again; they were constantly quarreling, and many had deserted the wagon train.

Brigham's party was anxious to take a look at the ferry that Bordeaux had mentioned. The fur trader replied he'd do even better than that; he'd give them a free sail in it. "We got on board the boat and had a pleasant ride about three miles down the Laramie fork to its mouth," Clayton remembered, "the current being very swift." The boat was then towed to camp for use the next day. After dinner, Clayton recrossed the river in the Mormons' *Revenue Cutter* and seined "sixty or seventy" fish—salmon and suckers—before returning to camp.

The Council of Twelve met that evening and decided to dispatch three of the Saints to the Mormon colony at Pueblo to bring back its well pioneers to follow the pioneer party to Utah. As a final entry in his journal that day, Clayton, always given to comparing local wildlife and plants with those he remembered in England, wrote: "I have seen three birds here which very much resemble the English magpie in size, shape and color, in fact I know no difference between the two. We passed a number of currant bushes quite thick with young, green currants."

Ferrying the Platte began the next morning. The first wagon was rafted across the river at 5 A.M. on the boat rented from Fort Laramie. Soon, one wagon was moving across every fifteen minutes. Brigham wanted an early start. Hundreds, perhaps thousands, of Gentile wagons were moving along the Platte's south bank, and each evening it would be a matter of jockeying for the best camp. Estimates of the number of other emigrants moving along the Oregon Trail varied. Clayton mentions that "there is a report . . . that there are 2,000 wagons on the road to Oregon, but a little distance behind," but he adds, probably correctly, that "we are satisfied that report is exaggerated." At the fort, Bordeaux's men had reported eighteen wagons camped about three miles downstream, and that "more than five hundred others" had been counted recently.

The ferrying began in cold weather, with a strong southeast wind which, according to Howard Egan, "made it easier crossing."

The crossing at Fort Laramie was a snap compared to its recrossing later in June, a grueling job that would require several days and considerable loss of equipment and risk of human life. It was organized in two divisions, Brigham leading one and John S. Higbee the second. To keep the job moving briskly, Brigham pitted the two divisions against each other, and at one point the spirit of competition was moving the wagons across at a rate of less than twelve minutes each.

Shortly before noon, the four men picked to return to Pueblo—A. Lyman, Thomas Woolsey, John H. Tippets and Roswell Stevens—got under way. Brigham and three others accompanied them as far as the Laramie fork, where all kneeled in prayer.

The crossing was delayed in the afternoon after a heavy hailstorm swept the old fort. Its thunder frightened the horses so badly they were herded inside a corral to prevent them from bolting. The Mormons hoped their livestock losses were at last diminishing. That day, William Clayton took stock of the animals lost or purposely removed from the column since Winter Quarters, and the toll was alarming. Two horses had been stolen by Pawnee Indians and two others killed in accidents. A mule had been traded for a pony by Stephen Markham; another mule and three horses had left with their riders for Pueblo. A horse had been traded by Porter Rockwell for three cows and two calves; John Pack had swapped another for three buffalo robes, Nathaniel Brown had exchanged still another for a pony, and there were a couple of other pony trades to boot. With the addition of animals of the Pueblo detachment by Robert Crow and his party of seventeen, who had joined up at Fort Laramie, the pioneers were now on their way with ninety-five horses, fifty-one mules, one hundred head of oxen, forty-one cows, three bulls, seven calves, an assortment of dogs and chickens, seventy-seven wagons and one cart. The ranks of the pioneers themselves had swelled to 161. The animals seemed sufficient to complete the trip; the only question was whether enough feed could be found for them on what was planned as a brisk, sustained march.

The Saints made seven and one half miles the following morning, June 4, after rafting the last of the wagons across the Platte by 8 A.M. They presently came to a downgrade so steep they had to lock all the wagon wheels and attach ropes to the rear of the wagons; holding the ropes, the men could drag back on the wagons to enable the descent to be made safely. It was the first time in weeks that such precautions were necessary, and an indication that the level Platte Valley was fading behind them. They camped that night just in time to crawl into their wagons to avoid an evening thundershower. They were heading into the wilderness and over a new terrain once again, and before retiring, William Clayton jotted down what he had seen that day after he had scaled a small hill to see what the trail looked like ahead:

> The bluffs come near the river and are very high, steep, and look like sand. From the top I could see Laramie peak very plainly and also some hills ailong way off to the northwest. The country looks very hilly as far as can be seen and the snow on the peaks looks quite plain.

Pratt's journal noted the trail's changing flora:

> The grass is very good. Timber much more plentiful than below Laramie. It consists of ash, cotton wood, willows, and box elder in low places, with mountain cherry, wild currants, pine and cedar thinly scattered upon the bluffs. The wild sage grows in great quantities, and increases in size as the country increases in elevation. The wild rose flourishes in great abundance. The principal herbs and plants of this elevated region are highly odoriferous, perfuming the atmosphere with their fragrance.

Daily now, the Saints noted other signs that they were entering mountain country. The grade was tougher, and on June 5, Clayton observed that the trail was studded with cobblestones, "which made it hard on the teams." Wagons jolted as their wheels rumbled over the stones, and at the bottom of a hill, Robert Crow's wagon bounced with such a heavy jerk it turned over. Although the vehicle was soon righted, it was only the first of a series of mishaps that plagued the Crows in the days ahead.

Although the Saints were at last on the well-established Oregon Trail, trod by hundreds of Gentile pioneers, Clayton thought it fitting that he should post periodic wooden markers every ten miles along the route to inform future emigrants that Mormons had also passed this way. That day, he planted the first such marker. Each listed the distance between that point and Fort John (Clayton always used Fort Laramie's former name).

The pioneers paused to rest at noon near a large warm spring Frémont had noted on his maps. They didn't linger long; they had gotten a late start that morning, because a number of oxen had wandered off during the night and had had to be retrieved. The overnight camping place, incidentally, was near Register Cliff, a favorite stopover for westbound emigrants, who carved their names and sometimes messages in its soft rock. Many of the names can be seen today, along with modern-day graffiti. The noon stop gave the Saints time to wash their clothes in what later became known as the "emigrants' laundry tub" when the spring's 70-degree water became popular with later pioneers. The warm springs lie a bit south of what is now Guernsey, Wyoming.

This was the day, also, that the Saints met the first Missourians. There were two of them, men on mules, who approached the noon camp and said their company of eleven wagons, headed west, was nearby. Two other companies were reported within twenty miles of Fort Laramie, and they, too were composed partly of Missourians. Moreover, according to the Saints' visitors, the other pioneers had come from areas very near where the Mormons had been severely persecuted the previous decade.

That night, when the Saints set up camp on the bank of a small stream, they noticed that the Missourians camped just a little farther east. There was no visiting between the groups that night, but contacts with Missouri parties increased in coming days.

Today's tourist can still find evidence of where the Mormons camped that night and where thousands of other emigrants passed through; the site is marked by wagon ruts cut four feet deep through the soft rock.

More Missourians were encountered the next day, Sunday, June 6. About 8 A.M., a group of eleven wagons passed the Mormons; just as a prayer meeting ended, a few hours later, four horsemen who said they were part of another Missouri party, of nineteen wagons, rode up. "Some of these [were] recognized by our brethren," Clayton said, "and they seem a little afraid and not fond of our company. They say the old settlers have all fled from Shariton,* Missouri, except two tavern keepers, and I feel to wish their fears may follow them even to Oregon."

The Mormons saw Missourians a third time that Sunday just after a midday worship service. The company passed by during a rainstorm (which had ended the services abruptly) and consisted of nineteen wagons and two carriages. The Mormons watched as the Missouri party moved past, noting that most of the wagons were pulled by five yoke of cattle, instead of the usual two used by pioneers.

Mormons and Missourians did not speak, but a non-Missourian guide from the west was friendlier; water was available about six miles ahead, he told the Mormons, and beyond that there was none for at least fifteen miles. Brigham, calculating that the Saints probably could not reach the second water by the next evening if they stayed put that Sunday, broke the Sabbath "day of rest" rule and ordered his wagons moved another five miles. With the Saints on the move, the Missourians now seemed more interested in conversation. "Several of [them] came to look at the roadometer, having heard from some of the brethren that we had one," Clayton recalled. "They expressed a wish to each other to see inside and looked upon it as a curiosity." Perhaps miffed that they didn't ask their questions of the roadometer's inventor, Clayton said: "I paid no attention to them."

Orson Pratt noted on the following day, June 7, that the Saints had "gained elevation very fast" since leaving Fort Laramie and were now within the climatic influence of Laramie Peak, twelve to fifteen miles distant. "Its top is whitened with snow that acts the part of a condenser upon the vapour of the atmosphere which comes within its vicinity, generating clouds which are precipitated in showers upon the surrounding country. This peak has been visible to our camp for eight or ten days, and I believe that almost every afternoon since, we have been visited by thundershowers." The grass was more luxuriant at this altitude; "the timber is cotton wood, willow, ash, and box elder; considerable quantities of pine grow on the higher ground."

The Saints made thirteen miles that day, stopping to camp at a fine site named Horseshoe Creek, which nestled in a grove of trees. The hunters bagged two fine black-tailed deer and one antelope during the day. Wilford Woodruff called the meal "the best feed we had . . . on the journey."

But it was not a happy day, nor was the next, for the accident-prone Robert Crow family. Crow's leg became tangled in a lariat as several Saints attempted to yoke two steers. One of the steers fell, and only by fast work was Crow "liberated without injury."

The following morning as she stood on a wagon tongue to get a drink from a water bucket, Harriet Crow took a bad spill and was run over when the team moved suddenly ahead. "The cattle . . . threw her under the wheel which passed

* Misspelling of Chariton.

over her leg below the knee and downwards," Clayton said, "passing over her foot above the toes. We thought her leg was broken, but were soon satisfied to the contrary."

Riding ahead as a scout, John S. Higbee sighted the Missouri companies that had passed the Mormons earlier in the day. He was surprised at the mess they had made before leaving camp. "In cleaning up breakfast," he said, "they strewed meal, salt, bacon, shortcake, beans and other things on the ground." When the main Mormon body reached the site, there was little left of the mess, however; hungry wolves were having themselves a feast on the leftovers.

The Mormons knew that another hazardous crossing of the Platte lay only another day or so ahead. This time they would cross it south to north to begin the main ascent into the Rockies. Late on June 8, a group of eastbound traders passed by and told the Saints they had left a boat made of buffalo hides hanging in a tree near the Platte. They had no further need for the boat, and the Mormons were welcome to it.

The news pleased Brigham; he doubted that the *Revenue Cutter* could handle the second Platte crossing by itself, and there was no other boat available for hire. He needed the buffalo boat, but there was a hitch: the Missourians, ahead of the Saints, probably would find it first. Brigham decided the Mormons would somehow simply get ahead of them.

On June 9, he organized nineteen teams and forty-nine pioneers and ordered them to march ahead of the pioneer party. They were to locate and secure the traders' boat; they were also to build a substantial raft of their own for a ferry, kill game and do whatever other work needed to be done in advance of the crossing. The advance party rolled out a half hour before the remainder of the company, which, after passing through a four-mile-long valley of unusually red sand and crossing a creek, camped after making a remarkable nineteen miles for the day—one of the best distances since leaving Winter Quarters.

The next day, the Saints reached the Platte again. They had marched seventy-seven miles since last sighting the river, nearly ninety since leaving Fort Laramie. By now the bountiful Platte had become an old friend. Some of the Saints tried their hand at fishing (Clayton caught "two dozen good fish," but Woodruff, hearing a noise in a riverbank bush and remembering stories of Indians, bears and wolves, "thought it wisdom to return to camp" empty-handed.)

More Missourians were seen on the trail that day after the pioneers broke camp at 7:30 A.M., passed by a rocky arch thirty feet high that later became a small state park known as Ayers Natural Bridge, covered eighteen miles, and settled down for the night in a lush stand of trees where, according to Thomas Bullock, "birds sang merrily and enlivened the grove." The Saints were in particularly good spirits that evening; not only had they made one of their best day's marches, but the good feed of the past few days had fattened their livestock again.

Clayton noted that the site "is rich and would doubtless yield good crops of grain and potatoes, etc."; the Saints also discovered a vein of coal there in the area of what later was to become the town of Glenrock, Wyoming. The town was an important one in Mormon history; it got its start in the early 1850s, when later Mormon emigrant companies established a way station where livestock could be rested and fed. Mormon Canyon, where Brigham sent a detachment of Saints in 1853 to establish another way station, lies just south of the present-day community.

While some of the Saints probed various places along the Platte for the next day's crossing, others hunted and fished. Elated from the previous day's bag of twenty-four fish, William Clayton crawled out of his bed at 4 A.M. but "caught only four." It mattered little; once again he was in country that reminded him of his native England. "The warbling of many birds, the rich grass, good streams and plenty of timber make it pleasant."

They were now approaching what is present-day Casper, Wyoming, a booming petroleum and mining center with oil refineries and intense activity. In 1847, however, it was merely a place to seek a good river crossing. Its terrain made the going tough because of the steep banks of several smaller creeks and the soft clay lining their sides. Clayton described the difficulty of moving that day (despite which they managed to cover seventeen miles): "We crossed a very crooked, muddy creek, about twelve feet wide and over a foot deep. The descent and ascent were both bad on account of a crook from one to the other. Five and three quarters miles farther another muddy creek about three feet wide was bad to cross on account of the clay being very soft in its banks. The balance of the road [is] good, but considerably crooked."

The Saints overtook two Missouri companies later that afternoon; they also were seeking a place to cross the Platte. The best place to ferry over, the Missourians felt, was about twelve miles farther; Brigham knew this was about where his advance party would be encamped, waiting for the main column. "These men," Clayton wrote of the meeting, "have got a light flat boat with them and have already got one load over. They say they have killed three bears between here and the bluffs. They have also killed a buffalo." The latter must have surprised the Saints, since they had seen only a single buffalo since leaving Fort Laramie. The Missourians also gave the Saints a "souvenir": it was a snowball.

They were all moving into high country.

The Saints and Missourians halted about a half mile apart that night, but there was no doubt which camp was the more disciplined. From a half mile away, Thomas Bullock said, "we could hear their bawling and profanity; they made ten times more noise than the whole [Mormon] pioneer camp."

The final crossing of the Platte caused the Saints the greatest delay of the entire trek. But the *Revenue Cutter* and a newly built raft not only aided them well, they helped them turn a badly needed profit.

On June 12, the Mormons' advance party was already at work building the raft.

(A reading of all journals fails to disclose what happened to the "buffalo boat" they had been offered earlier; very possibly, they never found it.) Meanwhile, a party of Missourians had arrived at the spot. They were impressed with the *Revenue Cutter* and its capability of carrying fifteen hundred pounds of cargo at a time. They bargained with the Saints to ferry their own supplies across; a price of $1.50 a load was agreed upon, with payment to be made in flour valued at $2.50 per hundred pounds, corn meal at fifty cents a bushel, or bacon at six cents a pound.

Most of the Missourians involved were from Jackson, Clay, Lafayette and Daviess counties, Missouri, where the Mormons had experienced so much trouble earlier. The Saints were doubtless a bit apprehensive about the bowie knives and pistols carried by their "customers," but the weapons were put away before the job of ferrying was completed. In fact, the Missourians cooked a hearty meal for their guests. During the mealtime conversation, the Saints were briefed on the fate that had befallen an old benefactor in the mid-1830s during the height of their Missouri troubles. Bill Bowman, a guard at the jail where Joseph Smith, his brother Hyrum, and others had been imprisoned, was one of those involved in letting the prisoners escape. The Mormons, on the run after that, never knew what had happened to Bowman. On June 12, they found out from Bowman's father, who was in the emigrant party encamped on the Platte. A mob headed by Obadiah Jennings, suspecting the young jailer of treachery, rode him "on an iron bar until they killed him." Jennings, incidentally, was believed to be the same man who led a mob that slaughtered seventeen Mormon men and boys in the infamous Haun's Mill attack.

The Missourians on the Platte had more than one reason to be hospitable that night. Earlier in the day, one of them had tried to swim the river fully clothed at a point where it was one hundred yards wide. "When he reached the current he became frightened and began to moan," Clayton remembered. "Some of our men went to him with the cutter and arrived in time to save his life."

On June 13, again the Sabbath, the pioneers paused to worship according to their custom, but daylight the following morning found them preparing to challenge the Platte, which was swollen by summer rains. The Missourians were across, now it was their own turn.

"We commenced at 5:00 o'clock in the morning and in four hours we had landed eleven wagons of goods upon the north shore with our little leather boat," Wilford Woodruff wrote, "and during the day we got over all the wagons belonging to our tens, there being eleven wagons in all. The rest of the encampment—being twelve tens—got over only the same number of wagons themselves. They floated their wagons by tying from two to four together, but the wagons turned clear over each other, bottom side up and back again, breaking the bows, covers, and boxes to pieces, and losing ploughs, axes, and iron that were left in the boxes." The Saints returned to ferrying only a single wagon across at a time. By the end of that first day—June 14—they had crossed over only twenty-three wagons; getting the rest across would require three more weary days.

To make matters worse, the weather turned sour. It rained hard that day, and the wind made the going even more difficult. "The rain was heavy indeed," Clayton remarked, "accompanied by hail and as strong a wind as I have ever witnessed." The Platte was rising, too; "the men have tried hard, much of the time being in the water and sometimes up to their armpits which is very fatiguing indeed."

Strong winds continued the next day, June 15. "The wind being so high they could not get along very fast," said Clayton in his journal that day. In the gusty, wet melee yet another horse had been lost. In the afternoon, "they commenced driving over some of the horses belonging to Brother Crow's company. They neglected to take the lariats off the horses and the buffalo horse was soon seen to be drowning." Some of the Saints tried to save the horse, from a skiff, but they were unsuccessful.

Loss of the horse caused immediate concern over what might happen to the Mormon cattle. "The current was very strong, the wind high and the river rising, which made it look dangerous." But time was precious; Brigham decided to move the cattle anyway. All made it safely, and by day's end, forty-three wagons—a little more than half of the total—were safely across the river.

Although the job had taken longer than anticipated, the organization of the Mormons had accomplished it without serious mishap. The Saints had, in fact, become skilled river crossers, and the tidy profit reaped from moving the Missourians across gave Brigham an idea. Why not, he wondered, leave a small detachment at the site to help ferry future emigrants across? He knew it would not be long before the main Saint population still at Winter Quarters would be moving west; in addition, there was a potential ferry business to be had in the increasing westward tide of Gentile pioneers as well. "By that means," Clayton explained later, "they will probably make enough to supply a large company with provisions."

That was the genesis of the famous "Mormon Ferry," which remained in business for many years. It also gave impetus for the founding of Casper, Wyoming. The ferry site today is designated by a marker at restored Fort Caspar, on the west end of Casper.

Meanwhile, the Saints had been experimenting with rafts and canoes. By the 16th, a group of men had been dispatched to the hills to chop down and hollow out two large logs to serve as pontoons to float the raft they had previously built. Brigham himself joined; stripped nearly to the skin, he "went to work with all his strength . . . and made a first-rate white pine and cottonwood raft," according to Thomas Bullock, but, as Clayton remembered, its maiden cruise across the Platte was a near disaster:

When they started over with Brother Goddard's wagon the wind was blowing stronger. James Craig and Wordsworth were on the raft with poles and when they got nearly half way across, Brother Craig's pole stuck in the sand and threw him overboard. He swam back to shore and in spite of Brother Wordsworth's exertions, the wind and current carried the raft about two miles down the river. It was finally landed by the help of the cutter and without accident.

At last, Thursday, June 17, the job of ferrying Mormon wagons and supplies across the Platte was finished. The last piece of equipment to be moved was the Saints' heavy cannon. But their feet would not be dry yet. Safely across themselves, the emigrants turned to the task of helping two newly arrived companies of Missouri pioneers over; the Missourians, apparently, just weren't up to the strenuous job of building their own raft, and the Mormons' ferry service—even for a price—seemed a better alternative. A contract was agreed upon with one group at a price of $1.50 per wagon. The second Missouri group, obviously in a hurry, offered to raise the ante by fifty cents per man for each of the ten Mormons operating the ferry. Brigham must have been tempted, but Albert P. Rockwood had already signed the agreement with the first Missourians at the lower rate. On June 17 it was Steven Markham's day to command the ferry, and he did not feel bound by Rockwood's contract. He took the second Missouri company first; working "all night until daylight," the second company was ferried.

It was time to move on, but Brigham decided to wait one more day; work was continuing on a larger ferry boat to be operated after the main body of Saints had gone. William Clayton did not mind the delay at all. He went fishing again and caught "sixty five very nice ones which would average half a pound weight each." Thomas Bullock and Porter Rockwell visited the Missouri camp to collect the provisions due the Saints for the ferry service. It came to a handsome profit indeed. From one company they received a bushel of beans, 153 pounds of flour, one heifer and $6.55 in cash. From another, the bill was five and one half bushels of meal, 916 pounds of flour, a peck of beans and some honey. From the third: 226 pounds of flour, 117 pounds of soap, six plugs of tobacco and one cow.

Brigham called a camp meeting that evening and agreed to let Eric Glines remain behind to run the ferry. Glines was not Brigham's choice; in fact, the church President wanted him to continue on with the pioneers. But when Glines insisted, Brigham gave in. He apparently was in no mood to chastise anyone that evening, although he did have a few words of counsel, as usual, for the entire camp. "The President preached a short sermon for the benefit of the young elders," Clayton wrote in his journal. "He represented them as being continually grasping at things ahead of them which belong to others. He said the way for young elders to enlarge their dominion and power is to go to the world and preach and then they can get a train and bring it up to the house of the Lord with them, etc."

On Saturday, June 19, 151 pioneers headed off from the Platte for the last time. It had sustained them well, this river, but now their course led toward another river, the Sweetwater, and the Rocky Mountains. Wasteland lay directly ahead. Their cattle had been fattened during the Platte crossing interlude, and that was a good thing; for three days, they would tramp through a region Clayton described as "the worst of the entire journey," and one part of it as "the most horrid, swampy, stinking place I ever saw."

Their destination on June 19 was a river about twelve miles ahead. Once there, they found it almost worthless. Wilford Woodruff in fact confided in his diary that Brigham might well name the place "Hell Gate." The country abounded with alkali, he said, "and the water was extremely nauseating." "The land [is] perfectly sandy and barren," Clayton wrote, "and nothing growing but wild sage and a small prickly shrub something like those on the moors in Lancashire, England . . . there are two small streams of water, one appears to come from the northwest and is not very bad water; the other comes from southwest and is so bad the cattle will not drink it. It is strong of salt or rather saleratus and smells extremely filthy. Its banks are so perfectly soft that a horse or ox cannot go down and drink without sinking immediately nearly overhead in thick, filthy mud."

The pioneers did not tarry. In fact, they made 21½ miles before making camp, the longest single day's march since Winter Quarters.

Even though the next day was the Sabbath, the Mormons had had their fill of the campsite. (Clayton mentions that mosquitoes were still another annoyance.) Skipping breakfast, they rolled at daybreak, cooking the morning meal four miles west by using sagebrush for fires, in the absence of wood. Heber C. Kimball and Ezra T. Benson rode ahead looking for better water and soon discovered that the Saints were not the only ones searching for better conditions. The Missourians were there again, and they resorted to a trick in an apparent effort to frighten the two Mormons and gain the best campsite for themselves.

> As they [Kimball and Benson] were riding slowly along [Clayton recorded later] they saw six men suddenly spring up from the grass to the left of the road. The men were clothed in blankets some white and some blue and had every appearance of being Indians and the brethren thought they were Indians. The six mounted their horses and started on a direction parallel with the road. The brethren also kept on course. In a little while one of the supposed Indians left the rest and rode toward the brethren and motioned with his hand for them to go back. They, however, kept on and paid no attention to his motion. When he saw them still coming, he wheeled round and joined the others who all put spurs to their horses and were soon out of sight behind a higher piece of land.

The Saints reached a ridge just in time to see the "Indians" enter a Missouri camp. "It is considered an old Missouri trick and an insult to the camp," Clayton fumed, "and if they undertake to play Indian again, it is more than likely that they will meet with Indian treatment."

Brigham had had his fill of both miserable landscape and phony Indians. Aware that several other Missouri companies were on the trail ahead, he ordered the Saints, as Clayton put it, "[to] press on and crowd them a little." As a result, despite the fact that June 19 was a Sunday, the Mormons moved twenty miles that day, sighting a vast range of hills and snow-covered peaks in the process, before camping at 8:30 P.M. The Sweetwater River, ahead, was a tempting target. "We had been in the hopes of reaching [the river] but it appears we are yet some miles from it," Clayton reported. "The whole country around is entirely destitute of timber, not a tree to be seen, nor a shrub larger than the wild sage which abounds in all this region of the country and will answer for cooking when nothing else is found."

Around the evening campfire, there was "some anxiety in camp" about Wilford Woodruff and John Brown, who had gone ahead fifteen miles to stake out a campsite. The pioneers built a huge bonfire as a beacon and fired the camp cannon. The two advance scouts had, in fact, accepted a Missouri company's invitation to camp overnight after a supper of bacon, buffalo meat, cornbread, coffee and milk. Woodruff duly recorded the hospitality in his diary, but could not resist comparing his own group with his hosts. "I found that there was a great difference between these Missouri companies and our own, where there was no thing as cursing, swearing, quarreling, contending with other companies, etc., allowed or practiced."

The next day, June 21, was a vastly improved one for the Saints. Not only did they finally arrive at the Sweetwater River, but they passed two noted Oregon Trail landmarks along the way: Independence Rock and Devil's Gate. The quality of the water improved immediately, wood was more available, and the spirits of the emigrants began to soar.

Independence Rock was sighted in the morning. "We have supposed this to be the rock of Independence," Clayton wrote. "After breakfast I went to view it and found that it was a vast pile of rock extending from south to north about five-hundred feet and in width, one-hundred feet. The rocks are large and seemed piled one on another with the edges up." The rock was devoid of soil, but it sustained life nevertheless. During his climb, Clayton spotted "a large mouse on the top which had a long bushy tail like a squirrel." He also sampled water from pools on the rock, and decided it had come from rainfall. Named by the first white travelers to see it, in 1812, Independence Rock, near the northwest corner of present-day Pathfinder Reservoir, is a remarkable example of geologic erosion; Clayton thought its granite ridges looked as if "giants in by-gone days had taken them in wheelbarrows of tremendous size" and dumped them on the ground.

There was plenty of evidence that previous emigrants had scaled the rock as Clayton had; on one corner were "hundreds of names painted there." He erroneously believed he was the first Mormon to scale its summit. Actually, that honor belonged to Woodruff and Brown, who had visited it after leaving the Missouri camp that morning.

Woodruff noted the names painted on the rock too, described a cavern in its side "that would contain thirty or forty persons" and found its summit a good place for prayer.

> Upon this rock we climbed to the highest point and offered up our prayers according to the order of the priesthood, praying earnestly for the blessing of God to rest upon President Young and his brethren the Twelve and all the Pioneer Camp, the Whole Camp and House of Israel in the wilderness, our wives, children, and relatives, the Mormon Battalion, and the churches abroad. While offering up our prayers the spirit of the Lord descended upon us.

From the summit, Woodruff and Brown could see the Saints approaching below. They had no way of knowing the emigrants were worried that they might be missing. They calculated it would take the main party until about noon to reach the rock, so they "rode to the foot of the mountain and traced the way to Devil's Gate, through which the Sweet Water runs."

Devil's Gate is a chasm three hundred thirty feet deep, with the Sweetwater River running between the cliffs for about two hundred yards. When he reached the site, Clayton found that the river at the bottom narrowed to less than fifty feet, "dashing furiously against huge fragments of rock."

Meanwhile, the pioneer party had found a bed of what they called "saleratus"—a kind of bicarbonate mineral that smelled like lime but "is said to raise bread equal to the best bought in eastern markets." Lorenzo Young gathered up a pailful of the strange substance to test it; large quantities could be picked up quickly, and Clayton said that "when pulverized it looks clean and nice." Norton Jacob found a similar pool at Soda Springs, nearby. He described it as a pool of clear water, about four hundred to five hundred yards in diameter, that "tasted of strong lye."

About noon, the main party reached the Sweetwater River. Forty-nine miles of hard march lay behind them since leaving the Platte. The Sweetwater was to be their new friend, and they crossed and recrossed it many times in the days ahead. The river at this point was twenty feet wide and three feet or more deep, Clayton found, its current "very . . . swift and the water a little muddy, but pleasant tasting."

For the next few days, the going was rough once again. Lorenzo Young's wagon broke an axletree on June 22. It was the worst possible place for such an accident, since there wasn't a stick of timber anywhere with which to make repairs. William Henrie, riding with the main company, returned to the Youngs to help, and finally found a piece of wood with which to mend the wagon. One of the Missouri companies came upon them as Young and Henrie worked and thought the heavy load might again damage the wagon. So until the Youngs could catch up with the main party, the Missourians took the cargo into their own wagons. Though they once had been sworn enemies, the Missourians and Saints had apparently found a mutual bond of need along the lonely expanses of the Oregon Trail. There were occasional grim reminders of what had preceded them on that tough trail. On June 23, for instance, shortly after breaking camp, the Saints found a grave and a wooden marker where a woman had died the previous year, in July 1846. The marker indicated that the victim of the trail was "Matilda Crowley," who had been born in July 1830. Clayton thought about it; this meant she was only sixteen when she died, and it gave him reason for solemn contemplation:

> On reflecting afterward that some of the numerous emigrants who had probably started with a view to spend the remainder of their days in the wild Oregon had fallen by the way and their remains had to be left by their friends far from the place of destination, I felt a renewed anxiety that the Lord will kindly preserve the lives of all my family, that they may be permitted to gather to the future home of the Saints, enjoy the society of the people of God for many years to come, and when their days are numbered that their remains may be deposited at the feet of the servants of God, rather than be left far away in a wild country.

Not far from where Clayton stood in reverence beside young Matilda Crowley's grave, an even greater tragedy befell an emigrant party nine years later. Pushing handcarts, the company of 576 men and women, headed by Howard Martin, got caught in early-winter storms and could move no farther. Before rescue arrived in the form of a wagon train from the West, one hundred died. Mormons all, converts to the church from England, they were members of the Mormons' Handcart Company, whose journey along the Mormon-Oregon trail was one of the saddest chapters in church history.

In June 1847, however, the Saints were struggling through sand at the foot of rocky hills near what is now Jeffrey City. Despite the hard going, they made seventeen miles before camping on the bank of the Sweetwater only a mile away from the camp of two Missouri companies.

The Saints and Missourians got together that night to exchange information on the trail ahead. One of the Missouri company's advance scouts had gone ahead to get a closeup look at famed South Pass, a wide valley that had become the main pathway into the Rocky Mountains, and had returned to report his findings. "He reports that he has been to the pass and that we shall find water about fourteen miles from here," Clayton recorded. "He has come from the pass in two nights and hid up in day time to avoid Indians, but had seen one. He says it is not over twenty eight miles to the pass from here."

In exchange for the information, Burr Frost set up his forge and repaired the wheels of one of the Missouri wagons. Other members of the camp ate dinner and watched the sun set over the towering mountains to the west. The nights had turned colder and there was occasional scattered snow. The Saints and Missourians were leap frogging each other now: on June 24, Brigham ordered the usual reveille bugle call discontinued so as not to alert the other emigrants that they had started, but the Missourians apparently had expected the ruse; they got started first that day.

During that morning—June 24—Norton Jacob found what he called a "great curiosity": an ice spring buried under the prairie, and more of the saleratus they had encountered earlier. Clayton described the discovery:

> The water in the hole smells strongly of sulphur or alkali and is not pleasant tasting, but under the water which is over a foot deep there is as clear ice as I ever saw and good tasting. Some of the brethren had broken some pieces off which floated and I ate some of it which tasted sweet and pleasant.

In other ways, the ground the Saints walked on offered up natural treasures. A supply of potash was discovered near the ice spring, and the pioneers found they could use it to raise bread as yeast would. Near the springs the Saints also found a supply of salt so pure it could be sprinkled directly on their food.

Brigham had other matters on his mind. Just before dark, as the emigrants were rounding up their horses for the night, John Holman accidentally shot the President's best horse. It was a fluke: Holman was using his rifle to hold back the horse when the animal bolted, and the trigger caught in Holman's clothing, discharging a bullet into the horse's flank. Brigham was distraught (the animal "appears to be in great pain the sweat falling from his forehead," Clayton put it) but he was just as concerned that Holman would blame himself unduly. The horse, the "best in camp," valued at one hundred fifty dollars, died the following morning, the second to be lost to accidental shootings during the trek.

Just after leaving camp the next morning, June 25, the Saints forded the Sweetwater River, crossed a smaller stream and began ascending a bluff to a site Clayton said was "a good place to camp." It was too early for the Saints to make camp at that hour, but Clayton rarely missed an opportunity to jot down such possibilities; they appeared later in his best-selling *Emigrants' Guide*. He was as attentive to ways the trail might be improved for future pioneers:

> After traveling a quarter of a mile near the river [his journal reads] we encountered another high sandy ridge, the road again winding to the north to cross it. The descent on the west side is very steep and unpleasant . . . it is the opinion of many that by fording the river twice at the foot of the ridge we could save a mile and they think it can be forded. Colonel Rockwood has paid

particular attention to the place and reports that one hour's labor for 100 men would dig down the foot of the ridge so as to make it good passing and save riding the ridge and a mile's travel without fording the river.

The Saints, pushed on, finding snow in shady ravines and scaling a ridge that Wilford Woodruff called the longest and highest hill to date. He measured snowbanks that were ten feet deep and remarked later in his diary that "I should almost have thought myself traveling over the beautiful prairies of Illinois and Missouri, except that the country was covered with more sage than prairie grass." He saw carnelian stones by the dozens. "I saw more in one hour this evening than ever during my whole life, either in the rude state or polished, in all the jeweler's shops I ever saw in my travels."

The Saints were soon at South Pass, the great natural, elevated corridor to their Zion. "We are evidently at the east foot of the pass," Clayton wrote on June 26, explaining that John Frémont could not have been certain either, "on account of the ascent being so gradual that they were beyond it before they were aware of it." The famous pass was discovered in 1812, but it wasn't until 1820 that early trappers began using it regularly. The first wagons passed through it in 1832; in the following three decades more than three hundred thousand emigrants plodded along its well-beaten trail. It was growing ever colder; Thomas Bullock reported that as the Saints got moving that morning, ice was in water buckets and milk in one wagon froze solid.

On June 27—a Sunday, the Sabbath, the Saints' holy day, and the third anniversary of the assassination in Carthage Jail of Prophet Joseph Smith and his brother Hyrum—the pioneers crossed the Continental Divide. They had arrived in the West, where Joseph Smith had sent them.

Joseph's death was certainly on the minds of the Pioneer Company when they crossed Little Sandy Creek, at a point where, in Clayton's words, "we have the satisfaction of seeing the current run west instead of east." Orson Pratt placed the altitude at 7,085 feet, and Clayton figured the distance from Fort Laramie at 280½ miles. Wilford Woodruff tasted some water from the muddy stream: "for the first time in my life [I have] tasted water running into the Pacific." It was yet another Sunday that Brigham decided to move the column instead of observing the Sabbath with rest. "It was the general feeling to spend the day in fasting and prayer," Clayton explained, "but the gentile companies being close in our rear and feed scarce, it was considered necessary to keep ahead of them." As for recalling the sad day at Carthage, he wrote: "Many minds have reverted back to the scenes [there] and it is a gratification that we have so far prospered in our endeavors to get from under the grasp of our enemies."

At Pacific Springs, a little farther along the trail, the pioneers met a noted mountain man named Moses "Black" Harris, a tough, grizzled outdoorsman who had tramped the West for twenty-five years at the elbow of such living legends as Jedediah Smith, Jim Bridger, Kit Carson and Bill Williams. He knew his mountains and he knew the West, and on this anniversary of their Prophet's death, the Saints listened to "Black" give a firsthand account of what they would find on the other side of the Divide. It wasn't altogether encouraging.

"From his description, ... " Clayton confided in his diary that night, ". . . we have little chance to hope for even a moderately good country anywhere in those regions. He speaks of the whole region as being sandy and destitute of timber and vegetation except wild sage. He gives the most favorable account of a small region under the Bear River mountains called the Cache Valley where they have practiced caching their robes, etc., to hide them from the Indians. He represents this as being a fine place to winter cattle."

Harris, whom Clayton found "to be a man of intelligence," presented the Saints with six Oregon newspapers dating from the previous February. He also gave them several issues of the California *Star*, published by Sam Brannan, who had safely delivered the *Brooklyn*'s Saints to California the previous year. The Saints listened intently, for they knew Harris spoke from long experience, but they were undeterred. This may have disappointed Harris a bit, since he was a professional guide among other things, and he was trodding the Oregon Trail looking for work among westbound emigrants. Harris remained the night as the Saints' guest, selling a few buckskin shirts to the pioneers at prices Clayton described as "high" and "discouraging," then left them the following morning.

That was the day—Monday, June 28—that the Saints met the most famous man of them all. Tough, profane and no stranger to the whiskey bottle, James Bridger nevertheless was another man whose descriptions of the West the Mormons would listen to, even if they chose later to ignore his advice. Bridger was not as discouraging about the Great Salt Lake Basin as Harris had been, but according to Brigham's journal:

> Bridger considered it imprudent to bring a large population into the Great Basin, until it was ascertained that grain could be raised; he said he would give $1,000 for a bushel of corn raised in that basin.

To which, church history says, Brigham replied, "Wait a little and we will show you."

That exchange is not found in William Clayton's diary, but a rather lengthy and detailed account of other parts of Bridger's long conversation with the Saints is. Although he noted that "it was impossible to form a correct idea" of either the route or the country "from the very imperfect and irregular way he [Bridger] gave his descriptions" (other diarists guessed that "Old Gabe" was probably drunk), Clayton said Bridger suggested that if the Saints insisted on settling in the basin, they choose Utah Lake as the best spot, despite two major problems:

The Utah tribe of Indians inhabit the region around [the lake] and are a bad people. If they catch a man alone they are sure to rob and abuse him if they don't kill him, but parties of men are in no danger. They are armed mostly with guns . . . . The soil is good and likely to produce corn were it not for the excessive cold nights.

Bridger told the Saints the basin did have merits. "There is a vast abundance of timber and plenty of coal. There is a tribe of Indians . . . who are unknown to either travelers or geographers. They make farms and raise abundance of grain of various kinds. He [sic] can buy any quantity of wheat there. This country lies southeast of the salt lake . . . *if ever there was a promised land, that must be it.*"

In return for his information, the Saints gave Bridger a free pass for the Mormon Ferry back on the Platte River. As if spurred by his talk of the Great Basin, their wagons rolled a record twenty-four miles in thirteen and a half hours the next day, June 29. Their first stop that day was on the banks of Big Sandy Creek. Later emigrants followed its banks closely to avoid a barren, thirty-five-mile stretch across open country, but Brigham's Saints were unaware of what lay ahead. By 6 P.M., when they normally would have made camp, scouts reported to Brigham that it would be another six miles before there was a place with sufficient feed for the cattle. "The teamsters spurred up in order to get through," Clayton said.

The Saints were pressing on Zion now. But as they finally made camp that evening, Clayton jotted in his journal an ominous note: "Many of the brethren have gone down sick within the past three days and a number more this evening. They generally begin with a headache, succeeded by violent fever, and some go delirious for awhile." He made specific reference to John S. Fowler, thirty-seven, the latest to be stricken with what the Saints later labeled "mountain fever."

"[He] was seized this afternoon and this evening is raving." Webster's describes mountain fever as "any febrile disease contracted in the mountains and believed locally to be the result of living in the mountains." In other words, it is a catch-all term for many feverish illnesses found in high elevations. The Saints, however, thought it specifically could be attributed to the alkali they had picked up en route and used in baking their bread. "It is considered poisonous," Clayton wrote. "Some consider also that we inhale the effluvium arising from it, which has the like effect."

However modern medicine may diagnose mountain fever, it was a constant bane to the pioneer party until they reached the Great Basin, a few weeks later. None died from the illness, but those stricken became so ill from its effects that they were laid in the wagons and had to suffer a jolting ride as well. Besides, it was difficult to breathe clean air inside the wagons; Clayton said on June 30—the day the Saints arrived at the Green River, a sylvan oasis in the wilderness—that while the road was good, "[it] was sandy and filling the wagons with dust."

Named not for its color but for an early trader the Green River could not be forded; the only way across was by raft. Brigham ordered the raft-building started after the midday meal, grumbling, perhaps, that while a company of Missourians ahead of them had built their own raft, they had "set [it] adrift, lest it should benefit us," as Norton Jacob wrote.

The river site was a pleasant place for the task, nevertheless. "There are . . . many patches of wild apple trees," Clayton said, "and rose bushes abound bearing pretty roses . . . . There is a narrow strip of land which might answer for farming on each bank of the river."

Such was the setting for the Saints' on-the-trail meeting with Sam Brannan. Knowing that Brigham was traveling overland to the West, he had left San Francisco on April 4, —coincidentally about the same time the Pioneer Company left Winter Quarters, —with two companions. The eastward overland trip gave Brannan some appreciation of what his brethren had endured; at one point, he told Brigham, he had passed the last campground of the Donner party. Human bones were scattered over the site, he said.

The Saints were pleased to see Brannan, who said the California Mormons were in a rich land, planting wheat and awaiting the main body of emigrants. They were delighted to hear of the progress in California and to catch up on other church news (Brannan told them, for instance, that Addison Pratt, doing missionary work in the Pacific's Society Islands, had converted three thousands islanders to the church.) But no recital of the virtues of California could change their minds. Brannan was persuasive; he had even brought along eleven issues of the California *Star*, printed on the presses shipped on the *Brooklyn* from New York. They, as he, extolled California's virtues. But although Brannan pled his case for several days on the trail, Brigham was adamant about the Great Basin.

Work on two rafts was completed the following day, July 1, but high winds prevented their use in crossing the Green River, swollen with runoff and running twelve to fifteen feet deep. The Saints tried the crossing anyway, but gave up when the wind made it impossible to continue. One of the rafts did not work well. It became waterlogged and was found to be too heavy for safety, so it was cut up for kindling.

By that day, the first of July, fifteen of the Saints were ailing with mountain fever. One was William Clayton, suffering "violent aching in my head and limbs." As a result, his once-voluminous journal entries dwindled for a few days to mere cursory jottings. Thomas Bullock was sick too, not from fever but from what he described as "over-exertion." Of the main diarists, only Wilford Woodruff appeared to be feeling well. When his wagon was ferried across the river after the wind abated, he rejoiced that "we are now in California." (In 1847, that included everything west of the Continental Divide.)

Rafting the Green River resumed at full schedule the following morning, July

2. On the opposite bank, the Twelve held a council, decided to send a small group of Saints back along the trail to guide Mormons known to have left Winter Quarters, and heard Brannan once again heap praises upon California. Clover grew there "as high as a horse's belly," he assured them; there were wild horses and geese in great abundance, and the rivers were alive with salmon, he said. The Twelve listened politely, but there were no takers; the Great Basin, drab by comparison though it may have been, was still the goal.

Camp business, weather and the hard work of ferrying the wagons delayed completion of the Green River crossing until Saturday, July 3. The last wagon was safely across by noon that day. The next day was the Sabbath, so Brigham ordered the column moved only far enough to find a good campsite; the Saints halted three miles farther on, where plenty of grass was found for the three hundred cattle. Rain poured down that afternoon, and thunder "spooked" the animals. And there were mosquitoes. "These insects," Clayton complained, "are more numerous here than I ever saw them anywhere, everthing was covered with them, making the teams restive in the wagons."

Once encamped, Brigham discussed the Saints' upcoming arrival at Fort Bridger and cautioned them to use restraint while trading at the fort. He expected to find prices at Bridger as inflated as they had been at Laramie. The eight apostles in camp held council and began compiling a packet of information on what the pioneers had learned so far about the trail from Winter Quarters. The information would be returned to the Nebraska settlement to aid those who would soon be moving west.

The mountain-fever sickness continued. One of those stricken, Norton Jacob, was advised by Heber C. Kimball to be baptized; blessed by Kimball in the waters of the Green River, he later reported the incident "had the desired effect and broke my fever."

On Sunday, July 4, five men, delegated to retrace the trail eastward to meet westward-moving Saints, left the camp. "At 2:30 P.M.," Clayton wrote, "the brethren returned from the [Green River] ferry accompanied by twelve of the Pueblo brethren from the army. They have got their discharge and by riding hard overtaken us. They feel well and on arriving in camp gave three cheers, after which President Young moved that we give glory to God which was done by hosannas."

As it was the Sabbath, the occasion was one for prayerful rejoicing. It was also an excuse for a rare treat; George Smith rode into the nearby mountains and returned with a large supply of snow. This was mixed with sugar, and the camp had ice cream that evening.

The day ended on a sad note. Robert Crow found one of his cows dead, apparently from some kind of poisioning.

The Saints apparently chose to ignore the fact that Sunday was also Independence Day. There is no reference to the holiday in the main camp journals. Perhaps the Saints had too many other matters on their mind to honor the day. Certainly they were not unpatriotic.

The Saints got rolling again the next day, though, as Clayton put it, "many of the brethren [were] still being sick [but] generally improving." Three and a half miles farther, they got a pleasant view of the snow-capped Bear River Mountains, far to the southwest, and they were moving through country Clayton described as "somewhat rolling, destitute of grass and some very steep places of ascent."

They camped that night on the left bank of Blacks Fork. The grass there was poor and there was little timber. Orson Pratt complained about the clouds of dust, which made life miserable for mountain-fever-stricken pioneers inside the wagons. He suggested, too, that extreme changes of temperature they had been experiencing may have affected the sick. "During the day it is exceedingly warm," he said, "while the snowy mountains which surround us on all sides, render the air cold and uncomfortable during the absence of the sun."

The Saints crossed rivers twice the next day, July 6. The first was Hams Fork, a fifty-foot-wide stream only two feet deep, which was forded with no difficulty. Clayton noted, for future emigrants, that its banks would be a good place to camp. The second was a larger river, Blacks Fork, a tributary of the Green River, which, although one hundred feet wide, was also crossed easily. Beyond Blacks Fork, the trail turned dusty and barren, uneven with gullies and ditches "caused by heavy rains washing the land." After a total march of eighteen miles, they camped on the west bank of the river at a spot that Clayton found inviting:

> At this place there is a fine specimen of wild flax which grows all around. It is considered equal to any cultivated, bears a delicate blue flower. There is also an abundance of the rich bunch grass in the neighborhood of the river bank and many wild currants. The prairies are lined with beautiful flowers of various colors—chiefly blue, red and yellow, which have a rich appearance and would serve to adorn an eastern flower garden.

Expecting to reach Fort Bridger, the pioneers broke camp at seven-thirty the next morning, crossed Blacks Fork a second time a few miles later, and by noon had covered nine miles. Finally they entered a lush valley dotted with Indian dwellings, in which the old trading post, Fort Bridger, was situated. The wagon train moved a mile past the fort, which one emigrant said was "not very impressive." In later years, however, it played an important role in Mormon history.

Clayton's roadometer showed that the Saints had traveled 397 miles from "Fort John," or Fort Laramie. Zion was almost within grasp.

Some of the toughest going of all lay ahead, for the mountains to the west were imposing ones. But only seventeen days remained before the hardy Mormons would reach the end of their journey.

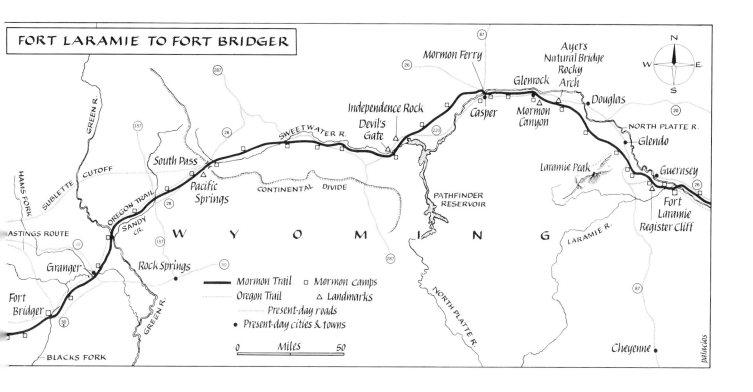

FORT LARAMIE TO FORT BRIDGER

GREEN R.

287

Mormon Ferry

26

Ayers
Natural Bridge
Rocky
Glenrock   Arch

87

N
W   E
S

187

28

SWEETWATER R.

Independence Rock
Devil's
Gate

220

Casper
Mormon
Canyon

Douglas

20

NORTH PLATTE R.

SUBLETTE   CUTOFF

South Pass

Pacific
Springs

OREGON TRAIL

CONTINENTAL   DIVIDE

PATHFINDER
RESERVOIR

Laramie Peak

Glendo

Guernsey

26

HAMS
FORK

28

SANDY
CR.

W   Y   O   M   I   N   G

Fort
Laramie
Register Cliff

HASTINGS ROUTE

187

LARAMIE R.

Granger

30

Rock Springs

30

Mormon Trail   □ Mormon Camps
Oregon Trail   △ Landmarks
          Present-day roads
      ● Present-day cities & towns

NORTH   PLATTE   R.

287

10

Fort
Bridger

30

GREEN R.

0   Miles   50

87

Cheyenne ●

BLACKS FORK

palacios

Photographer's Notes

About two miles north of Fort Laramie a gravel road takes off to the west. This road closely parallels the old Oregon Trail. Trail ruts can be seen clearly on the south side of the road for the first few miles. Several miles west over this road and just a mile or so from a Continental Oil Company tank farm, there is a gravel ranch road that leads north. This road crosses the trail about one-half mile from the junction. Overgrown trail ruts are clearly visible, and there is an Oregon Trail marker on the west side of the road, but better still is the hulk of a Model A Ford on the east side which probably expired making its way west along the trail about forty or more years ago.

If, after backtracking to the east-west gravel road you left to see the trail ruts, you turn west, the trail will dead-end a few miles down the road at an improved north-south thoroughfare. Turn north on this road; it intersects the Oregon Trail a few hundred yards south of the North Platte River. A sign a few hundred yards south of the river will indicate a turn to the west to reach the ruts. One would wonder perhaps why the pioneers did not take the easier road at the base of the bluffs, rather than go over the sandstone escarpment. It must be remembered that this area, now well drained, was an impassable marsh when the pioneers went through. The sign at the intersection of the trail to the Guernsey Ruts indicates a distance of one-half mile to the ruts. It is closer to a mile.

The Oregon Trail crossed to the north side of the North Platte at Casper. It is possible to follow the trail closely for the next sixty miles, but the journey is quite rough, since most of it is over a gravel road that may see a road grader no more than once a year. To get on this road, take the Poison Spider Creek road west out of Casper. It will be an improved road for approximately ten miles and then gravel or dirt for the next fifty or so miles. To make matters more confusing, there are no signposts (although there are Oregon Trail markers from time to time) and the occasional ranch road will lead off to the left or right and may even look better than the road you are traveling on. The official Wyoming state map shows this unimproved road but does not show crossroads or junctions. Furthermore, the state map leads you to believe that the road is relatively straight—this is certainly not the case. It is wise to obtain a reasonably current county map that has considerable detail, before striking off across country. I made the trip only twice. Both times, I found myself doing a certain amount of backtracking. Twice when I had lost my way I was lucky enough to find a rancher who was able to direct me.

Overgrown trail ruts looking west from a point six to seven miles west of Fort Laramie.

From the trail looking north (about seven miles west of Fort Laramie). A storm can be seen making up.

Register Cliff.

A mile west of Register Cliff. Rugged bluffs on the south side of the trail.

The Guernsey Ruts—a famous landmark on the Oregon Trail.

The pioneers first saw Laramie Peak from Fort Laramie. This photograph was made from a point along Highway 25 near Glendo.

Near Douglas. Mule deer on sage range.

Natural Bridge. "The creek on which we camped last night is named A La Pierre [actually A La Prele] and about a mile from where the road crosses, it runs through a tunnel from ten to twenty rods under the high rocky cliffs. The tunnel is high enough for a man to stand upright in it, and when standing at the entrance one can see the light through on the other side. It seems as though this tunnel has been formed by some strange feat of nature." Clayton evidently did not see this feature himself but used someone's account for his journal; it is much more bridge-like than tunnel-like.

The Ayers Natural Bridge State Park, showing the red bluffs.

Made from the trail about fifteen miles west of Casper. "There is some interesting scenery on top of this bluff, especially a range of rough, coarse sandy rocks of a dark brown color."

Independence Rock.

"On the top there are a number of pools of water."

Pioneer signatures on top of Independence Rock.

Looking southeast from the top of Independence Rock at the alkali lakes noted in William Clayton's journal. "This place looks swampy and smells bad. The beds of saleratus smell like lime, but the saleratus itself is said to raise bread equal to the best bought in eastern markets."

Looking north from the Sweetwater River a short distance west of the ford site.
A herd of antelope in the foreground.

Newborn twin antelopes.

The meandering Sweetwater River, from the top of Independence Rock looking east.

Photographer's Notes

The east side of Devil's Gate lies on the Dumbell Ranch while the west side is on Sun Ranch property. Even though most of this land is owned by the federal government, it is courteous when visiting to check in at ranch headquarters and ask permission. The old Highway 220 was laid practically on top of the Oregon Trail through much of these two ranches. The new improved highway passes a mile or two to the south of the original trail, but it is possible to travel the trail for quite a distance on the old blacktop road. This road takes off from the new highway a few miles east of Devil's Gate in the form of a two-lane blacktop spur. There is a cattle gap to cross and then you can stay on the road for several miles. Through the Sun Ranch there are five or six cattle gates that must be opened and closed each time you pass through. On the east side of Devil's Gate the road to the Dumbell Ranch headquarters takes you to a bridge over the Sweetwater River. After crossing the bridge, the driving is satisfactory for a few hundred yards, from which point it is a short walk to Devil's Gate. It is also possible to walk to Devil's Gate from the west, or Sun Ranch, side.

The east side of Devil's Gate looking west.

Martin's Cove (the valley to the left in the photograph) as seen from the trail on the south side of the Sweetwater. It was here that a handcart company led by Will Martin encountered an early blizzard. Many perished.

Split Rock. A famous landmark not mentioned by William Clayton. It was first seen by pioneers after they passed Devil's Gate.

7

Zion

For mountain man Jim Bridger, the arrival of the Mormons at his fort, on July 7, was a mixed blessing. In partnership with Louis Vasquez, Bridger had built the fort only five years earlier, in the declining years of the fur trade. He figured that its geographical position along the major pioneer roadway to the West would turn it into a prosperous provisioning center for the mushrooming emigrant trade. Bridger guessed correctly. The arrival of the Saints, on July 7, 1847, was only the first trickle of a Mormon flood to follow. The California gold rush of 1849 touched off another wave of emigrants that even Bridger had not counted on; by the end of the 1840s and until 1855, when the Mormon Church bought the outpost from him, "Old Gabe" was well on his way to a retirement nest egg.

But to Bridger that was, as they say, "the good news." What he had not counted on was that in settling in and developing the Great Salt Lake Basin, just over the Rockies, the Mormons, with their well-disciplined, polished mercantile organization and business sense, accomplished what the mountain man could not. So the Mormon settlements scattered throughout Utah Territory soon took away much of Fort Bridger's business, including Indian business.

Until its purchase by the federal government in 1857 (it is presently owned by the state of Wyoming), Fort Bridger enjoyed a varied history. It figured prominently in the history of the Shoshone and Bannock Indians, the Oregon Trail, the development of the Hastings cutoff, which proved so disastrous to the Donner party in 1846, and in the so-called "Utah War" of 1857–58. When Bridger met the Mormons, they became friends and partners; years later, Bridger hated the Saints bitterly; on one occasion, he even accused them of a death plot against him, an accusation that proved utterly without foundation.

But this, of course, all came much later. On July 7, 1847, the fort was small and Spartan, the final outpost of civilization the Saints came upon before trudging the last hundred miles—and the toughest hundred miles—to Zion.

To William Clayton, Fort Bridger was pleasingly situated. "The grass is very plentiful in the neighborhood and much higher than we have generally seen it. The whole region seems filled with rapid streams all bending their way to the principal fork. They doubtless originate from the melting of the snow on the mountains and roar down their cobbly beds till they join Black's Fork." The fort itself, he wrote,

> is composed of two double log houses about forty feet each and joined by a pen for horses about ten feet high constructed by placing poles upright in the ground close together. . . . There are several Indian lodges close by and a full crop of young children playing around the door. These Indians are said to be of the Snake River tribe, the Utahs inhabiting beyond the Mountains. The latitude of Fort Bridger is 41° 19′ 13″ and its height above the level of the sea according to Elder Pratt's observation is 6,665 ft. It is doubtless a very cold region and little calculated for farming purposes.

Brigham Young had elected to lay over at the fort a few days to let his pioneers rest, wash their clothes and repair equipment, primarily worn wagon wheels. It was chilly and windy the morning of July 8 and the Saints found ice on their water buckets. But the cold did not keep them from visiting the fort to trade, nor Wilford Woodruff from his favorite pastime of fishing. Woodruff angled wherever he could along the trail, and residents of the fort had mentioned a good trout stream nearby. It seemed a good place to try out a fishing rod and some dry flies he had brought back from England but had not previously used. He found a group of other fishermen at the stream; they had baited their hooks with fresh meat and grass-hoppers. None seemed to be having much luck, so Woodruff decided to stick with his own equipment.

> I threw my fly into the water and it being the first time that I ever tried the artificial fly in America or ever saw it tried, I watched as it floated upon the water with as much interest as Franklin did his kite when he was experiment-ing in drawing lightning from the sky; and as he received great joy when he saw electricity descend on his kite string, so I was highly gratified when I saw the nimble trout dart at my fly hook, and run away with the line. I soon worried him out and drew him to shore.

Woodruff fished "two or three hours" during the morning and evening, catching twelve trout in all. He considered it a triumph. "One half of them would weigh three fourths of a pound each, while all the rest of the camp did not catch three pounds in all, which was taken as proof that the artificial fly is by far the best to fish with."

When he wasn't fishing, Woodruff joined the others in bartering at Fort Bridger. He was luckier than many of the others, who found few takers for offers of Mormon goods to be traded; Woodruff "traded off my flint-lock rifle for four buffalo robes which were large, nice, and well-dressed," but like the others, "found things generally at least one-third higher than I had ever known them at any other trading post I ever saw in America."

Brigham and Heber Kimball bought a few buckskins, and Howard Egan swapped two rifles for "19 buckskins, three elk skins and other articles for making moccasions."

The Mormons had a legal problem on their hands during their brief stay at Bridger. Earlier, a fur trapper, Tim Goodale, had apparently stolen some Mormon horses and mules from the Mormon Battalion sick detachment at Pueblo. A warrant had been issued for Goodale's arrest. By coincidence, Goodale was at Fort Bridger when the Saints arrived. Sergeant Tom Williams of the battalion had the warrant in hand, but Brigham urged him not to serve it; what would the Mormons do with the trapper if they took him prisoner? The Saints felt that justice should be served, however, and Brown found a way: he seized one of Goodale's own horses, gave him a receipt, and suggested that he recover his loss "from your own people."

The pioneers wrote letters that a trapper had agreed to carry east to relatives on the trail or at Winter Quarters, and Sam Brannan and Sergeant Williams were detached to intercept members of the Mormon Battalion coming from Pueblo.

Thus rested, their wagons mended, their larder replenished, the theft of their animals vindicated, and Woodruff's fishing creel stuffed to its brim, they set out on the final leg of the journey.

The Saints were moving into almost virgin territory. The route they proposed to take over the mountains to the Great Basin had been followed by only fifty-seven other wagons: the Harlan-Young and Donner-Reed parties, of the previous year. Jim Bridger had been of little help in giving them specific directions. Instead they had to rely on the *Emigrant's Guide to Oregon and California*, compiled by Lansford W. Hastings, a lawyer and entrepreneur who had purportedly discovered a cutoff on the route to California that would save hundreds of extra miles required by the well-beaten Oregon Trail. Although Bridger had found considerable merit in Hastings' new route (after all, his trading post lay squarely at its eastern terminus), its promoter later was judged guilty of downright criminal irresponsibility. The Donner-Reed party, of the previous year, following Hastings' route, had taken a full month to go from Fort Bridger to Salt Lake Valley. They were marooned by an early snowstorm in the high Sierra, and more than half of the party's eighty-seven members died as a result. The remainder kept alive only by eating the flesh of their dead companions.

The Mormon camp was aroused by the usual daybreak bugle on July 9, and the wagons began rolling westward from Bridger at 8 A.M. The Saints were now without a river to act as a guide, and the wagon ruts of 1846 had all but been erased by a year of snow, rain and wind. At the outset, the trail was "tolerably level," then became tough going to reach a plateau the descent from which, Clayton remembered, was "the steepest and most difficult we have ever met with." In midafternoon the pioneers crossed Muddy Fork, which became known as "Big Muddy." They formed an encampment on the west bank; after days of traveling more than fifteen or twenty miles a day, this one had netted them but thirteen. The early halt, however, was attributed as much to the availability of good "bunch grass" as to the ruggedness of the terrain.

Bunch grass resembles wheat, with a head on top, and grows nearly as tall as wheat. It made excellent browsing for the animals, and it became even more common as the Mormon wagontrain trudged westward. Mountain fever persisted in the camp. Wilford Woodruff was the latest victim; he had to retire to his wagon "with distressing pain in my head, back, joint bones, marrow and all through my system, attended with cold chills and hot flashes through the body"; a dosage of cayenne and "vegetable pills" had him feeling better by morning. Despite the weariness of the new trail and the persistent mountain malady, however, spirits were high in the camp that night; the Saints serenaded Brigham with religious hymns before turning in.

The going was no easier the next day, July 10; if anything, it was tougher. Before, the wagons somehow managed to overcome obstacles on the trail by the sheer strength of their teams and the iron will of their masters. Now the Saints had to mend the trail itself as they moved along. Past a spring that tasted coppery and ran over strangely red sand, the Saints struggled up another high ridge and discovered they could not descend on the west side without somehow rearranging their path. "About halfway down," Clayton wrote, "there is a place over huge rocks, leaving barely enough room for a wagon to get down, but by labor it was soon made possible. A little farther, the brethren had to dig a place considerably to make a pass between the mountains." No one, not even Brigham and Heber Kimball, was omitted from the task; "President Young and Kimball labored hard with a number of others," Clayton remembered, "and in about a half hour made a good road."

About 1:45 P.M., the Saints halted to rest their cattle. Thomas Bullock named the place "Gunpowder Springs," because its bubbly water "tastes like gunpowder and smells like rotten eggs."

Another "very high" mountain lay directly ahead; Pratt's instruments made its height 7,700 feet, and it was ascended via a crooked road and a hefty amount of sheer manhandling. Wagon wheels were locked together for the descent, on the other side, and when bottom was reached, Thomas Bullock looked back and remarked that "it seemed like jumping off a house."

From trapper Bordeaux, at Fort Laramie, the Saints had heard of another mountain man, named Miles Goodyear, who lived in the Great Basin and whose cabin was near the present-day Utah city of Ogden. They had hoped to gain some information from Goodyear, and that night, after making camp, they got their chance. Goodyear had been hired as a guide by a group of emigrants returning from California, and their camp on July 10 was not far from the Mormons. As the Saints huddled around their campfire, Goodyear paid them a visit:

> He [Goodyear] says it is yet seventy five miles to his place [Clayton wrote] although we are now within two miles of Bear River. His report of the valley is more favorable than some we had heard but we have an idea he is anxious to have us make a road to his place through selfish motives.

There were two forks in the trail ahead, near Sulphur Springs, Goodyear told the Saints, and he advised them to take the right-hand one. They did so, but not right away, for the following day was Sunday, July 11, and on this Sabbath they would again halt to pray and rest.

They also went exploring.

"After prayers," William Clayton noted in his journal, "we . . . discovered a very strong sulphur spring. The surface of the water is covered with flour of sulphur and where it oozes from the rocks is perfectly black. The water in the creek shows sulphur very clearly and smells bad."

The Saints also discovered oil that day. As Clayton described it,

> The substance which rises out of the ground resembles tar and is very oily. Some have oiled their gun stocks and it and oiled their shoes, others have gone to fill their tar buckets and are sanguine it will answer well to grease wagons.

Clayton then grew contemplative about the trail ahead and how the Saints were reacting after so many weeks of march:

> There are some in camp who are getting discouraged about the looks of the country, but thinking minds are not much disappointed, and we have no doubt of finding a place where the Saints can live which is all we ought to ask or expect. It is evident the country grows much better as we proceed west, and vegetation is more plentiful and looks richer.

When the Saints came to the fork they had been told about, they had to decide which branch to take. Goodyear had proposed the northern road to the Salt Lake Valley, which he said was shorter. The Twelve met that evening and expressed doubts that the shortest trail was necessarily the safest. The majority, however, voted to take it anyway. "Such matters," Clayton wrote, "are left to the choice of the camp so that none may have room to murmur at the Twelve hereafter."

The pioneers reached the Bear River the next morning after breaking camp at seven-thirty and moving two miles. Clayton described it as "a very rapid stream about six rods wide and two feet deep, bottom full of cobble stones, water clear, banks lined with willows and a little timber, good grass, many strawberry vines and the soil looks pretty good." Pratt took an instrument reading and announced that the elevation was 6,836 feet.

The river was forded easily. Just beyond, the column began moving along the north trail of the fork. Almost immediately, the few scant signs of their pioneer predecessors disappeared. "There is scarcely any wagon track to be seen," Clayton wrote, "only a few wagons of Hastings' Donner-Reed Party company having come this route; the balance went the other road and many of them perished in the snow; it being quite late in the season and much time was lost quarreling who would improve the roads, etc."

The Saints had tolerated various outbreaks of mountain fever for several days. On July 12, however, Brigham Young himself became ill, and his sudden incapacity to lead changed the character of the march the rest of the way to the Great Basin. The road up the mountains was rough enough; now, with their leader too sick to walk, too sick even to be carried at full pace in his wagon, the company began to split up. After a two-hour halt to take stock of the situation, the main company moved ahead as eight others, led by Heber C. Kimball, remained behind to care for the ailing church president.

This marked the beginning of a division that split the Saints into three groups: an advance guard, the main body, and a few wagons delegated to remain behind with Brigham and other victims of the fever. The main body that day covered a total of sixteen miles before camping beside a small creek near which Clayton saw many antelope "but [which is] destitute of timber." Just west of the campsite, R. Jackson Redden found a cave. Four to six feet high and about thirty feet deep, it seemed to be a place where trappers had stored goods and provisions. It became known as Cache Cave.

Heber Kimball and Howard Egan rode up from the rear-guard party shortly before noon the next day, July 13, to report on Brigham's condition. "He [Kimball] reported that President Young is a little better this morning, but last evening was insensible and raving," Clayton wrote. "Colonel [Albert P.] Rockwood is also very sick and deranged." It was disquieting news; the Saints called a hasty meeting to decide what to do. The session ended quickly when a sudden thundershower doused the camp, but was soon resumed, and Heber C. Kimball then proposed how the company should proceed. An advance guard would be formed under the leadership of Orson Pratt "and endeavour to find Mr. Reid's [sic] route across the mountains for we had been informed that it would be impracticable to pass through the canyon on account of the depth and rapidity of the water." Pratt selected twenty-three wagons and forty-three men for his detachment, and moved out in the early afternoon. To these men would go the honor of being the first to enter the Salt Lake Valley. That evening, Willard Richards, Wilford Woodruff and George A. Smith went into the hills near their campsite and prayed for Brigham Young's health; according to Woodruff, "we received a testimony that he would recover from that very hour."

Orson Pratt's wagons meanwhile were moving steadily ahead. By the end of the following day, July 14, they had left the ailing Brigham and the main company nearly fourteen miles behind, camping that evening at the junction of Red Ford (Echo Creek) and the Weber River. "Our journey down Red Fork," Pratt said, "has truly been very interesting and exceedingly picturesque. We have been shut up in a narrow valley from 10 to 20 rods wide, while upon each side the hills rise very abruptly from 800 to 1200 feet, and the most of the distance we have been walled in by vertical and overhanging precipices of red pudding-stone, and also red sand-stone, dipping to the northwest in an angle of about 20 deg." Weber's Fork was a "rapid current" at that point, "whose crossing was quite rough because of its stony bottom."

The rugged gorge they passed through that day was Echo Canyon. Two days later, William Clayton, traveling with the main company, suggested how it got its name:

> There is a very singular echo in this ravine, the rattling of the wagons resembles carpenters hammering at boards inside the highest rocks. The report of a rifle resembles a sharp crack of thunder and echoes from rock to rock for some time. The lowing of cattle and braying of mules seem to be answered beyond the mountains. Music, especially the brass instruments, have a very pleasing effect and resemble a person standing inside the rock imitating every note. The echo, the high rocks on the north, high mountains on the south, with the narrow ravine for a road, form a scenery at once more romantic and more interesting than I have ever witnessed.

In the main camp on that day, Brigham was improving, though only slightly, but Rockwood remained very sick. "There are one or two new cases of sickness in our camp," Clayton wrote, "mostly with fever which is very severe on the first attack, generally rendering its victims delirious for some hours, and then leaving them in a languid, weakly condition. It appears that a good dose of pills or medicine is good to break the fever. The patient then needs some kind of stimulant to brace his nerves and guard him against another attack." Those in the main camp did not pass the day idly. Some caught up on washing and cooking, while others bagged five antelope in the nearby hills.

Wilford Woodruff considered that his carriage was the "easiest in camp." The next morning, July 15, he brought it back for Brigham and Rockwood to ride in, and found both men in improved health. By noon, riding in greater comfort, Brigham's rear guard caught up with the main body at the head of Echo Canyon. The march that day extended but four and a half miles, but at least the entire Pioneer Company was on the move once again. Its rear half had been delayed two precious days because of fever.

Meanwhile, Orson Pratt's advance guard crossed the Weber River again, from its right to its left bank, and camped for the night near the present site of Henefer, Utah.

Some of Pratt's group, including Orson, rode ahead on horseback to search for the Donner-Reed trail. "We soon struck the trail," Pratt remembered, "although so dimly seen that it only now and then could be discerned; only a few wagons having passed here one year ago, and the grass having grown up, leaving scarcely a tree." Pratt followed the trail another six miles. "There is some cotton-wood timber fringing the shores of Weber's Fork," he reported back, "and also thick clusters of willows, making very close thickets for bears which, from their large tracks and the large holes they have made in digging for roots, must be very numerous."

The main party had considerable difficulty getting through Echo Canyon the next day, July 16. Clayton, whose thirty-third birthday it was that day, remarked that "the mountains seemed to increase in height and come so near together as to barely leave room for a crooked road." But there was heartening news; Porter Rockwell, riding back from the advance party, now twenty miles ahead, came to tell them that the Donner-Reed trail had been found.

The news must have especially cheered Clayton on his birthday, for after writing about a broken wagon earlier in the day (Harvey Pierce's), of teams having to double up to make the grade, and of other nuisances of the trail, he now found more pleasant news to record:

> . . . we saw patches of oak shrubbery though small in size. In the same place and for several miles there are many patches or groves of the wild currant, hop vines, alder and black birch. Willows are abundant and high. The currants are yet green and taste most like a gooseberry, thick rind and rather bitter. The hops are in blossom and seem likely to yield a good crop. . . . Grass is plentiful most of the distance and seems to grow higher the farther we go west. At this place the grass is about six feet high, and on the creek eight or ten feet high. There is one kind of grass which bears a head almost like wheat and grows pretty high, some of it six feet.

By another Sabbath, July 18, only a little more than thirty miles remained. Clayton wrote that snow was seen for the first time, the previous day, since Fort Bridger, and the ground was covered with a white frost in the early-morning hours, although even at that elevation it was very warm during the midday hours. Neither company moved that day. Pratt's journal entry was only four sentences long, but in the main camp there was considerably more activity. Brigham was still "a very sick man," Clayton wrote, and there was growing concern among the Saints how the final miles would be mastered with their leader still in bed.

> Kimball proposed to the brethren that instead of scattering off, some hunting, some fishing, and some climbing mountains, etc., that they should meet together and pray and exhort each other that the Lord may turn away the sickness from our midst and from our President that we may proceed on our journey.

At the sound of the bugle, the Saints assembled as requested at 10 A.M. and heard Kimball propose that most of the wagons—except Brigham's and eight or ten others—should travel the next day toward the Great Basin, to "find a good place to plant potatoes, etc., as we have little time to spare." Kimball called for a vote, and his plan was unanimously agreed to. The pioneers adjourned the meeting until early afternoon, when they convened again to hear Kimball encourage them about the days ahead. "The bishops broke bread and sacrament was administered. Good feelings seem to prevail," Clayton wrote. Kimball said the Lord had answered the prayers earlier that day, and while a number of the Saints remained sick, "we expect all will soon recover." As were all the pioneers, Clayton was anxious to get moving again; doubtless with some relief, he confided to his journal before retiring that night, "Elder Kimball consented for me to go on tomorrow with the company that goes ahead."

"Tomorrow" was July 19, and for some members of the Pioneer Company (though not Clayton) it was the grandest day since leaving Nauvoo. For that was the day they got their first glimpse of the Salt Lake Valley.

But not the main company. Kimball's wagons slogged ahead that day over a road Clayton described as "very rough on account of loose rocks and cobblestones," entered Main Canyon, climbed a ridge known as Horseback Summit, then zig-zagged down the other side at great risk to their teams and wagons; the wheels of one wagon—George A. Smith's—in fact collapsed during the descent. Woodruff called it "the worst road of our journey," and the exhausted pioneers finally made camp in a grove of willows on East Canyon Creek five miles from Hogsback. Clayton erected a stake at the site; it was eighty miles from Fort Bridger.

Orson Pratt's day had been considerably easier and its conclusion far more rewarding. While others in the advance party moved slowly with their wagons, Pratt and John Brown rode on ahead on horseback up a gradual incline. Four miles farther, they staked their mounts and continued up the slope on foot. From the summit, they could at last see Zion. "Both from the ridge where the road crosses, and from the mountain peak, we could see over a great extent of the country," Pratt related later. "On the south-west we could see an extensive level prairie, some few miles distant, which we thought must be near the [Great Salt] Lake."

It was the first level stretch of real estate any of the Saints had seen since entering the Rocky Mountains. The two Saints then returned to their wagons, only six and a half miles from the site of their morning encampment, the short mileage due both to the ruggedness of the road and the fact that they paused frequently to move boulders and otherwise improve it for the benefit of pioneers of the main body who were following.

Although all three groups—Pratt's, the main body and Brigham's "sick detachment"—were moving at a snail's pace now, the distance between them was narrowing.

Clayton reported on July 20 that the sick were improving, but the going was among the most difficult of the entire trip. They were deep in the Wasatch Mountains, and the Saints had to fight and claw their way up and down every inch of terrain. Orson Pratt's advance company moved but six miles, crossing Big Mountain, at times being delayed along the way because of straying cattle. The start of the main company was slow too, delayed until 11 A.M. because repairs had to be made on wagons damaged in the previous day's journey. Some time was spent making a coal pit so that Burr Frost, the blacksmith, could repair the wheels of George Smith's wagon.

One of the pioneers from Pratt's detail rode back to report rough going up ahead, which Clayton later confirmed:

We found the road exceedingly rough and crooked and very dangerous on wagons . . . teams sweat much and it has been a pretty hard day's travel. Several accidents have happened to wagons today. . . . The sick are getting better.

Some of the ill may have been improving, but the scourge of mountain fever was far from over. Three more pioneers came down with it—Henry G. Sherwood, Benjamin Franklin Dewey and James Case—and their three wagons were left behind as the main company moved on. It was growing late to plant crops in the Valley of the Great Salt Lake, and the Saints simply could not dawdle any longer, sickness or no.

Clayton walked ahead of the party for about four miles and picked "many gooseberries nearly ripe." At places, he noted that stands of willows had become so thick (sometimes they towered over twenty feet and were tangled with other bushes) they became a real obstacle. "Although there has been a road cut through, it is yet scarcely possible to travel without tearing the wagon covers." Eleven times, his company crossed a creek that Orson Pratt had named Canyon Creek, "and the road is one of the most crooked I ever saw, making sharp turns in it and the willow stubs standing make it very severe on wagons." Clayton added:

> As we proceed up, the gap between the mountains seems to grow still narrower until arriving at this place where there is room to camp, but little grass for teams. There are many springs along the road but the water is not very good. In one place about a mile back there is a very bad swamp where the brethren spent some time cutting willows and laying them to improve it. . . . at this place the ground around is represented as being swampy and dangerous for cattle. . . . we have passed through some small patches of timber today where a few house logs might be cut, but this is truly a wild looking place.

Brigham's rear guard broke camp at 5:30 A.M. that day so as "to travel in the cool of the morning," as Howard Egan put it, and managed to cover twelve miles, catching up before nightfall with the three wagons left behind by the main company.

The following day, July 21, two of the Saints—Orson Pratt and Erastus Snow—set foot in the Salt Lake Valley for the first time. Snow had been dispatched ahead of the main party to deliver a letter of instructions on how the valley should be entered and how the first crops should be planted; he and Pratt then rode ahead and made their way four and a half miles down Emigration Creek, which Pratt called Last Creek, to the mouth of what is now Emigration Canyon. To avoid the rugged canyon mouth, the Donner-Reed party, the previous year, had struggled up what Pratt called "a steep and dangerous hill"; known as Donner Hill today, the mountain was their undoing. Not having to manhandle heavy wagons up its slopes, however, Pratt and Snow reached its summit easily, and the sight that lay beyond was occasion for unbridled joy:

> . . . a broad valley, about 20 miles long and 30 long [Pratt's journal reads] lay stretched out before us, at the north end of which the broad waters of the Great Salt Lake glistened in the sunbeams, containing high mountainous islands from 20 to 30 miles in extent.

The Saints could hardly contain their spirit of thanksgiving. "After issuing from the mountains among which we had been shut up for many days," Pratt recalled, "and beholding in a moment such an extensive scenery open before us, we could not refrain from a shout of joy which almost involuntarily escaped from our lips the moment this grand and lovely scenery was in our view." They did not linger to stare long. "We immediately descended very gradually into the lower parts of the valley, and although we had but one horse between us . . . [we] traversed a circuit of about 12 miles before we left the valley to return to our camp."

It was nearly 9 P.M. when Snow and Pratt reported their find to other members of the advance party. By now, the main company was encamped only one and a half miles east. Their day had not been as inspiring as Pratt's and Snow's. "Much of the time," Clayton said, "was spent cutting down tree stumps, heaving out rocks and leveling the road. It is an exceedingly rough place." Kimball's wagons were clawing up an ascent now, "the last mile [of which] is very steep and nearer the top the steeper it grows"; going down the other side, the pioneers again had to lock their wagon wheels for safety. The hill was Big Mountain, and from its summit, before the descent, "we can see an extensive valley to the west but on every other side high mountains, many of them white with snow." Clayton seemed certain that "only a few hours of travel" would bring them out of the mountains, but his estimate was too optimistic; not until the next day, even with the help of trail-clearing by Orson Pratt's advance company, did their wagons at last roll on level ground once again. For President Brigham and the "sick detachment" remaining with him, Zion was even farther from reach; he was again too sick to move, and his camp remained immobilized in Echo Canyon through July 21.

Except for Brigham and his small group, all the pioneers entered the Salt Lake Valley the next day, July 22. Orson Pratt had, of course, been there the day before with Erastus Snow. Taking George A. Smith, Porter Rockwell, J. C. Little, John Brown, Joseph Matthews and John Pack with him, he rode in again for some more-detailed exploring. They rode toward the Great Salt Lake for about five miles, then swung north to check out farming possibilities. Meanwhile, Pratt had left forty-two members of the advance party at the mouth of Emigration Canyon to clear away timber and thick underbrush.

> For 3 or 4 miles near the lake we found the soil of a most excellent quality. Streams from the mountains and springs were very abundant, the water excellent, and generally with gravel bottoms. A great variety of green grass, and very luxuriant, covered the bottoms for miles where the soil was sufficiently damp, but in other places, although the soil was good . . . the grass had nearly dried up for want of moisture. We found the drier places swarming with very large crickets, about the size of a man's thumb. The valley is surrounded with mountains, except on the north: the tops of some of the highest being covered with snow.

Every mile or two they traveled, streams emptied into the valley from the mountains to the east, "many of which were sufficiently large to carry mules and other machinery."

> As we proceeded towards the Salt Lake the soil began to assume a more sterile appearance, being probably at some seasons of the year overflowed with water.

We found . . . great numbers of hot springs issuing from near the base of the mountains. These . . . were highly impregnated with salt and sulphur: the temperature of some was nearly raised to the boiling point.

Pratt's party turned eastward to the mountains after a fifteen-mile ride, and encountered wagons of the advance company camped five miles into the valley. Still plodding down Emigration Canyon with the main company, William Clayton climbed a hill to gain his first view of the valley and was "much cheered" by what he saw. "There is an extensive, beautiful, level looking valley from here to the lake, which I should judge from the numerous green patches must be fertile and rich." Like many others, he was disappointed by the valley's lack of timber. "There is no prospect for building log houses without spending a vast amount of time and labor, but we can make Spanish bricks and dry them in the sun; or we can build lodges as the Pawnee Indians do in their villages." The lack of trees did not escape Thomas Bullock's scrutiny either. "But there is an ocean of stone in the mountains, to build stone houses and walls for fencing."

On the morning of July 23, two riders were dispatched to the mountains to brief the church president on what they had found; the advance and the main companies were together at last, encamped near a stream they called City Creek. At 9:30 A.M. they assembled to offer a prayer. It was a brief service (Clayton sums it up in half a sentence: "At the opening, the brethren united in prayer and asked the Lord to send rain on the land, etc."), for there was work to be done quickly.

With the dust of their wagons barely settled, the Saints set immediately to work. Before noon, their plows had turned the first furrows of future farms; crops to be planted were potatoes, corn, beans and buckwheat. The pioneers thought these would have the best chance of maturing before winter; it was already extremely late in the growing season.

Work assignments were issued. To Charles A. Harper, Charles Shumway and Elijah Newman went the responsibility of seeing that plows and drags were available for the planting (already a few plows had broken down in the hard ground). Stephen Markham was directed to ensure that fresh teams were available every few hours for the plowing. Others set to work building a dam across City Creek for irrigation and digging ditches to bring water. By 2 P.M., with the first full day in the valley barely half over, water was already flowing from City Creek onto the farm land.

Back in the mountains, Brigham's "sick detachment" slowly worked its way down Emigration Canyon. They had started at 6:45 A.M. from East Canyon, climbing Big Mountain, and then, as had the advance and main companies before them, descended inch by inch down the precipitous slope on the other side. After a brief rest, they worked their way to the top of Little Mountain and halted at 5 P.M. for the night on the bank of Emigration Creek.

For Brigham and his small group, it must have been one of the longest nights of their lives.

The next morning, July 24, 1847, after a six-mile march down Emigration Canyon, they at last entered the valley. "We gazed with wonder and admiration upon the vast fertile valley spread out before us for about twenty five miles in length and sixteen in width," Wilford Woodruff said, "clothed in a heavy garment of vegetation, and in the midst of which glistened the waters of the Great Salt Lake, with mountains all around towering to the skies, and streams, rivulets and creeks of pure water. . . ."

From Nauvoo, the Saints had marched nearly fifteen hundred miles, "through flats of the Platte River and plateaus of the Black Hills and Rocky Mountains and over the burning sands, and eternal sage regions, willow swails and rocky regions, to gaze upon . . . the grandest scenery and prospect we could have obtained on earth."

Brigham Young was riding in Woodruff's carriage. Although the trek's diarists noted that the church president arrived in the valley that day, officially completing the trek, nothing was recorded about Brigham's reaction. On July 24, 1880, however—the thirty-third anniversary of the day—Wilford Woodruff delivered a sermon in which he recalled the occasion:

> On the twenty-fourth I drove my carriage, with President Young lying on a bed in it, into the open valley, the rest of the company following. When we came out of the canyon, into full view of the valley, I turned the side of the carriage around, open to the west, and President Young arose from his bed and took a survey of the country. While gazing on the scene before us he was enwrapped in a vision, and upon the occasion he saw the future glory of Zion and Israel, as they would be planted in the valleys and the mountains.

When the vision had passed, Brigham said quietly, "It is enough. This is the right place. Drive on."

*   *   *

Postscript

Charles Shumway and his son, Andrew, entered the Salt Lake Valley on July 22, 1847—the day after Orson Pratt's advance company, two days ahead of Brigham Young. It had been exactly one year, five months and twenty-three days since Shumway ferried the first wagon across the ice-clogged Mississippi River to launch the exodus west.

In those historic, weary, meaningful days and months of 1846–47, he had shared both the joy and the agony of his fellow Mormon pioneers. He had experienced personal tragedy at Winter Quarters when two of his family perished in the bitter Nebraska winter. As had others in the Pioneer Company, he had marveled at the huge, majestic herds of buffalo that blackened the plains of the Platte, felt the chill of countless dawns at bugle's reveille, watched in wonderment as noon sun and sunset shadows wove their pastel tapestries on such Mormon-trail landmarks as Chimney Rock, Devil's Gorge, and the vise-like chasm of Emigration Canyon. In good times along the trail, he had joined in singing around the campfire, rejoiced when, with God's benevolence, the pioneers managed fifteen, twenty or more miles per day with their wagons, accepted with resignation those other days when weather and terrain limited progress to only three or four. He shared the concern of the others when, struggling up the eastern face of the Rocky Mountains, one by one their members fell ill with mountain fever. On June 27, when he heard Moses "Black" Harris speak as disparagingly about the Salt Lake Valley as he did favorably about the Cache Valley as a place to settle, little did he realize the role he was to play in the settlement of both in one of the largest colonization programs in world history.

In the history of the Mormon Church of the nineteenth century, Charles Shumway's own life becomes a convenient timetable by which many key events may be remembered.

After reaching Zion, on July 24, 1847, the pioneer Saints turned quickly to the task of establishing Salt Lake City. Only four days after entering the valley, the Twelve met to designate the site of Temple Block, to lay out the grid for what would become one of the most important communities in the West, to lay plots for homes, shops and farms to accommodate an eventual seventy thousand other Mormon emigrants who crossed the Plains by wagon and handcart before the nation was linked by railroad in 1869. Charles was in the valley on August 7, when, as a gesture of thanksgiving and a symbol of their desire to start their lives afresh in this Zion, the church leadership concluded that all the pioneers should be rebaptized; Charles, in fact, was invited to help perform the ceremony. He was there to share the joy of the valley's first Mormon birth, a girl, Elizabeth Steele, on August 9, and to mourn its first Mormon death, two days later, by drowning, of George Therlkill, age three.

Five days after the arrival of the Pioneer Company, the Salt Lake population increased by two hundred with the arrival of the Mormon Battalion sick detachment, which had wintered at Pueblo. The Mississippi Saints followed. But there were hundreds more back along the trail, in Winter Quarters, and in the semipermanent camps strung across Iowa. On August 30, a detachment of eighty men was designated by Brigham to return east to guide the others to Utah. Charles Shumway, already at work building a carpenter shop, was among them.

Brigham himself led another detachment back to the Missouri River later in

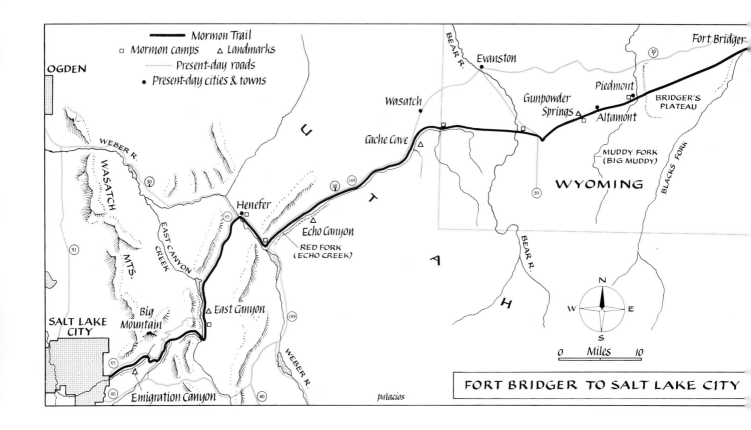

Mormon Trail
□ Mormon camps   △ Landmarks
Present-day roads
● Present-day cities & towns

OGDEN

Fort Bridger

BEAR R.

Evanston

30

Wasatch

Gunpowder
Springs

Piedmont

BRIDGER'S
PLATEAU

Altamont

Cache Cave

WEBER R.

WASATCH

30

189

30

Henefer

65

EAST CANYON CREEK

Echo Canyon

RED FORK
(ECHO CREEK)

91

MTS.

Big
Mountain

△ East Canyon

SALT LAKE
CITY

65

△

40

Emigration Canyon

40

189

WEBER R.

palacios

U   T   A   H

WYOMING

MUDDY FORK
(BIG MUDDY)

BEAR R.

89

BLACKS FORK

N
W   E
S

0   Miles   10

FORT BRIDGER TO SALT LAKE CITY

Snow in a draw a few miles east of the Sweetwater campsite.

Approximate location of the Sweetwater River campsite and the last crossing of the river.

Sunrise. Looking back towards the Sweetwater crossing from South Pass.

The Wind River Mountains from South Pass.

Trail ruts at South Pass.

South Pass. Huge herds of antelope in the snow.

Photographer's Notes

In good weather it is possible to drive from Farson west almost to the site of the Mormon ferry on the Green River over a gravel road that takes off from US 187 about one and one-half miles north of Farson. This road parallels the Oregon Trail closely. It is on the north side of Sandy Creek. At a junction in the road about twenty-five miles west of Farson a sign indicates Fontanelle to the right and Green River to the left. There is a bridge over the Green River at Fontanelle, but it involves a detour of approximately thirty miles. There is, however, another bridge over the river at Stauffer Soda Ash plant, on the east bank of the Green River. This is a railroad bridge that doubles as an automobile bridge. There is no marker on any of the ranch roads indicating this bridge and it is not easy to find. The plume of steam from the soda-ash plant is visible on clear days from a great distance. Getting to the facility is, however, a different matter. If you miss this road and still keep bearing south on the gravel trail you have been on, it will take you to Green River. You will have traveled along the crest of a range of bluffs for most of the distance. The pioneers crossed the river by ferry a short distance from the confluence of Sandy Creek and the Green River.

Badlands east of the Green River ferry site.

The Green River ferry site (approximate location). "We arrived on the banks of the Green River, having traveled eight miles and formed our encampment in a line under the shade of cottonwood timber."

Antelope on the crest of a hill near Lyman.

Fort Bridger. The fort has been restored and looks today very much as subsequent parties of Mormons found it, about 1885.

Uinta Range from Fort Bridger.

Echo Canyon. "There is a very singular echo in this ravine, the rattling of the wagons resembles carpenters hammering at boards. . . . The echo, the high rocks on the north, high mountains on the south with the narrow ravine for a road, form a scenery at once romantic and more interesting than I have ever witnessed."

Weber Canyon, "Witches' Rocks."

Main Canyon.

A cottonwood grove beside Canyon Creek, in Main Canyon.

The view from Main Canyon.

Whitetop growing alongside the road on the descent into Emigration Canyon.

Emigration Canyon, near the opening to the Valley of the Great Salt Lake, at sunrise.

"The president signifying a wish to ascend a high peak to the north of us, after some hard toil and time we succeeded in gaining the summit, leaving our horses about two-thirds the way up. Some of the brethren feel like naming this Ensign Peak. From this place we had a good view of the Salt Lake and could see the waters extend for a great many miles to the north of us."

The Great Salt Lake.

The Promontory Range across a part of the Great Salt Lake, taken from the Bear River Wildlife Sanctuary.

The sun setting over the Bear River. Taken from the Bear River Wildlife Sanctuary.

"This is the place."

Wild teasel alongside a road near Farmington. The Wasatch Mountains in the background.

Antelope Island .

Approximately one hundred miles south of Salt Lake City are the white sand hills called the Little Sahara Recreational Area.

Ophir, once a prosperous mining town, is now a ghost town. The house shown here is very much like many built by the early pioneers.

California gulls.

The Valley of the Great Salt Lake.

The Handcart Company Memorial, at Temple Square, in Salt Lake City.

Salt Lake City today.

The Temple.

1847, returning to Zion the following year with companies totaling two thousand Saints and four thousand animals of various kinds.

For the rest of his life, Charles Shumway, like many of the early pioneers, was involved in the colonization of what are now several western states. It was never the plan of the Mormons' westward movement to settle only the Great Salt Lake Valley. When the President issued his call for Saints throughout the world to gather to Zion in the mountains, his plan embraced an area three times the present size of Utah. It was to be called the State of Deseret.

To establish Deseret, many of the pioneer party, including Charles Shumway, were on the move most of their lives. To Brigham, this was the test of a man's faith: to be willing to uproot himself and his family whenever asked, to serve wherever needed.

Charles Shumway passed the test. At various times, he was called to serve in Sanpete County; at Payson, where he built a sawmill and the community's first adobe house; in South Cottonwood, where he built a gristmill, and in the Cache Valley. He was one of the original founders of Mendon, Utah, and spent his declining years in an Arizona town he also helped found and which today bears his name.

Charles served briefly on a mission to Canada, and watched his now-grown son, Andrew, leave on a similar mission to England. In the summer of 1849, Brigham dispatched Charles to the Platte River to help run the famous Mormon Ferry. He served in the Utah Territorial Legislature. He was also appointed a lieutenant in the newly organized Nauvoo Legion, a private defense militia whose importance soared in the bloodless so-called "Utah War" of 1857, when the United States sent troops to quell a nonexistent "rebellion" in Utah Territory.

The grant of territorial status to Utah had dashed the Mormons' hopes for their State of Deseret, and life in Zion was never quite the same afterward. With the peace they had so vainly sought in the East still eluding them, with their hopes for an isolated theocratic society destroyed by hordes of Gentile emigrants pouring west after the California gold discovery, frictions with their neighbors increased. The main issue was still polygamy, but the Mormons' political and economic controls over the territory, in which Brigham had been appointed governor, were also factors. Even after a fifteen-hundred-mile flight across the wilderness, the Mormons could not be let alone.

Some church leaders were jailed. Others went into hiding. (In June 1858, when Charles Shumway paid a visit to Salt Lake City, he found only a handful of Saints there; most of the others, alerted to an impending U.S. Army "invasion," had fled south to Provo.) Church property was confiscated, and members were deprived of their right to vote or hold office.

A series of court decisions, and finally the Manifesto of 1890, outlawed the practice of polygamy forever. Eventually the Mormons were restored their rights, and their property was returned. Only when Utah was finally admitted to the Union, in 1896, however, were the Saints finally rid of what many called the "carpetbag government" staffed by political appointees almost unanimously hostile to everything Mormon.

Charles Shumway did not live to see the end of the nineteenth century, when old animosities finally began to fade and the walls of mistrust to crumble. He did not live to see a Mormon elected governor of a Gentile state and come close to being nominated for the presidency; he did not live to see a Mormon girl become a Miss America. But he did live to see many of the seeds of the early struggles bear fruit.

One of Charles Shumway's greatest personal thrills, according to a family biography, was when he was invited to participate in ceremonies in Salt Lake City on July 24, 1897, the fiftieth anniversary of the Pioneer Company's triumphant entry into the Salt Lake Valley. Shumway could not attend; then eighty-nine, the oldest living survivor of the Pioneer Company, he was too ill to leave his home, in Shumway, Arizona, but the honor of being asked to unveil a statue of Brigham Young, whose leadership he had so faithfully followed, was heartwarming nonetheless.

Worldwide, Mormon Church membership today totals more than four million; it is one of the world's fastest-growing religions. It is no longer alone a "Salt Lake City church," but has stakes in virtually every major country around the globe. The Salt Lake Valley was only a beginning; the gathering that began there within only days began moving in other directions, and the church founded by six members only one hundred fifty years ago has become international in scope.

Charles Shumway died May 21, 1898, in Shumway, Arizona. No matter how many more years he might have lived, he doubtless would have continued to serve his church. Doubtless, too, each day he would have felt a renewed faith in the Lord, who had sustained the Saints in their most trying days of 1846–47 and from whom they had drawn their strength and determination.

And as much as anything else, he would have felt a never-ending pride in having crossed the Plains and climbed the mountains with the Mormon pioneers.

Appendix

THE
LATTER-DAY SAINTS'
EMIGRANTS' GUIDE:
BEING A
TABLE OF DISTANCES
SHOWING ALL THE
SPRINGS, CREEKS, RIVERS,
HILLS, MOUNTAINS,
CAMPING PLACES, AND
ALL OTHER NOTABLE PLACES,
FROM COUNCIL BLUFFS,
TO THE
VALLEY OF THE GREAT SALT LAKE.
ALSO, THE
LATITUDES, LONGITUDES AND
ALTITUDES
OF THE PROMINENT POINTS
ON THE ROUTE.
TOGETHER WITH REMARKS ON
THE NATURE OF THE LAND,
TIMBER, GRASS, &c.
THE WHOLE ROUTE HAVING BEEN
CAREFULLY MEASURED BY A
ROADOMETER, AND THE DISTANCE
FROM POINT TO POINT, IN
ENGLISH MILES,
ACCURATELY SHOWN.
BY W. CLAYTON.
ST. LOUIS:
MO. REPUBLICAN STEAM POWER
PRESS—CHAMBERS & KNAPP.
1848

PREFACE

When the author first compiled the following work, it was not with a design to publish it, although well aware of the advantages which emigrants, traveling to the *Valley of the Great Salt Lake*, would continually realize by having it in their possession. However, there were so many who applied for copies of it— and the labor of writing a copy being considerable, as well as requiring much time—it was concluded to publish it in its present form, by which means it can be afforded at a price which will bring it within reach of any person wishing to have it.

Many works have been published, and maps exhibited for the instruction of emigrants, but none which ever pretended to set forth the particulars contained in this work, so far as regards the route from Council Bluffs to the Great Salt Lake. The distances from point to point are shown as near as a *Roadometer* can measure; and by this means the traveler can know, each day, the kind of country lying before him, and how far he must go in order to find a suitable place to camp at night.

Emigrants have lost many of their teams in the neighborhood of the *Alkali lakes*, in consequence of not knowing the distance from any one of these lakes to good water. By paying attention to the *remarks* in this work, a person need run *no risk*, inasmuch as all the Alkali lakes, which are near the road, are mentioned—and, also, the places where an encampment can be formed with safety.

The author feels a delicacy in saying much in favor of the *"Guide,"* but is well aware that, when its merits have been tested by experience, no person will repent of having purchased it. It is, therefore, submitted cheerfully to the consideration of an intelligent public.

AUTHOR

St. Louis, Mo., 13th March, 1848

EXPLANATION

In the following table, the *large type* shows the prominent points and places which will naturally be noticed by the emigrant. The *first* column of figures shows the distance from point to point, in English miles. The *second* column of figures shows the total distance of each point to Winter Quarters; and the *third* column, the total distance of each point to the Temple Block, in the *City of the Great Salt Lake.* As, for example:

How far is it from Winter Quarters to Pappea?*

Answer. (page 5, second line) 18 miles.
How far from Pappea to the Elk Horn river?

Answer. (page 5, second and third lines) 9 miles, &c.

Again: How far is it from Raw Hide Creek to Fort John?

Answer. (page 11, last line) 12 miles.
How far is Fort John from Winter Quarters?

Answer. (p. 12, first line) 522 miles.
How far is Fort John from the City of the Great Salt Lake?

Answer. (p. 12, third column of figures) 509 miles.

The *small type,* in this table, contains the various *remarks* touching the nature of the road, lands, and its adaptation for camping purposes, &c. For example:

What is said concerning the "La Bonte river?" Page 13, second line.

Answer. "It is a good place to camp—being plenty of timber, grass and water"—the necessaries for camping purposes, and consequently can be depended on. But, if thought advisable to go a little further, "there is a good camping place a mile further," consequently you have choice of the two good places, within one mile of each other.

What is said of a branch of the La Bonte? Page 13, third line.

Answer. "Doubtful about water;" consequently not safe to depend on for a camp ground. It is also said that the "banks are steep," which shows that it is not very good to cross, &c.

*The page numbers that follow are those of the original edition. The respective page numbers in this edition are pages 156 and 157 for page 5, page 164 for pages 11 and 12, page 165 for page 13.

EMIGRANTS' GUIDE

PROMINENT POINTS AND REMARKS	DIST. MILES.	FROM W QRS. MILES.	FROM C OF GSL MILES.
Winter Quarters, Lat. 41° 18′ 53″			1031
The road good, but very crooked, following the ridges and passing over a continual succession of hills and hollows.			

PROMINENT POINTS AND REMARKS	DIST. MILES.	FROM W QRS. MILES.	FROM C OF GSL MILES.
Pappea, ten feet wide, high banks.	18	18	1013
Some timber on the creek, but it is difficult to water teams. After this, the road is crooked and uneven to the Elk Horn.			

PROMINENT POINTS AND REMARKS	DIST. MILES.	FROM W QRS. MILES.	FROM C OF GSL MILES.
Elk Horn, nine rods wide, three feet deep	9	27	1004
Current rather swift, and not very pleasant to ferry. Plenty of timber on its banks. (See Note 1.)			
Creek, ten feet wide, steep banks.	$\frac{3}{4}$	$27\frac{3}{4}$	$1003\frac{1}{4}$
This creek has a good bridge over it, but little timber on the banks. There is a high post, erected near the bridge, for a guide to it.			
Platte river and Liberty Pole.	$11\frac{1}{4}$	39	992
Plenty of timber, but you will probably have to go to the river to water—distance about a quarter of a mile. The nearest and best road to water is round the east point of the timber.			
Small Lake (narrow) south side the road.	$3\frac{1}{2}$	$42\frac{1}{2}$	$988\frac{1}{2}$
No timber on the Lake.			
Circular Lake, or pond, close to the road, (south.)	$\frac{3}{4}$	$43\frac{1}{4}$	$987\frac{3}{4}$
No timber. In the neighborhood of this, the road runs alongside a number of small lakes, or ponds, for two miles; but there is little timber near them.			
R. R. and T., road joins the river, Lat. 41° 27′ 5″	9	$52\frac{1}{4}$	$978\frac{3}{4}$
This is a point where a branch of the river runs round an island, on which is plenty of timber. Not much water in the channel, but plenty for camping purposes.			
Indian Grave, north side the road.	$7\frac{1}{2}$	$59\frac{3}{4}$	$971\frac{1}{4}$
This is a large pile of			

PROMINENT POINTS AND REMARKS	DIST. MILES.	FROM W QRS. MILES.	FROM C OF GSL MILES.
earth, about eighty yards north of the road.			
R. R. and T., road joins the river.	$\frac{1}{2}$	$60\frac{1}{4}$	$970\frac{3}{4}$
Plenty of timber and water, without leaving the road.			
Shell creek, 12 feet wide, three feet deep.	2	$62\frac{1}{4}$	$968\frac{3}{4}$
This creek is bridged, and a few rods lower is a place to ford. Plenty of timber on it. After this you will probably find no water for twelve miles, without turning considerably from the road.			
Small lake, south side of the road.	$5\frac{3}{4}$	68	963
Plenty of water in the Spring season, but none in Summer. It was entirely dry, October 18, 1847.			
R. and R., road joins the river.	$6\frac{1}{2}$	$74\frac{1}{2}$	$956\frac{1}{2}$
After this point you will have four or five miles of heavy, sandy road.			
Long Lake, south side the road.	$\frac{1}{2}$	75	956
There is a little timber where this lake joins the river, and it is a good camping place.			
Forks of road to new and old Pawnee villages.	$5\frac{1}{2}$	$80\frac{1}{2}$	$950\frac{1}{2}$
The left hand road leads to the Pawnee location of 1847; the other to the old village. The latter is your route.			
Lake, south of the road.	$\frac{1}{2}$	81	950
Plenty of timber close to the road. The banks of the lake are high, but there is a small pond near, where teams can water.			

PROMINENT POINTS AND REMARKS	DIST. MILES.	FROM W QRS. MILES.	FROM C OF GSL MILES.
Loup Fork—lake and timber.	5	86	945
Opposite to where the Pawnees were located, in the Spring of 1847, and is a good place to camp.			
Lake and timber, south of the road.	8¼	94¼	936¾
Looking-glass creek, 16 feet wide, 2 deep.	1	95¼	935¾
There is a poor bridge over this creek. It is, however, not difficult to ford. Plenty of timber on and near it.			
Long Lake, south side the road.	2	97¼	933¾
Some timber on the south bank, but none on the north side.			
Beaver river, 25 feet wide, 2 feet deep: Lat. 41° 25′ 13″; Long. 98° 0′ 15″...	6½	103¾	927¼
Plenty of good timber on both sides. There are two fording places. The upper one is good going in, but steep on the opposite side. The lower one not good going down, but good on the other side.			
Plumb creek, five feet wide: Lat. 41° 24′ 29″; Altitude, 1,090 feet.	6¾	110½	920½
On this creek the old Pawnee mission station stands, but is not a very good place to camp, being near the Pawnee cornfields. The creek was dry, October 16, 1847.			
Ash creek, 12 feet wide, one foot deep.	2½	113	918
Some timber, but not a very good chance to camp.			
Ford of the Loup Fork:			

PROMINENT POINTS AND REMARKS	DIST. MILES.	FROM W QRS. MILES.	FROM C OF GSL MILES.
Lat. 41° 22′ 37″; Long. 98° 11′ 0″...	1¼	114¼	916¾
This is the pioneer's ford, but is considered not so good as the upper ford. River about 300 yards wide.			
Old Pawnee village. ...	½	114¾	916¼
Formerly occupied by the Grand Pawnee and Tappas bands; but burned by the Sioux, in the Fall of 1846.			
Cedar creek, 8 rods wide, 2 feet deep.	1½	116¼	914¾
Some timber, and plenty of willow. After this, the road runs on the bottom, through high grass for some distance, and gradually rises to higher land.			
Road descends to low land again.	3	119¼	911¾
You will now find some deep ravines to cross, but none difficult.			
Road leaves the river, and turns up a ravine.	1¾	121	910
After ascending the higher land, the road is good and level, except crossing the deep, dry ravines.			
Road descends into a ravine.	½	121½	909½
You travel up this ravine a quarter of a mile, mostly through high grass.			
Old Pawnee village, south side the road.	5½	127	904
On the banks of the Loup Fork, but mostly destroyed.			
Road descends from the bluffs.	½	127½	903½
After descending here, you cross a creek twelve feet wide, and one foot deep—banks soft, but not			

PROMINENT POINTS AND REMARKS	DIST. MILES.	FROM W QRS. MILES.	FROM C OF GSL MILES.
difficult. You then travel through high grass and small bushes.			
Road ascends the bluffs.	$\frac{1}{4}$	$127\frac{3}{4}$	$903\frac{1}{4}$
After traveling about four miles, then turning left from the road, so as to strike the timber you see ahead where it meets the river, the road can be shortened at least a half mile.			
Upper ford of the Loup Fork.	6	$133\frac{3}{4}$	$897\frac{1}{4}$
You will find the water in some places near 3 feet deep, and will have to travel down the river about half a mile, to avoid deep holes, and find a good place to get out. (See Note 2.)			
Road ascends the bluffs.	$5\frac{3}{4}$	$139\frac{1}{2}$	$891\frac{1}{2}$
After ascending the bluffs you will find a heavy, sandy road for five or six miles.			
Prairie creek, 12 feet wide 1½ feet deep.	18	$157\frac{1}{2}$	$873\frac{1}{2}$
Plenty of water and grass, but no timber. Banks, some soft and miry. By taking a south-west course from this creek, you would strike Wood river six or eight miles above the old crossing place, and thence crossing to the Platte, by a course a little west of south, the road may be shortened at least five miles.			
Dry creek.	1	$158\frac{1}{2}$	$872\frac{1}{2}$
Dry creek.	$\frac{1}{2}$	159	872
Main Platte river.	$6\frac{3}{4}$	$165\frac{3}{4}$	$865\frac{1}{4}$
You do not come within two miles of the river, untill you arrive at Wood river.			
Wood river, 12 feet wide, one foot deep.	$3\frac{1}{4}$	$169\frac{1}{4}$	$861\frac{3}{4}$
Plenty of timber, and a			

PROMINENT POINTS AND REMARKS	DIST. MILES.	FROM W QRS. MILES.	FROM C OF GSL MILES.
good place to camp. Banks descending, steep, and some soft—but good going out. The road now generally runs from one to two miles distant from the main Platte.			
Road descends to lower land.	14	$183\frac{1}{4}$	$847\frac{3}{4}$
The road now runs near the timber for two miles. The grass is high, and a good chance to camp, without turning off the road.			
Road ascends to higher land.	2	$185\frac{1}{4}$	$845\frac{3}{4}$
You will probably have to turn off the road some, for the next camping place.			
Deep ravine—steep descent.	$22\frac{3}{4}$	208	823
Deep ravine.	$\frac{1}{4}$	$208\frac{1}{4}$	$822\frac{3}{4}$
Two and a quarter miles beyond this, is a good place to camp, there being plenty of grass and water, on a low bench, about twenty rods south of the road. There is, however, no timber but willow.			
Deep dry creek.	$3\frac{1}{2}$	$211\frac{3}{4}$	$819\frac{1}{4}$
No timber on it.			
Creek or slough, south side the road.	$1\frac{3}{4}$	$213\frac{1}{2}$	$817\frac{1}{2}$
Plenty of willows and grass, but doubtful for water.			
Deep, dry creek.	$4\frac{1}{4}$	$217\frac{3}{4}$	$813\frac{1}{4}$
The head of Grand Island is about opposite to this creek, but the road now runs so far from the river, we could not ascertain exactly.			
Elm creek.	$3\frac{1}{4}$	221	810
Deep banks, plenty of timber, but no water, October 9, 1847.			

PROMINENT POINTS AND REMARKS	DIST. MILES.	FROM W QRS. MILES.	FROM C OF GSL MILES.
Road leaves the river near timber.	$6\frac{3}{4}$	$227\frac{3}{4}$	$803\frac{1}{4}$
This is a pretty good camping place.			
Buffalo creek, south side the road.	$\frac{1}{2}$	$228\frac{1}{4}$	$802\frac{3}{4}$
A wide creek, with deep banks, but no timber except a few willow bushes. The road runs alongside this creek for three and a half miles.			
Crossing of Buffalo creek.	3	$231\frac{3}{4}$	$799\frac{1}{4}$
R. and R., road runs near the river.	7	$239\frac{1}{4}$	$791\frac{3}{4}$
Pretty good chance to camp.			
R. and R., road runs near the river.	$5\frac{1}{4}$	$244\frac{1}{2}$	$786\frac{1}{2}$
Plenty of buffalo-grass, and short prairie-grass. Plenty of timber on an island, close by.			
Willow Lake, south of the road.	7	$251\frac{1}{2}$	$779\frac{1}{2}$
Good place to water teams, but no timber for camping purposes.			
Ptah lake, south of the road.	$7\frac{3}{4}$	$259\frac{1}{4}$	$771\frac{3}{4}$
The lake is long and very crooked. About a mile before you arrive at it, the road runs near the river a little piece, then leaves it again.			
Deep, dry creek.	$2\frac{1}{2}$	$261\frac{3}{4}$	$769\frac{1}{4}$
Low, sandy bluffs, extending to the river.	14	$275\frac{3}{4}$	$755\frac{1}{4}$
R. and R. near the Sandy Bluffs: Latitude 41° 0' 47".	3	$278\frac{3}{4}$	$752\frac{1}{4}$
After leaving this place, the road leaves the river, and runs near the foot of the bluffs, to avoid a bad			

PROMINENT POINTS AND REMARKS	DIST. MILES.	FROM W QRS. MILES.	FROM C OF GSL MILES.
swamp. You will not strike the river for sixteen miles, but will have no difficulty in finding feed and water.			
Skunk creek, six feet wide.	2	$280\frac{3}{4}$	$750\frac{1}{4}$
Crossing of Skunk creek.	5	$286\frac{1}{4}$	$744\frac{3}{4}$
Banks some soft, but not difficult. No timber.			
Lake or marsh, south of the road.	1	$287\frac{1}{4}$	$743\frac{3}{4}$
Lake, south of the road.	1	$288\frac{3}{4}$	$742\frac{1}{4}$
Plenty of grass and water, but no timber nearer than five or six miles.			
Good spring of cold water.	$4\frac{1}{4}$	293	738
At the foot of the bluffs, north of the road, and at the head of the Pawnee swamps.			
Low, sandy bluffs.	$1\frac{1}{4}$	$294\frac{1}{4}$	$736\frac{3}{4}$
This is opposite to the junction of the north and south forks of Platte river. Lat. 41° 7' 44"; Long. 100° 47' 15"; Altitude 2,685 feet.			
Carrion creek, 10 feet wide, one foot deep.	$3\frac{1}{2}$	$297\frac{3}{4}$	$733\frac{1}{4}$
Good place for grass, but no timber near.			
R. R. and T., road, river and timber.	$4\frac{3}{4}$	$302\frac{1}{2}$	$728\frac{1}{2}$
Good place to camp.			
Last timber on north side the river.	$3\frac{3}{4}$	$306\frac{1}{4}$	$724\frac{3}{4}$
You will find no more timber on the north side the river for two hundred miles, except one lone tree. Your only dependence for fuel will be buffalo chips and drift wood.			
Wide, deep creek.	$2\frac{1}{4}$	$308\frac{1}{2}$	$722\frac{1}{2}$
Plenty of water, October 4, 1847. The banks are high but not bad to cross.			

PROMINENT POINTS AND REMARKS	DIST. MILES.	FROM W QRS. MILES.	FROM C OF GSL MILES.
R. R. and lake, road and river near a bayou.	1¼	309¾	721¼

Opposite to this place are several islands, covered with willow bushes, which will answer for fuel, and there is little difficulty in getting to it.

Black mud creek.	2	311¾	719¼

Plenty of water, October 3, 1847, but little feed for teams.

R. and R., road joins the river.	2	313¾	717¼

After this, the road again leaves the river, until you arrive at the north Bluff Fork. Road good, but poor feed.

Small creek.	3½	317¼	713¾

Steep banks, but very little water.

North Bluff Fork, 6 rods wide, 2 feet deep.	3½	320¾	710¼

Swift current, muddy water, low banks, quicksand bottom, but not bad to cross. Poor place for grass.

Sandy Bluffs, east foot.	1½	322¼	708¾

The road over these bluffs is very crooked, but not bad. If a road can be made up the bed of the river, it would save at least two miles travel.

Sandy Bluffs, west foot.	4½	326¾	704¼

By following the foot of the bluffs, after this, the road may be shortened at least a mile, and be equally as good a road as to follow the river.

2d. Sandy Bluffs, east foot.	4	330¾	700¼

These bluffs are hard on teams, being mostly soft sand.

2d. Sandy Bluffs, west

foot.	1¼	332	699
Bluff Creek, 4 feet wide, 1 foot deep.	¼	332¼	698¾

After this, the road may be made considerably shorter, by following the foot of the bluffs.

3d. Sandy Bluffs, east foot.	6¼	338½	692½

These bluffs are sandy, and heavy on teams. Near the west side you will find several steep places to descend, but not difficult, the sand being soft.

Small creek, running between the bluffs.	¼	338¾	692¼

Many small Lizards on the sandy places, but they appear to be perfectly harmless.

Sandy Bluffs, west foot.	2	340¾	690¼
Bluff Spring and small creek 200 yards, and one a quarter of a mile.	¼	341	690

In the neighborhood of these creeks the land is swampy and soft. The road was made close to the bluffs, to avoid the swamps.

Petite creek, 4 feet wide, 9 inches deep.	1	342	689

Plenty of water, some muddy, October 1, 1847. Latitude 41° 12' 50".

Picanninni creek, 3 feet wide.	1¼	343¼	687¾

Good spring water, and plentiful, October 1, 1847.

Goose creek, 30 feet wide, 3 inches deep.	¾	344	687

After crossing this, you pass over a low range of bluffs, very sandy, but only a quarter of a mile wide;

PROMINENT POINTS AND REMARKS	DIST. MILES.	FROM W QRS. MILES.	FROM C OF GSL MILES.
then you descend on the bottom land again, but will find it soft and springy.			
Small spring creek. ...	1¼	345¼	685¾
Many springs of cold water at the foot of the bluffs.			
Small creek, 4 feet wide.	1¼	346½	684½
Plenty of clear cold water, October 1, 1847.			
Duck-weed creek, 10 feet wide.	¼	346¾	684¼
Abundance of good, cold spring water, Oct. 1, 1847.			
Shoal stream, 3 feet wide.	2	348¾	682¼
Dry, October 1, 1847.			
Rattlesnake creek, 20 feet wide, 1½ ft. deep.	3¾	352½	678½
Swift current, sandy bottom, but not bad to cross.			
Cedar Bluffs.	1½	354	677
On the south side the river. Lat. 41° 13′ 44″ Long. 101° 52′.			
Creek, six feet wide. ..	5	359	672
Water plenty, September 30, 1847. Land, in this neighborhood, sandy.			
Creek, four feet wide. .	½	359½	671½
Plenty of water, September 30, 1847.			
Crooked Creek, five feet wide.	¼	359¾	671¼
Plenty of water, September 30, 1847.			
Camp Creek, eight feet wide.	4	363¾	667¼
Two creeks here, about the same size, but a few rods apart—water cold and plenty, September 30, 1847. No doubt they rise from springs.			
Creek, three feet wide.	4	367¾	663¼
Plenty of water, May 20,			

PROMINENT POINTS AND REMARKS	DIST. MILES.	FROM W QRS. MILES.	FROM C OF GSL MILES.
but dry, September 30, 1847.			
Pond Creek, four feet wide.	¼	368	663
Dry, September 30, near the river, but further north many ponds and tall grass.			
Wolf Creek, 20 feet wide.	1½	369½	661½
At the east foot of Sandy Bluffs, which are bad to cross, you will probably have to double teams, if heavy loaded.			
Sandy Bluffs, west foot.	¾	370¼	660¾
Two hundred yard further, is a creek five feet wide.			
Watch Creek, 8 feet wide, and 2 feet deep.	3½	373¾	657¼
After this, the road runs pretty near the river banks, to avoid some swamps near the bluffs.			
"Lone Tree," north side the river.	4¼	378	653
About three hundred yards south from the road.			
Ash Hollow, south side the river.	2¾	380¾	650¼
So named from a grove of Ash timber growing on it. It occupies a space of about fifteen or twenty acres, and is surrounded by high bluffs.			
Castle Creek, 6 rods wide, 2 feet deep.	3	383¾	647¼
Swift current, quick-sand bottom, water muddy. Low banks, but not good to cross, on account of quick-sands.			
Castle Bluffs, south side the river.	4¼	388	643
You cross no more creeks			

PROMINENT POINTS AND REMARKS	DIST. MILES.	FROM W QRS. MILES.	FROM C OF GSL MILES.
of water, until you arrive at Crab creek, twenty-five and a half miles from here. The road good, except in one place, where you travel three-fourths of a mile over sand.			
Sand Hill creek, 12 feet wide, south side the road.	$\frac{3}{4}$	$388\frac{3}{4}$	$642\frac{1}{4}$
Near some sandy mounds, on the north side the road.			
Creek or slough. ...... Dry.	$1\frac{1}{2}$	$390\frac{1}{4}$	$640\frac{3}{4}$
Creek or slough. ...... Dry.	$7\frac{1}{2}$	$397\frac{3}{4}$	$633\frac{1}{4}$
Sandy Bluffs, east foot.	3	$400\frac{3}{4}$	$630\frac{1}{4}$
Sandy Bluffs, west foot.	$\frac{1}{2}$	$401\frac{1}{4}$	$629\frac{3}{4}$
Dry creek.	$\frac{1}{4}$	$401\frac{1}{2}$	$629\frac{1}{2}$
Dry do.	$\frac{3}{4}$	$402\frac{1}{4}$	$628\frac{3}{4}$
Dry creek, 30 feet wide.	4	$406\frac{1}{4}$	$624\frac{3}{4}$
The road runs near the river, from here to Crab Creek.			
Crab Creek, 20 feet wide, very shoal. .	3	$409\frac{1}{4}$	$621\frac{3}{4}$
Two miles further you will see some high bluffs on the right. By ascending one of the highest you will see Chimney Rock, to the west.			
Small lake, south of the road.	$1\frac{1}{4}$	$410\frac{1}{2}$	$620\frac{1}{2}$
Good chance to camp, without turning from the road.			
Cobble Hills, east foot.	5	$415\frac{1}{2}$	$615\frac{1}{2}$
You cross three dry creeks before you arrive here and then you travel over another range of sandy bluffs—ascent pretty steep, but not very sandy.			
Cobble Hills, west foot.	$2\frac{1}{4}$	$417\frac{3}{4}$	$613\frac{1}{4}$
After you descend on the low land, you will find it			

PROMINENT POINTS AND REMARKS	DIST. MILES.	FROM W QRS. MILES.	FROM C OF GSL MILES.
mostly sandy for ten miles, and in some places very heavy drawing.			
"Ancient Bluff Ruins," north side the road. Latitude 41° 33′ 3″.	$1\frac{1}{4}$	419	612
Resembling the ruins of ancient castles, fortifications, &c.; but visitors must be cautious, on account of the many rattle-snakes lurking round, and concealed in the clefts of the bluffs.			
R. and R., road joins the river.	$10\frac{1}{2}$	$429\frac{1}{2}$	$601\frac{1}{2}$
Good place to camp. After this, the road runs near the river, until you arrive at the next low sandy ridges.			
Low sandy bluffs, east foot.	$7\frac{1}{2}$	437	594
Low sandy bluffs, west foot.	1	43^8	593
After this, the land for several miles, is soft in wet weather, but good traveling in dry weather.			
"Chimney Rock," (meridian) south side the river.	$14\frac{1}{4}$	$452\frac{1}{2}$	$578\frac{1}{2}$
The higher land now begins to be sandy and barren. Many Prickly-pears and Wild Sage, which continue mostly through the remainder of the journey.			
Scott's Bluffs, (mer.) south side the river.	$19\frac{1}{4}$	472	559
The road here is near enough to the river to camp Lat. of meridian. 41° 50′ 52″.; Long. 103° 2′.			
Spring Creek, 10 feet wide, 8 inches deep.	4	47^6	555

PROMINENT POINTS AND REMARKS	DIST. MILES.	FROM W QRS. MILES.	FROM C OF GSL MILES.
South of the road. You do not cross it, but travel half a mile alongside. Good water, and many trout in it. R. and R., road runs near the river.	$12\frac{1}{2}$	$488\frac{1}{2}$	$542\frac{1}{2}$
Good chance to camp. Low sandy bluffs, north side the road.	$2\frac{3}{4}$	$491\frac{1}{4}$	$539\frac{3}{4}$
You travel at the foot of these bluffs, but will find the road sandy and heavy on teams. Creek, about 200 yards south of road.	2	$493\frac{1}{4}$	$537\frac{3}{4}$
By ascending one of the highest bluffs near, you have a view of "Laramie Peak" in the Black Hills. Timber, north side the river.	$11\frac{1}{2}$	$504\frac{3}{4}$	$526\frac{1}{4}$
Road here about a quarter of a mile from the river — after this, generally from one to two miles distant. The road, to Laramie, very sandy. "Raw Hide" creek, 1 rod wide.	$5\frac{1}{4}$	510	521
Plenty of water, June 1st, but dry, Sept. 15, 1847. "Fort John" or Laramie ford.	12	522	509
The fort lays about one and a half miles west from the river. The ford is good in low water. River 108 yards wide. (See Note 3.) Steep hill to descend. .	$7\frac{1}{4}$	$529\frac{1}{4}$	$501\frac{3}{4}$
The descent being over rock, and very steep, makes it dangerous to wagons, but it is not lengthy. Steep hill to ascend and descend.	$4\frac{1}{2}$	$533\frac{3}{4}$	$497\frac{1}{4}$
In traveling over this hill, you will find the road rocky in places, and about half way over there is a sudden turn in the road over rough rocks, which is dangerous to wagons, if care is not taken. Road leaves the river. .	$\frac{3}{4}$	$534\frac{1}{2}$	$496\frac{1}{2}$
At this point, the road bends to the south-west, leaving the river. You will not come to the river banks again for eighty miles. "Warm Springs," Lat. 42° 15′ 6″.	$1\frac{3}{4}$	$536\frac{1}{4}$	$494\frac{3}{4}$
This is a very strong spring of clear water, but it is warmer than river water, at all seasons of the year. Very steep bluff, half a mile up.	$1\frac{1}{4}$	$537\frac{1}{2}$	$493\frac{1}{2}$
Before arriving at this, you pass through a narrow ravine, between bluffs. The ascent is unpleasant, on account of cobble stones. "Porter's Rock," left of the road.	$4\frac{3}{4}$	$542\frac{1}{4}$	$488\frac{3}{4}$
A mile beyond this, you descend to the lower land again. The descent is steep, lengthy and sandy. Bitter Creek and Cold Spring.	$4\frac{1}{4}$	$546\frac{1}{2}$	$484\frac{1}{2}$
This was dry, September 13. Here is plenty of timber, and if there is no water, you will find plenty three and a half miles further. Bitter Creek—second crossing.	$\frac{3}{4}$	$547\frac{1}{4}$	$483\frac{3}{4}$
Bend in the road.	2	$549\frac{1}{4}$	$481\frac{3}{4}$
Road turns south about two hundred yards, to avoid a deep ravine, then back again the same distance. Dead Timber creek, 10 feet wide.	$\frac{3}{4}$	550	481
Plenty of timber, grass and water.			

PROMINENT POINTS AND REMARKS	DIST. MILES.	FROM W QRS. MILES.	FROM C OF GSL MILES.
Creek, south side the road.	$1\frac{1}{2}$	$551\frac{1}{2}$	$479\frac{1}{2}$
You don't cross this creek, but go just above it. It is a good chance to camp.			
Small creek and spring: Lat. 42° 21′ 51″. . .	$7\frac{3}{4}$	$559\frac{1}{4}$	$471\frac{3}{4}$
Not safe to depend on for a camping place. Little grass and not much water— dry, September 13, 1847.			
Steep hill, quarter mile up.	$\frac{1}{4}$	$559\frac{1}{2}$	$471\frac{1}{2}$
Pleasant view of the surrounding country from the summit. The descent steep in several places, and many cobblestones in the road.			
"Horse Creek" and Heber's Spring. . .	$5\frac{1}{2}$	565	466
The spring lays a little to the right of the road, at the edge of timber. If it is dry, there is water in the creek, about one hundred yards north from this spring.			
Bluff $\frac{3}{4}$ths of a mile to the summit.	$2\frac{1}{2}$	$567\frac{1}{2}$	$463\frac{1}{2}$
Difficult to ascend on account of six or seven steep places, where you will probably have to double teams.			
Small creek: Lat. 42° 29′ 58″.	$2\frac{1}{4}$	$569\frac{3}{4}$	$461\frac{1}{4}$
After crossing this, you cross five others, about a mile apart, but none of them safe to depend on for a camping place, being little grass, and less (if any) water.			
5th small creek from the last.	$4\frac{3}{4}$	$574\frac{1}{2}$	$456\frac{1}{2}$
After crossing this, you ascend a high bluff, the top of which is a succession of hills and hollows for five			
miles. The road is good, but crooked.			
"La Bonte" river, 30 feet wide, 2 ft. deep. . .	$8\frac{1}{4}$	$582\frac{3}{4}$	$448\frac{1}{4}$
Good place to camp— plenty of timber, grass, and water. There is also a good chance, a mile further. Plenty of wild mint on the creek.			
Branch of La Bonte, 10 feet wide, 18 inches deep.	5	$587\frac{3}{4}$	$443\frac{1}{4}$
Doubtful about water. Steep banks. You have now traveled near a mile over this dark, red sand, and will find it continue three and a half miles further.			
Very small creek.	$6\frac{1}{4}$	594	437
Little chance for grass, and less for water. One mile beyond this, you ascend another bluff, but the road is tolerably straight and good. Look out for toads with horns and tails.			
Very small creek.	$6\frac{1}{4}$	$600\frac{1}{4}$	$430\frac{3}{4}$
Very poor chance for camping.			
Very small creek.	$\frac{1}{2}$	$600\frac{3}{4}$	$430\frac{1}{4}$
The road runs down the channel of this creek, near two hundred yards, but there is little grass on it.			
A La Prele river, one rod wide, 2 ft. deep. . .	$1\frac{1}{2}$	$602\frac{1}{4}$	$428\frac{3}{4}$
Current rapid—good place to camp. Land between creeks mostly sandy and barren. Road from here to the Platte very uneven, being a succession of hills and hollows.			
Small creek.	$4\frac{1}{4}$	$606\frac{1}{2}$	$424\frac{1}{2}$
No place to camp— doubtful for water.			
Box Elder creek, 5 feet			

PROMINENT POINTS AND REMARKS	DIST. MILES.	FROM W QRS. MILES.	FROM C OF GSL MILES.
wide.	1	607½	423½
Clear water, and plenty— but not much grass. Not very good to cross, banks being steep. Some timber on it.			
Fourche Boise river, 30 feet wide, 2 feet. deep: Lat. 42° 51' 5".	3¼	610¾	420¼
Current rapid. Plenty of good grass and timber.			
North fork of Platte river.	4	614¾	416¼
Not much grass here. You will now find a sandy road and heavy traveling.			
"Deer Creek," 30 feet wide, two feet deep: Lat. 42° 52' 50": Altitude, 4,864 feet.	5	619¾	411¼
Lovely place to camp. Swift current, clear water, and abundance of fish. Nice grove of timber on the banks, and a coal mine about a quarter of a mile up, on the east side. After this, you will find sandy roads for nine miles, but not much grass.			
Deep hollow, or ravine— steep banks.	2½	622¼	408¾
Sudden bend in the road.	5¾	628	403
To avoid a deep ravine.			
Grove of timber on the banks of the river.	1	629	402
Good chance to camp. Lat. 42° 51' 47".			
Crooked, muddy creek, 12 ft. wide, 1 deep.	1	630	401
Not good to cross—steep banks. Plenty of grass, but no wood.			
Muddy creek, 3 feet wide.	5¾	635¾	395¼

PROMINENT POINTS AND REMARKS	DIST. MILES.	FROM W QRS. MILES.	FROM C OF GSL MILES.
Soft banks and bad to cross. Considerable small timber, but little grass. After this, good but crooked road.			
Deep gulf.	2¾	638½	392½
Creek, two feet wide. .	1½	640	391
No place to camp.			
Muddy creek, 5 feet wide, 1½ feet deep.	1	641	390
No chance to camp.			
2 ravines, near together: Lat. 42° 51' 44". . .	3	644	387
Opposite here there is a fording place, where companies generally have forded the river.			
Creek five feet wide. . .	3	647	384
Abundance of fish, early in the season, but little grass and no timber.			
Upper Platte ferry and ford.	1½	648½	382½
Plenty of feed and some timber on both sides the river (See Note 4.) Lat. 42° 50' 18". Altitude 4,875 feet.			
Road turns south, and rises a long hill. . . .	7	655½	375½
Ascent gradual. Many singular looking rocks on the south side. Descent rough and crooked. Towards the foot, road very uneven.			
Mineral spring and lake.	5½	661	370
Considered poisonous. No bad taste to the water, unless the cattle trample in it. In that case it becomes black, and is doubtless poisonous. No timber near.			
Rock avenue and steep descent.	7½	668½	362½
The road here passes between high rocks, forming a kind of avenue or gateway, for a quarter of a mile.			

PROMINENT POINTS AND REMARKS	DIST. MILES.	FROM W QRS. MILES.	FROM C OF GSL MILES.
Alkali swamps and springs.	2	$670\frac{1}{2}$	$360\frac{1}{2}$
This ought to be avoided as a camping ground—it is a small valley, surrounded by high bluffs. The land exceeding miry, and smells bad. There is a creek of good water north-west. No timber and little grass. Next mile, rough road.			
Small stream of clear spring water.	4	$674\frac{1}{2}$	$356\frac{1}{2}$
Good camping place. Plenty of grass, but no wood.			
"Willow Spring."	$2\frac{3}{4}$	$677\frac{1}{4}$	$353\frac{3}{4}$
About three rods west of the road, at the foot of willow bushes. Water cold and good—grass plenty, but creek some miry.			
"Prospect Hill," (summit.)	1	$678\frac{1}{4}$	$352\frac{3}{4}$
Pleasant view of the surrounding country, to the Sweet Water mountains.			
Bad slough.	$3\frac{1}{4}$	$681\frac{1}{2}$	$349\frac{1}{2}$
Plenty of grass, but little water. A mile further is a hill, both steep ascending and descending.			
Creek, 300 yards south of road.	$1\frac{3}{4}$	$683\frac{1}{4}$	$347\frac{3}{4}$
Plenty of grass, but no wood.			
Small creek, left of the road.	$2\frac{1}{2}$	$685\frac{3}{4}$	$345\frac{1}{4}$
Grass plentiful, but doubtful for water, and no wood. The road runs alongside this creek for half a mile.			
Grease-wood creek, 6 feet wide 1 ft. deep.	$1\frac{3}{4}$	$687\frac{1}{2}$	$343\frac{1}{2}$
Very little grass, and no fuel but wild sage. Road from here to the Sweet			

PROMINENT POINTS AND REMARKS	DIST. MILES.	FROM W QRS. MILES.	FROM C OF GSL MILES.
Water sandy, and very heavy.			
Alkali springs and lakes.	$6\frac{1}{4}$	$693\frac{3}{4}$	$337\frac{1}{4}$
Here gather your Saleratus from a lake, west of the road. Land swampy, and smells bad. Water poisonous.			
"Sweet-water river," 8 rods wide, 2 ft. deep.	$4\frac{1}{4}$	698	333
Swift current—good water. Grass plentiful, but little timber. (See Note 5)			
Independence Rock and ford.	$\frac{3}{4}$	$698\frac{3}{4}$	$332\frac{1}{4}$
On the north side of the river—about six hundred yards long, and a hundred and twenty wide, composed of hard Granite. (See Note 5.)			
Devil's Gate.	$5\frac{1}{4}$	704	327
A little west from the road. The river here passes between perpendicular rocks four hundred feet high.—This is a curiosity worthy of a traveler's notice.			
Creek two feet wide. . .	$\frac{1}{2}$	$704\frac{1}{2}$	$326\frac{1}{2}$
Not good to cross. The road runs near the river banks for ten miles after this.			
Creek, 6 feet wide.	$\frac{1}{2}$	705	326
Good to cross. Water and grass plenty, but lacks timber. You will find grass all along on the banks of the river, but very little wood.			
Deep ravine and creek.	$6\frac{1}{4}$	$711\frac{1}{4}$	$319\frac{3}{4}$
Plenty of grass and water, but no wood.			
Deep ravine and creek.	$\frac{3}{4}$	712	319
Doubtful for water.			
Road leaves the river: Lat. 42° 28′ 25″. . .	3	715	316

PROMINENT POINTS AND REMARKS	DIST. MILES.	FROM W QRS. MILES.	FROM C OF GSL MILES.
Road after this, sandy and heavy, and passes over a high bluff. Land barren for seven and a half miles. (See Note 6.)			
Alkali Lake.	$\frac{1}{2}$	$715\frac{1}{2}$	$315\frac{1}{2}$
On the left of the road.			
Sage creek.	$4\frac{3}{4}$	$720\frac{1}{4}$	$310\frac{3}{4}$
No grass. High banks. Doubtful for water, but Wild Sage plentiful. One and three-quarter miles further you arrive on the river banks again.			
Creek, three feet wide.	4	$724\frac{1}{4}$	$306\frac{3}{4}$
Doubtful for water, but the road runs close to the river.			
High gravelly bluff. . . .	$1\frac{1}{4}$	$725\frac{1}{2}$	$305\frac{1}{2}$
Left of the road, and a very good place to camp.			
Bitter-cotton-wood creek.	$1\frac{1}{2}$	727	304
Doubtful for water and grass. Some timber on it. After this, the road leaves the river for six miles.			
Road arrives at the river.	$6\frac{1}{4}$	$733\frac{1}{4}$	$297\frac{3}{4}$
Leave the old road and ford the river.	$\frac{1}{4}$	$733\frac{1}{2}$	$297\frac{1}{2}$
By fording here, the road is shorter, and you avoid much very heavy, sandy road. Lat. 42° 31′ 20″.			
Road turns between the rocky ridges.	$1\frac{1}{2}$	735	296
After this, you ford the river twice—but it is easily forded. Then the road leaves the river again.			
Ford No. 4—good camping place. . . .	8	743	288
After this, the road leaves the river again, and you will probably find no water fit to drink for sixteen and a half miles.			
Ice Spring.	$5\frac{3}{4}$	$748\frac{3}{4}$	$282\frac{1}{4}$

PROMINENT POINTS AND REMARKS	DIST. MILES.	FROM W QRS. MILES.	FROM C OF GSL MILES.
This is on a low, swampy spot of land on the right of the road. Ice may generally be found, by digging down about two feet. There are two alkali lakes a little further.			
Alkali springs.	$\frac{1}{4}$	749	282
On the left of the road.			
Steep descent from the bluffs.	$9\frac{1}{2}$	$758\frac{1}{2}$	$272\frac{1}{2}$
Ford of Sweet-water, No. 5.	1	$759\frac{1}{2}$	$271\frac{1}{2}$
Plenty of good grass and willow bushes. River about three rods wide, and two feet deep.			
Creek a rod wide.	$\frac{1}{4}$	$759\frac{3}{4}$	$271\frac{1}{4}$
Doubtful for water.			
Bluff or hill, $1\frac{1}{2}$ miles to summit.	$\frac{1}{4}$	760	271
The ascent gradual, though steep in some places.			
Road joins the river, and fords it.	$3\frac{1}{2}$	$763\frac{1}{2}$	$267\frac{1}{2}$
The river is forded here, to avoid crossing the next high, sandy ridge, making the road much better, and some shorter.			
Ford back.	$\frac{1}{2}$	764	267
River banks and stream, 25 feet wide.	$\frac{1}{2}$	$764\frac{1}{2}$	$266\frac{1}{2}$
This appears to be a branch of the river, running round a piece of land, about a quarter of a mile wide.			
Creek, two feet wide: Lat. 42° 28′ 36″. . .	3	$767\frac{1}{2}$	$263\frac{1}{2}$
A good cold spring, a little to the right of the road and a soft swamp just below, but it is a good place to camp.			
Road leaves the river. .	2	$769\frac{1}{2}$	$261\frac{1}{2}$
Good camping place. After this, the road winds			

PROMINENT POINTS AND REMARKS	DIST. MILES.	FROM W QRS. MILES.	FROM C OF GSL MILES.
around and over a succession of hills and hollows, for three miles.			
Rough, rocky ridges. . .	2½	772	259
Dangerous to wagons, and ought to be crossed with care.			
Soft swamp and very small creek.	3	775	256
No place to camp.			
Creek, a foot wide.	1¾	776¾	254¼
Creek, two feet wide. .	¼	777	254
Strawberry creek, five feet wide.	2	779	252
Plenty of grass and water, and some willows. Good place to camp. There is a poplar grove about a mile below.			
Quaking-aspen creek. .	1	780	251
This rises in a small grove of timber on the south side the road, but is not safe to depend on for water.			
Branch of Sweet-water, 2 rods wide, two feet deep.	2¾	782¾	248¼
Good place to camp. Water good and cold. Grass and willows, plenty.			
Willow creek, 8 feet wide, 2 feet deep.	2¼	785	246
Good camping place for grass, water and willows. The ford is near three rods wide.			
Sweet-water, 3 rods wide, 3 feet deep.	4¾	789¾	241¼
Good place to camp. After traveling seven miles beyond this, and passing between the Twin mounds, you will find a good camping place a quarter of a mile north of the road.			
South Pass, or summit of dividing ridge. . . .	9¾	799½	231½
This is the dividing ridge			

PROMINENT POINTS AND REMARKS	DIST. MILES.	FROM W QRS. MILES.	FROM C OF GSL MILES.
between the waters of the Atlantic and Pacific. Altitude, 7,085 feet.			
Pacific creek and springs.	3	802½	228½
Abundance of grass any where for a mile. Good water, and plenty of Wild Sage for fuel.			
Pacific creek (crossing) three feet wide: Lat. 42° 18′ 58″: Long. 108° 40′ 0″.	1½	804	227
Not good to cross. Pretty good place to camp, except for wood. After you leave here you will find a good road, but very little water.			
Dry Sandy.	9	813	218
The water brackish, and not good for cattle. Very little grass, but no wood.			
Junction of California and Oregon roads.	6	819	212
Take the left hand road. Good road a few miles, afterwards sandy and heavy.			
Little Sandy, 20 feet wide, 2½ feet deep.	7¾	826¾	204¼
Muddy water—swift current. Plenty of willows and wild sage. Abundance of grass down the stream. After this, barren and sandy land.			
Big Sandy, 7 rods wide, 2 feet deep: Lat. 42° 6′ 42″.	8¼	835	196
Good chance to camp. A few miles further, you will find a short piece of rough road, over rocks and cobble stones. No grass or water after this for near 17 miles.			
Big Sandy.	17	852	179
Good chance to camp. After this, barren, sandy land, and heavy road till you			

PROMINENT POINTS AND REMARKS	DIST. MILES.	FROM W QRS. MILES.	FROM C OF GSL MILES.
arrive at Green river.			
Green river ford, 16 rods wide.	10	862	169
Good camping anywhere on the banks, and plenty of timber. It is not difficult fording in low water; but if too high to ford, the best crossing place is up stream. Latitude—2 miles above—41° 52' 37"; Long. 109° 30'. Alt. 6,000 feet.			
Good camping place on Green river.	$1\frac{1}{2}$	$863\frac{1}{2}$	$167\frac{1}{2}$
Plenty of grass here. But no other very good chance to camp on this side the river.			
Road leaves Green river.	$3\frac{1}{2}$	867	164
No grass nor water after this for fifteen and a half miles. Land rolling, barren—mostly sandy, and several steep places to pass.			
Black's fork, 6 rods wide, 2 feet deep.	$15\frac{1}{2}$	$882\frac{1}{2}$	$148\frac{1}{2}$
Good chance to camp, and a nice place, though not much timber.			
Ham's fork, 3 rods wide, 2 feet deep.	$3\frac{3}{4}$	$886\frac{1}{4}$	$144\frac{3}{4}$
Rapid current, cold water, plenty of bunch grass and willows, and is a good camp ground.			
Black's fork again.	$1\frac{3}{4}$	888	143
Not much grass, but plenty of willows. You will now have some uneven road, with many ravines.			
Small creek, 2 feet wide.	$10\frac{3}{4}$	$898\frac{3}{4}$	$132\frac{1}{4}$
No grass, and probably no water.			
Black's fork, third time.	2	$900\frac{3}{4}$	$130\frac{1}{4}$
After crossing you will find a good camping place. Plenty of bunch grass; also, wild flax.			

PROMINENT POINTS AND REMARKS	DIST. MILES.	FROM W QRS. MILES.	FROM C OF GSL MILES.
Black's fork, fourth time.	$2\frac{1}{4}$	903	128
You ford again at a good camping place.			
Stream 2 rods wide, 2 feet deep.	$2\frac{3}{4}$	$905\frac{3}{4}$	$125\frac{1}{4}$
Very swift current, and plenty of bunch grass. Road pretty rough after this.			
Stream—good camping place at a bend. . . .	$3\frac{1}{2}$	$909\frac{1}{4}$	$121\frac{3}{4}$
You do not cross the stream, but there is a good camping place, where the road passes a bend of the creek.			
"Fort Bridger:" Lat. 41° 19' 13"; Long. 110° 5'; Altitude, 6,665 feet.	$8\frac{1}{4}$	$917\frac{1}{2}$	$113\frac{1}{2}$
You cross four rushing creeks, within half a mile, before you reach the Fort, and by traveling half a mile beyond the Fort, you will cross three others, and then find a good place to camp.			
The Fort is composed of four log houses and a small enclosure for horses. Land exceeding rich—water cold and good, and considerable timber.			
Cold Springs, on the right side the road.	$6\frac{1}{4}$	$923\frac{3}{4}$	$107\frac{1}{4}$
There is timber here, and it is a pretty good camping place.			
Small creek and springs.	$1\frac{1}{4}$	925	106
No feed here, and no place to camp.			
Summit of High Ridge: Lat. 41° 16' 11". . .	1	926	105
After this, you travel several miles on tolerably level land, then you descend to lower land by a steep, tedious route.			
Muddy Fork, 12 feet			

PROMINENT POINTS AND REMARKS	DIST. MILES.	FROM W QRS. MILES.	FROM C OF GSL MILES.
wide.	$4\frac{1}{2}$	$930\frac{1}{2}$	$100\frac{1}{2}$
Plenty of bunch grass and willows. Water clear, and not bad tasted. After this, you will probably find no good water for eleven miles.			
Copperas, or Soda Spring.	$3\frac{3}{4}$	$934\frac{1}{4}$	$96\frac{3}{4}$
Left of the road at the foot of a hill. The road now begins to ascend another high ridge.			
Summit of Ridge: Altitude 7,315 feet. . .	$1\frac{3}{4}$	936	95
The descent is lengthy, and some tedious. About half way down you pass over rough rocks, and the pass being narrow, makes it dangerous to wagons.			
Copperas, or Soda Spring.	1	937	94
Cattle will drink this water, and there is plenty of grass around it. A little further the road turns to the left and passes down a narrow ravine.			
Spring of good water, south side the road.	$4\frac{1}{2}$	$941\frac{1}{2}$	$89\frac{1}{2}$
This is surrounded by high grass, close to the creek side. There is another spring a little further on the north side the road, which will probably be the last water you will find till you arrive at Sulphur creek.			
East foot of dividing ridge.	1	$942\frac{1}{2}$	$88\frac{1}{2}$
Dividing ridge between the waters of the Colorado and Great Basin. Ascent very steep and crooked— narrow summit and steep descending. After this, crooked road between mountains. Altitude of			

PROMINENT POINTS AND REMARKS	DIST. MILES.	FROM W QRS. MILES.	FROM C OF GSL MILES.
ridge, 7,700 feet.			
Sulphur creek, 10 feet wide.	6	$948\frac{1}{2}$	$82\frac{1}{2}$
Plenty of grass and some willows; also, small cedar at the foot of the mountain. (See Note 7.)			
Bear river, 6 rods wide, 2 feet deep.	$1\frac{3}{4}$	$950\frac{1}{4}$	$80\frac{3}{4}$
Swift current—clear cold water; plenty of timber and grass. Altitude at ford, 6,836 feet.			
Summit of Ridge.	$2\frac{3}{4}$	953	78
Half a mile further you cross a small ridge, then descend into, and travel down a nice narrow bottom, where is plenty of grass.			
Spring of clear, cold water.	$1\frac{3}{4}$	$954\frac{3}{4}$	$76\frac{1}{4}$
On the south side the creek, about two rods from the road. The spring is deep—water clear, cold and good. Perhaps it will not be easy to find, being surrounded by high grass.			
Yellow creek, cross at foot of rocky bluffs.	$4\frac{3}{4}$	$959\frac{1}{2}$	$71\frac{1}{2}$
You will soon cross this again, and about a mile further you ascend another long ridge, the ascent being pretty steep and tedious.			
Summit of Ridge.	$1\frac{3}{4}$	$961\frac{1}{4}$	$69\frac{3}{4}$
Descent pretty steep. About three-fourths of a mile down from the summit, is a spring of good cold water, on the left of the road.			
Cache Cave and head of Echo creek: Altitude, 6,070 feet. . .	$3\frac{3}{4}$	965	66
Cave in the bluffs north. Several springs along the road, before you arrive			

PROMINENT POINTS AND REMARKS	DIST. MILES.	FROM W QRS. MILES.	FROM C OF GSL MILES.
here, and one, a quarter of a mile south from the Cave. Plenty of grass, and a good place to camp.			
Cold spring, on the right of the road.	2	967	64
This also is a good place to camp, being plenty of grass.			
Cold spring, south side the road.	$2\frac{1}{4}$	$969\frac{1}{4}$	$61\frac{3}{4}$
At the foot of a high hill. Good place to camp. After this, you travel down a narrow ravine, between high mountains, till you arrive at Weber river. Not much difficulty for camping down it.			
Deep ravine.	$1\frac{1}{4}$	$970\frac{1}{2}$	$60\frac{1}{2}$
Steep on both banks. After this, you will cross Echo creek a number of times, but in no place very difficult.			
Red fork of Weber river: Alt. 5,301 feet. . . .	16	$986\frac{1}{2}$	$44\frac{1}{2}$
There is a good camping place a mile before you arrive here. Also, almost any where on the banks of the river. Plenty of timber. The stream abounds with spotted trout.			
Weber river ford, 4 rods wide, 2 ft. deep. . .	4	$990\frac{1}{2}$	$40\frac{1}{2}$
Good to ford. Plenty of grass and timber on both sides the river.			
Pratt's Pass, to avoid the Kanyon.	$\frac{1}{2}$	991	40
The Kanyon is a few miles below, where the river runs between high mountains of rocks. Some emigrants have passed through, but it is dangerous.			
East foot of Long hill. . .	1	992	39
There is a small creek descends down the hollow,			

PROMINENT POINTS AND REMARKS	DIST. MILES.	FROM W QRS. MILES.	FROM C OF GSL MILES.
up which the road is made. There are several springs near the road.			
Bridge (over the creek.)	$2\frac{1}{4}$	$994\frac{1}{4}$	$36\frac{3}{4}$
Not a bad place to camp.			
Summit of Ridge.	$2\frac{1}{2}$	$996\frac{3}{4}$	$34\frac{1}{4}$
The country west looks rough and mountainous. The descent is not pleasant, being mostly on the side hill.			
Small creek, left of the road.	$1\frac{3}{4}$	$998\frac{1}{2}$	$32\frac{1}{2}$
Good place to camp. Plenty of grass, water and willows. The road here turns north a quarter of a mile, then west, and ascends a steep hill.			
Kanyon creek, 1 rod wide, 1 foot deep: Lat. 40° 54' 7". . . .	$2\frac{3}{4}$	$1001\frac{1}{4}$	$29\frac{3}{4}$
You have to cross this creek thirteen times, besides two bad swamps. The road is dangerous to wagons, on account of dense, high bushes, trees, and short turns in the road. Good place to camp. (See Note 9.)			
Leave Kanyon creek. . .	8	$1009\frac{1}{4}$	$21\frac{3}{4}$
Here you turn to the right, and begin to ascend the highest mountain you cross in the whole journey. You travel through timber, some on side hills, and cross the creek a number of times.			
Small spring, left of the road.	3	$1012\frac{1}{4}$	$18\frac{3}{4}$
You will probably find water in several places, but it is uncertain where, as it runs but a little way in a place, and then sinks in the earth.			

PROMINENT POINTS AND REMARKS	DIST. MILES.	FROM W QRS. MILES.	FROM C OF GSL MILES.
Summit of mountain: Altitude, 7,245 feet.	1	1013¼	17¾
You have now a view of the south part of the Valley of the Great Salt Lake. The descent is steep, lengthy, and tedious, on account of stumps in the road.			
Bridge over a deep ravine.	¾	1014	17
This is dangerous to cross, and a wagon may be easily upset. The road lays through a forest of small timber, and is unpleasant traveling.			
Brown's creek and spring.	¾	1014¾	16¼
Not a bad place to camp, but there is a much better one, half a mile lower down.			
Cold spring on Brown's creek.	2¼	1017½	13½
Within a rod of the road, on the east side, under a grove of Black Birch bushes. Good place to camp, but some miry. Good camping any where for two miles lower.			
Leave Brown's creek. .	1¾	1019¼	11¾
You now ascend another high mountain, by a steep and crooked road. On both sides this mountain, there are many Serviceberry bushes.			
Summit of last ridge. ...	1	1020¼	10¾
The descent is very steep, all the way, till you arrive on the banks of Last creek.			
Last creek.	¾	1021	10
You cross this creek nineteen times. Several of the crossings are difficult. There are several side hills which require care in teamsters. Three camping places on it, but the road is rough.			
Mouth of the Kanyon. .	5	1026	5
You now enter the Velley of the Salt Lake. The road at the mouth of the Kanyon bad, and rough with stumps. Afterwards, descending and good.			
City of the Great Salt Lake.	5	1031	

The city is located within three miles of the mountains, which enclose the east side of the valley—within three miles of the Utah Outlet, and twenty-two miles of the Salt Lake. The land is gradually sloping, from the mountain to within a mile of the Outlet, and is of a black, loose, sandy nature. A stream of water rushes from the mountains east of the city, and, at the upper part, it divides in two branches, both of which pass through the city to the Outlet. The water is good, and very cold, and abundance for mill purposes, or for irrigation. The air is good and pure, sweetened by the healthy breezes from the Salt Lake. The grass is rich and plentiful and well filled with rushes, and the passes in the mountains afford abundance of good timber, mostly *balsam Fir.*

The valley is about forty miles long, and from twenty to twenty-five miles wide. It is beautifully surrounded on the west, south, and east by high mountains. Salt Lake extends from a point a little south of west, from the city, to about eighty miles north, forming the north-western boundary of the valley. There are two sulphur springs a mile and a half north from the *Temple Block;* the water is salt, and a little warmer than blood: two miles further north there is a sulphur spring of boiling water. There is not much land on the north part of the valley fit for cultivation; but the east side is well adapted for farming, being well watered by several large creeks, and the soil beautiful. The land on the west of the Utah Outlet, is also good for farming, and easily irrigated from the south end of the Outlet.

The latitudes, longitudes, and altitudes are copied from the observations and calculations made by Elder O. Pratt.

The variation of the magnetic needle, at the City of the Great Salt Lake, 15° 47′ 23″ east, as determined on the 30th July, A. D. 1847, by the mean of several observations, and calculations of the Sun's Azimuths and Altitudes.

NOTES

Note I. If the Elk Horn river is fordable, you leave the main road a mile before you strike the river, and turn north. After leaving the road *three-fourths* of a mile, you will cross a very bad creek or slough, being soft and miry; but, by throwing in long grass, it will be good crossing. You then travel three-fourths of a mile further, and arrive at the ford. You will go up stream when fording, and gradually come nearer to the opposite shore, till you strike a piece of low land on the west side; you then pass by a narrow, crooked road, through the timber, till you arrive on the open prairie. You will then see a *post* erected in near a south direction, about a mile distant. Go straight to that post, and you will find a good bridge over the creek—and there, again strike the main road. From here, you have before you near five hundred miles travel over a flat, level

*Latitude of northern boundary of Temple Block, 40° 45′ 44″.
Longitude of northern boundary of Temple Block, 111° 26′ 34″.
Altitude of northern boundary of Temple Block, 4,300 feet.

country, and a good road, with the exception of several sandy bluffs mentioned herein. The road generally runs from one to two miles from the Platte river, but not too far to turn off to camp in case of necessity. All camping places, which lay near the road, are mentioned in this work. You will find near two hundred miles without timber, but in that region you will find plenty of buffalo chips, which are a good substitute for fuel. Buffalo are numerous after you arrive at the head of Grand Island, and continue two hundred miles.

Note II. The descent to the ford is steep, and at the bottom very sandy. Your best chance to ford will, probably, be to enter the river opposite to where you descend from the bluff; then go near a straight course, but inclining a little down stream, till more than half way over, when you will find a sand-bar. Follow this, down stream near half a mile, and you will then see a good place to go out on the south side. In this river the channels often change—the old ones fill up, and new ones are made—hence, the wisdom and necessity of having several men go across on horses, to find the best route, before you attempt to take wagons over. If this precaution is not taken, you may plunge your wagons from a sand-bar into a deep hole, and do much damage. If you ford up stream, and come out higher than where you enter, after crossing, strike for the bluffs, in a direction a very little west of south, till you arrive on the old road.

On arriving at Prairie creek, if you take a south-west course, a short day's drive will bring you to Wood river, six or eight miles above where the old road crosses; and by keeping the same course after crossing Wood river, you will strike the Platte ten or twelve miles above where Wood river empties into it. By this means the road would be shortened at least five miles, and probably much more.

Note III. Fort "John, or Laramie," lays about one and a half miles from the river, in near a south-west course, and is composed of a trading establishment, and about twelve houses, enclosed by a wall eleven feet high.

The wall and houses are built of *adobes*, or Spanish brick. It is situated on the Laramie Fork, and is a pleasant location: the latitude of the Fort is 42° 12′ 13″; longitude 104° 11′ 53″, and altitude above the sea, 4,090 feet. After leaving here you begin to cross the "Black Hills," and will find rough roads, high ridges, and mostly barren country. There is, however, not much difficulty in finding good camping places, each day's travel, by observing the annexed table.

There is a road follows the river, instead of crossing the Black Hills, and it is represented as being as near, and much better traveling if the river is fordable. By following this road you have to cross the river three times extra, but will find plenty of grass, wood, and water. If the river is fordable at Laramie, it is fordable at those three places, and you can go that route safely.

Note IV. The best place to ford will probably be a little below the bend in the river. After this you have fifty miles to travel, which is dangerous to teams, on account of Alkali springs. Great care should be taken to avoid them, by selecting a camping place where none of these springs are near.

Note V. In low water the river is easily forded opposite to the Rock Independence; but, if not fordable here, a good place can be found a mile higher up the river.

Independence Rock is one of the curiosities to be seen on the road, mostly on account of its peculiar shape and magnitude. There are many names of visitors painted in various places, on the south-east corner. At this corner most travelers appear to have gone up to view the top; but there is a much better place on the north side, about half way from end to end. Latitude 1½ miles below 42° 30′ 16″.

The road along the Sweet Water is mostly sandy and heavy traveling. You will find many steep places, and as you approach the Rocky Mountains, you will find some high hills to travel over.

After crossing the mountains the country is level, but still barren, and, if possible, more sandy. You will have to make some long drives to obtain water for camping. There is great lack of timber, from the Upper Platte ferry to Fort Bridger, and in fact scarcely any kind but willows. In all this region the willows and wild sage form your chief ingredient for fuel.

Note VI. It is supposed that a good road can be made here, by following the banks of the river. If so, these high bluffs, and much sandy road, would be avoided.

Note VII. At the foot of the mountain, on the south side the road, and at the edge of the creek, there is a strong sulphur spring. A little above the spring, on the side of the mountain, is a bed of stone coal. At the foot of the bluff, west of where you cross the creek, is a noble spring of pure, cold water; and about a mile from this place, in a south-west course, is a "Tar," or "Oil Spring," covering a surface of several rods of ground. There is a wagon trail runs within a short distance of it. It is situated in a small hollow, on the left of the wagon trail, at a point where the trail rises a higher bench of land.

When the oil can be obtained free from sand, it is useful to oil wagons. It gives a nice polish to gun-stocks, and has been proved to be highly beneficial when applied to sores on horses, cattle, &c.

Note VIII. From the summit of this ridge, you will see to the west, a ridge of high, rough, peaked rocks. The road runs at the south foot of that ridge, and there crosses Yellow creek. From the place where you now stand, the road runs through a beautiful narrow valley, surrounded by gently rolling hills, and is pretty straight and pleasant traveling, till you arrive at that ridge of rocks. There is little difficulty in finding a good camping place, between here and the ridge in view, except for fuel, which is scarce. There are several springs of good water along the creek.

Note IX. On this creek is a very rough piece of road; the bushes are high, and road narrow, in consequence of which wagon covers are liable to be torn and bows broke. There are many short turns in it, where wagon tongues are liable to be broke. Some of the crossing places are bad. There is a good camping place where first you strike the creek—one about half way up, and one a quarter of a mile before you leave the creek.

The ascent up the next mountain is both lengthy and tedious, mostly through high timber, and there are many stumps in the road. It is a chance whether you will find any water till you descend on the west side.

From this creek to the valley is decidedly the worst piece of road on the whole journey, but the distance is short, and by using care and patience, it is easily accomplished.

Index